John Stoughton

Shades and Echoes of Old London

John Stoughton

Shades and Echoes of Old London

ISBN/EAN: 9783337428808

Printed in Europe, USA, Canada, Australia, Japan

Cover: Foto ©ninafisch / pixelio.de

More available books at **www.hansebooks.com**

SHADES AND ECHOES

OF

OLD LONDON

BY

JOHN STOUGHTON, D.D.,

AUTHOR OF

'HOMES AND HAUNTS OF LUTHER,' 'FOOTPRINTS OF THE ITALIAN REFORMERS,' ETC.

LONDON
THE RELIGIOUS TRACT SOCIETY
56, PATERNOSTER ROW; 65, ST. PAUL'S CHURCHYARD
AND 164, PICCADILLY
1889

PREFATORY NOTE.

THE chapters included in this volume originally appeared in the *Leisure Hour*. They have been revised; but in many cases there are references to buildings not now standing. It has been thought better to leave some of these references as interesting details of the London of the past now so rapidly disappearing. The volume is issued in popular form in the hope that the mass of interesting information in it will both amuse and instruct the circle of readers to which this series of books appeals.

CONTENTS.

	PAGE
INTRODUCTION	9

SHADES OF THE DEPARTED:—

I.—MILTON		21
II.—RICHARD BAXTER		38
III.—ISAAK WALTON AND HIS FRIENDS		56
IV.—ANDREW MARVELL AND LORD WILLIAM RUSSELL		73
V.—MARGARET GODOLPHIN		88
VI.—JOSEPH ADDISON		101
VII.—SIR ISAAC NEWTON		121
VIII.—ISAAC WATTS		136
IX.—OLIVER GOLDSMITH		161
X.—SIR JOSHUA REYNOLDS		179
XI.—DR. SAMUEL JOHNSON		199
XII.—EDMUND BURKE		223
XIII.—JOHN HOWARD		242

ECHOES OF WESTMINSTER HALL:—

I.—AXE AND HAMMER		265
II.—ROYAL FEASTINGS		277
III.—MEN OF THE MARBLE CHAIR		289
IV.—OLD PARLIAMENTS AND POLICY		304
V.—BENCH AND BAR		318
VI.—STATE TRIALS		336
VII.—THE SEVEN BISHOPS AND SACHEVERELL		350
VIII.—JACOBITES AND AN INDIAN VICEROY		367

INDEX	381

LIST OF ILLUSTRATIONS.

	PAGE
THE SAVOY CHAPEL	*Frontispiece*
MILTON HOUSE, BARBICAN	25
OLD ST. PAUL'S CATHEDRAL	41
OLD CHARTERHOUSE, FROM THE GREEN	103
ABNEY HOUSE	137
A PARTY AT THE HOUSE OF SIR JOSHUA REYNOLDS	189
DR. JOHNSON'S HOUSE IN BOLT-COURT	215
JOHN HOWARD VISITING A PRISONER	251
WESTMINSTER HALL, IN QUEEN ANNE'S REIGN	270
THE SEVEN BISHOPS ON THEIR WAY TO THE TOWER	354

Shades and Echoes of Old London.

INTRODUCTION.

Time was, when, in the belief of almost everybody, the green woods were haunted by fairies; sylphs might be seen dancing on the banks of fresh running streams by moonlight; and in the courtyards of old castles, in the chambers of old towers, and in certain memorable parts of old cities, there were strange spirits of the past to be met with at the midnight hour. The village maiden, as she came back from her walk in the churchyard at sunset, fancied she saw some Robin Goodfellow sitting under the hedge, or coming out to salute her. The baron's daughter, in her chamber watching the embers on a winter's evening, with her foot on the rude andirons, and, just as the castle clock struck twelve—lifting up her bright eyes to the grim portrait of the man in armour over the fireplace—was sure to think that she saw, as plain as plain could be, the stalwart figure step out of the canvas, and, striding toward the door, open it with a mysterious key, and then, with his iron boot, go thump, thump, along the echoing corridor. The very warder, as he kept watch at the still hour of night, if he saw nought else, would see something not of mortal mould: a crusader, not of flesh and blood, but one impalpable; or a lady fair, all clothed in white, no more to be touched than the moonbeam shining through the turret loophole.

Those days are gone by, and we are not sorry. People now are neither pleased nor troubled with apparitions of that kind. Yet we should not at all like to have this world of ours reduced to such a prosaic, matter-of-fact condition, as, in no sense, ever to see anything but what, according to the law of optics, was painted on the retina of the eye. To say nothing now of great spiritual realities, which encircle our globe and interpenetrate the scenes of our whole life, we must confess that we should be very sorry not to have communion sometimes with the shades of the mighty dead, as well as to shake hands and talk with the humble living. There are shades of a certain kind which we are glad to see. When some of them haunt us it is very pleasant; when others of them appear it is very grand; and they are all more accommodating than were those of the olden time. Then, when folks called for spirits from the 'vasty deep,' there was room to ask, 'But will they come?' Now the shades *we* invoke always come when they are called for. By day as well as by night, they come. In the crowded street as well as the silent solitude, they come. To others they may be invisible, but to us they come. They are *the Memories of Great Men;* and if there be one place more than another haunted by them, it is OLD LONDON.

Many, many changes have occurred in our mother city. Over and over again it has been built and rebuilt. The very soil we walk upon is an accumulation of remains, in many parts some twenty feet above the pavement trodden by the Roman masters of that colony which gave it its time-honoured name. But the ages, as they have rolled over London, have left behind them memories not subject to the laws of change. The fire of 1666 destroyed many a goodly church, and hall, and mansion; but not one of the names rendered famous by noble achievements, virtuous deeds, or historical associations, could it consume or blacken. Streets alter, public edifices disappear, houses are pulled down and new ones take their place; but the monuments which consist of the recorded actions, and deeds, and thoughts of the great and good, defy the accidents of time, and are as imperishable as the heavens. Fiction tells us of a city in an African desert where the inhabitants were turned to stone, and there they stood the memorials of their once living selves. And in Athens there was a *second* population besides the evanescent one that crowded her streets and climbed her Acropolis; even the statues which stood in marble beauty by the steps of the temples and the thresholds of the houses. London has more enduring memorials of some who once lived within her walls; and has a *second* population, nobler than the sculptures of Greece and the gods of her mythology. Almost defying calculation as the material wealth of our metropolis may be, unparalleled as 'the value of its shipping and its stores,' its commerce and its money, its estates and their treasures, its arts and its manufactures, its antiquities and its curiosities—all that is surpassed by the moral wealth of its names and memories. 'No material interests, no common welfare can so bind a community together and make it strong of heart, as a history of rights maintained, and virtues incorrupted, and freedom won; and one legend of conscience is worth more to a country than hidden gold and fertile plains.'

Buildings, dingy and dilapidated, or tastelessly modernized, in which great geniuses were born, or lived, or died, are, in connection with such events, transformed into poetic bowers; and narrow, dirty streets, where they are known often to have walked, change into green alleys, resounding with richer notes than ever trilled from bird on brake. Tales of valour and suffering, of heroism and patience, of virtue and piety, of the patriot's life and the martyr's death, crowd thickly on the memory. Nor do opposite reminiscences, revealing the footprints of vice and crime, of evil passions and false principles, fail to rise, fraught with salutary warnings and cautions. The broad thoroughfare is a channel within whose banks there has been rolling for centuries a river of human life, now tranquil as the sky now troubled as the clouds, gliding on in peace, or lashed into storms.

The history of London is the history of our commerce. Here is seen gushing up, in very early times, that stream of industry, activity, and enterprise, which from a rill has swelled into a river, and has borne upon its bosom our wealth and our greatness, our civilization, and very much of our liberty.

The history of London is a history of our literature. Time would fail to tell of all the memorials of genius with which London abounds: memorials of poets, philosophers, historians, and divines, who there have lived, studied, toiled, suffered, and died. No spot in the world, perhaps, is so rich in associations connected with the history of great minds. There is scarcely one of the old streets through which you ramble, or one of the old churches which you enter, but forthwith there come crowding over the minds of the well-informed, recollections of departed genius, greatness, or excellence.

The history of London is the history of our constitution and our laws. There thicken round it most of the great political conflicts between kings and barons, and lords and commons; between feudalism and modern liberty; between the love of ancient institutions and the spirit of progress, from which under God have sprung our civil government and social order.

The history of London is the history of our religion, both in its corrupted and in its purified forms. Early was it a grand seat of Roman worship; numerous were its religious foundations in the latter part of the mediæval age. Here councils have been held, convocations have assembled, controversies have been waged, and truth has been exalted or depressed. St. Paul's Churchyard and Smithfield are inseparably associated with the Reformation. The principles proclaimed from the stone pulpit of the one could not be destroyed by the fires that blazed round the stakes of the other. The history of the Protestant establishment ever since is involved in that of our city; places connected with its grand events, its advocates, and its ornaments, are dear to the hearts of its children; while other spots in London, little known to fame, are linked to the memory of the Puritans, and, reverently traced out by those who love them, become hallowed ground.

The shadows of great kings cross our path as we go through the streets of ancient London. For example, one sees in the dim distance of the fourteenth century, Edward the Black Prince returning from the victory at Poitiers, with John of France as captive; the city making gala day—displaying triumphal arches, tapestry, plate, and arms—and thousands of faces peering out at windows, from the roofs of houses and down church steeples. Then there come gorgeous processions of the prince's father, with knights and squires, on his way to the jousting place in Smithfield; and again the same crowned head is seen with three others—John of France, David of Scotland, and the King of Cyprus—riding down to Henry Picard's mansion in the Vintry, to do the city honour by feasting at the Lord Mayor's hospitable board. Henry the Sixth, too, meets us on London Bridge, and by the help of John Lydgate's MS. of 'the cominge of the king out of France to London,' we are enabled to see all the show; and brave it is: Lord Mayor clothed in velvet, sheriffs and aldermen in scarlet cloaks, crafts of the city in white liveries, the king and nobles in polished armour, the bridge decked out with towers, and cloth of arras, and giants, and emblematical empresses, Nature, Grace, and Fortune, and seven maidens full of mystic meaning, and other quaint devices, through which the inborn spirit of poetry in those romantic times sought to express itself. And later, Queen Elizabeth sweeps along Cheapside, in her progress from the Tower to Westminster. Accompanied by her lords and ladies ' all in crimson velvet, and their horses trapped with the same,' the new sovereign is escorted through the metropolis of her dominions. The city puts itself to great expense that its love and joy may be expressed in pageants, fountains of wine, music, speeches, verses, and the like. And near 'the little conduit at the upper end of Cheapside,' an old man, having a scythe and wings, representative of Father Time, issues from an artificial cave, leading by the hand another personage 'clothed in white silk, gracefully apparelled,' who represents Truth, Time's daughter, having in her hands a book, on which is written *Verbum Veritatis* (the Word of Truth). The lady in white makes a speech to the maiden queen, and hands her the sacred volume, which is taken by a gentleman, and placed in the royal hands. And as soon as she receives it, she kisses it, and holding it up, lays it on her breast, and thanks her faithful Londoners for this present, saying 'she would often read over that book.'

Then follow shadows of great poets. There is Chaucer down at the Tabard Inn, eyeing, from the straggling gallery round the yard, the motley group preparing for their pilgrimage to Canterbury—and beginning already to imprint for all coming ages, the forms and ways and words of those average specimens of English folks in the fourteenth century, who peopled the houses or paced up and down the thoroughfares of London and Southwark. One searches in vain for the place of his birth, though he was a citizen of the metropolis; but a glimpse is caught of him mixed up in municipal strife, as a friend of the famous John of Northampton; and also as beating a Franciscan friar in Fleet Street, for which the poet had to pay a fine of five shillings. Political entanglements brought him to the Tower a prisoner, and some time afterwards we find him quietly renting a house near Westminster Abbey.

Next we observe his friend, 'the moral Gower,' an inhabitant of Southwark—his bones now mouldering in St. Mary Overies—taking boat from some stairs on the Borough side, and meeting Richard II. in his stately barge. The monarch invited the minstrel on board, and desired him to write 'some new thing,' whence arose the 'Confessio Amantis;' and so a production of one of England's early poets becomes associated with the silent highway, and his visions are seen floating over those wide waters.

Shakespeare spent a considerable portion of his time in London, and, in the few authentic notices we have of his life story, his name is indissolubly associated with the Globe, Bankside, and with Blackfriars: but the scanty materials for his biography which the most diligent antiquaries have brought together, afford us scarcely any other local memories of the Stratford bard. Yet in his works there is evidence enough of his acquaintance with London; and the scenes sketched by his magic pencil throw his shadow over Eastcheap, old St. Paul's, Smithfield, Crosby House, the Tower, the Abbey at Westminster, and the London streets, full of the men and women whom he depicts with lifelike touches. And do not the stirring times in which he lived—when England was threatened with the Armada—when London provided her levies— when the masculine queen harangued her troops at Tilbury Fort—appear in such passages as the following?—

> '*King John.* What earthly name to interrogatories
> Can task the free breath of a sacred king?
> Thou canst not, cardinal, devise a name
> So slight, unworthy, and ridiculous,
> To charge me to an answer, as the pope.
> Tell him this tale; and from the mouth of England,
> Add thus much more,—that no Italian priest
> Shall tithe or toll in our dominions;

But as we under heaven are supreme head,
So under Him, that great supremacy,
Where we do reign, we will alone uphold,
Without the assistance of a mortal hand:
So tell the pope; all reverence set apart,
To him and his usurped authority.

  K. Phil. Brother of England, you blaspheme in this.

  K. John. Though you, and all the kings of Christendom,
Are led so grossly by this meddling priest,
Dreading the curse that money may buy out;
And, by the merit of vile gold, dross, dust,
Purchase corrupted pardon of a man,
Who, in that sale, sells pardon from himself;
Though you, and all the rest, so grossly led,
This juggling witchcraft with revenue cherish;
Yet I, alone, alone do me oppose
Against the pope, and count his friends my foes.

    *   *   *   *   *   *

  K. John. The legate of the pope hath been with me,
And I have made a happy peace with him;
And he hath promised to dismiss the powers
Led by the Dauphin.

  Bast. O inglorious league!
Shall we, upon the footing of our land,
Send fair play orders, and make compromise,
Insinuation, parley, and base truce,
To arms invasive?

    *   *   *   *   *   *

This England never did, nor never shall,
Lie at the proud foot of a conqueror,
But when it first did help to wound itself.
Now these, her princes, are come home again,
Come the three corners of the world in arms,
And we shall shock them: nought shall make us rue,
If England to itself do rest but true.'

'This royal throne of kings, this sceptered isle,
This earth of majesty, this seat of Mars
This other Eden, demi-paradise,

> This fortress, built by Nature for herself,
> Against infection and the hand of war;
> This happy breed of men, this little world;
> This precious stone set in the silver sea,
> Which serves it in the office of a wall,
> Or as a moat defensive to a house,
> Against the envy of less happier lands;
> This blessed plot, this earth, this realm, this England.'

> 'All furnished, all in arms;
> All plumed, like estridges that with the wind
> Bated,—like eagles having lately bathed,
> Glittering in golden coats,—like images;
> As full of spirit as the month of May,
> And gorgeous as the sun at midsummer:
> Wanton as youthful goats; wild as young bulls.'

In such majestic verses we find gathered up the burning words of defiance against papal domination, which went from lip to lip through London when awful days of evil seemed coming on. Here, too, we have a picture of the goodly array which went out at the city gate towards Tilbury—and here the proud patriotism which inspired both hosts and queen.

Shadows of Reformers, too, in goodly numbers rise before us; Wicliff, Latimer, Ridley, and many more less known to fame. St. Paul's Churchyard, for example, and Smithfield, are fraught with ennobling reminiscences. We love to think of Henry Monmouth, the alderman who befriended Tyndale, our great translator of the Scriptures; we love to think of the people who gathered round the old cross, and there caught the fire and inspiration of the Reformed faith; we love to think of those who crowded to hear the Bible-readings, and, when the book was proscribed, secreted it in their dwellings, and read it at the risk of liberty and life; we love to think of those who stood and saw the Bible-burnings, and heard the proud anathemas against the study of Heaven's own records, and still went on reading its pages, and drinking in its consolations—

> 'Fierce whiskered guards that volume sought in vain,
> Enjoyed by stealth, and hid with anxious pain;
> While all around was misery and gloom,
> This showed the boundless bliss beyond the tomb.
> Freed from the venal priest, the feudal rod,
> It led the weary sufferer's steps to God;
> And when his painful course on earth was run,
> This, his chief wealth, descended to his son.'

We love to think of those who had piety and courage sufficient to brave the horrors of Lollards' Tower and other dark dungeons, and whose faith and firmness enabled them to triumph over the last fiery trial; we love to see them, while multitudes look upon the painful scene—some mocking the sufferers, some awe-struck at their constancy, some strangely turned by a touch of sympathy at the sight of so much agony and heroism—lift up their placid countenances and hope-beaming eyes to the heaven of liberty and love, whose opening portals invite them to enter.

But we must conclude these general recollections, and proceed to notice certain illustrious names of later times, which have left their imprint very distinctly in London localities with which everybody is familiar.

SHADES OF THE DEPARTED.

I.
MILTON.

MILTON's memory is one of our most frequent and cherished visitants, as we ramble through the streets of London. He meets us in many a spot, which his name, like a spiritual presence, has hallowed; for from first to last of his earthly history he belonged to the mother-city of his native land. It was the scene of his birth and burial, and in various localities within its precincts he also spent the greater portion of his manhood. His love of the beautiful and sublime in Nature was not the outgrowth of scenes that encircled his infant senses, but was itself a living root of poetry in his soul, producing, like leaves and flowers in their springtide freshness and abundance, those aspirations after the beautiful and sublime in Nature which led him to go forth in quest of them; for he could have said, in the words of one gifted with the like endowments,

'I was reared
In the great city—pent mid cloisters dim,
And saw nought lovely but the sky and stars.'

We turn out of the tumultuous traffic of Cheapside into Bread Street—rather comfortless and melancholy-looking, as it strikes us—and soon reach, on the left hand, the site of what was the dwelling of John Milton, scrivener; some old house, we fancy, which rose like inverted steps, story projecting beyond story, till the top, with beetling brows, overshadowed no small portion of the narrow street. We know that a sign hung over the door, bearing the armorial badge of the family, a spread eagle; and under it we seem to stand, on a cold December day, the 28th of the month, in the year of grace 1608, while there issues from the oak-carved doorway the citizen-inhabitant with his wife, a woman known and loved all round the parish for her benevolence; and a nurse bearing in her arms a boy, of whose high mental destiny no one of the little party on their way to the church of Allhallows could ever dream. The Allhallows church of that day was destroyed in the Fire of London; it was replaced by an edifice built by Sir Christopher Wren, which was demolished in 1875. At the side of this church, in Watling Street, was fixed a tablet containing Dryden's lines, and a memorial as follows:—

> 'Three poets in three distant ages born,
> Greece, Italy, and England did adorn;
> The first in loftiness of thought surpast;
> The next in majesty; in both the last.
> The force of Nature could no further go,
> To make a third she joined the other two.
>   JOHN MILTON
> was born in Bread Street on Friday, the 9th day of December, 1608, and was baptized in the parish church of Allhallows, Bread Street, on Tuesday, the 28th day of December, 1608.'[1]

---
[1] This tablet is now fixed in the wall outside Bow Church, Cheapside.

Leaving the shade of the infant, we meet in the close vicinity of his paternal abode the shade of the schoolboy. In St. Paul's Churchyard, opposite the east end of the cathedral, stood St. Paul's School, transferred to a new Gothic building in the Hammersmith High Road in 1884. For more than a century it was familiar to passers-by as a dark imprisoned court, under a stone colonnade, which made itself known from time to time as the playground for the boys in St. Paul's School, by the sportive shouts and the bursts of glee which issued from between the close iron rails. But St. Paul's School, in the first quarter of the seventeenth century, was quite another sort of building. A Gothic edifice in the Tudor style then stood upon the site, probably with open courts patched over with a little green; and thither wended the boy from the Spread Eagle, 'with satchel on back,' to play with his long-since forgotten schoolfellows. He was studious, and, when only twelve years of age, many a time did he sit up till midnight, conning his books, thus not only laying the foundation of his marvellous scholarship, but of his blindness too. Nor was his muse unfledged even then. Ere eleven summers had rolled over him, he would sing of 'the golden-tressed sun,' 'the spangled sisters of the night,' and 'the thunder-clasping hand of the Almighty.' When a youth he must have had a countenance of majestic beauty, judging by what he was in manhood; and with this agrees the legend of the Italian lady, who fell in love with him as she saw him asleep one day beneath a tree.

Descending Ludgate Hill to St. Bride's Churchyard, the shade revisits us, now risen into manliness, and just returned from Italy full of ripe learning and rich taste. Milton took lodgings at the house of one Russel, a tailor, and there educated his two nephews. And in that noisy lodging-place he formed acquaintance with Patrick Young, the librarian of Charles I.; the Republican and the Royalist sympathizing in a common love for literature.

Wherever we meet with the memory of Milton in old London, we find the place so changed that we have to bring back the shades of departed scenes, as well as of the departed man, to give anything like vivid reality to our image of him. Manuscripts in the Middle Ages were defaced and written over again, but antiquaries have deciphered in some cases the original writing, and thus restored the book to what it was of old. A like process Fancy performs in reference to London streets and houses, in these literary perambulations. Ancient scenes defaced, and covered with modern architecture, we endeavour by a little imaginative power to reproduce. It requires rather an effort to do this in the next locality sacred to Milton. 'He made no long stay at his lodging in St. Bride's Churchyard; necessity for having a place to dispose of his books in, and other goods fit for the furnishing of a good handsome house, hastening him to take one; and accordingly *a pretty garden house* he took in Aldersgate Street, at the end of an entry, and therefore the fitter for his turn, by reason of the privacy, besides that there are few streets in London *more free from noise than that.'* Aldersgate Street free from noise! a garden house there! Well, after all we can

MILTON HOUSE, BARBICAN.

fancy it, and there we see him plunging into prose authorship, and writing eloquent books on ecclesiastical reform. He unwisely marries a lady 'accustomed to a great deal of company, merriment and dancing,' and little fitted therefore to sympathize with him in his severe tastes and classic sort of life; so in that garden house there is domestic strife, over which we sorrowfully draw a veil. But he continues still to write and study, and receives more pupils, when storms assail him from without, aroused by the displeasure of the Presbyterian clergy. Then comes domestic reconciliation with Mrs. Milton, at the house of a relative in St. Martin-le-Grand, after which we find him settling in a new house in Barbican. This house, No. 17, was not taken down until 1864, although it had undergone considerable alteration since Milton's time. A modern warehouse occupies its site.

Wandering up High Holborn, again the poet meets us, issuing from his new dwelling, the back of which opened into Lincoln's Inn Fields. His removal there occurred just after the march of the army to London to put down an insurrection which had been excited by Massey and Brown.

Charing Cross, and the region round about, are abundant in associations connected with the Commonwealth. Whitehall was the residence of Cromwell. In 1649 Milton was appointed Latin Secretary to the Council of State, and composed those despatches and documents in his favourite tongue which show what a master he was of its style and rhythm.[1] His biographer Symmons informs us, that, on his appointment, he removed to a lodging in the house of one Thompson, at Charing Cross, and afterwards to apartments in Scotland Yard. Scotland Yard is connected with Whitehall, and perhaps we should identify Milton's residence in the former place with the lodgings in the palace once occupied by Sir J. Hippesley.

This glimpse of the poet is vague and indistinct; and not much more can be said of our view of Milton in his next abode. He removed to Petty France, Westminster, to a 'house next door to the Lord Scudamore's, and opening into St. James's Park.' Petty France is now York Street, but the place where Milton dwelt, lately known as No 19, is no longer to be found; the site being occupied by modern dwelling houses, built on the 'flat' principle. The garden formerly opened upon the park, in what is now called Birdcage Walk. It was never a large house, and shows that the illustrious Secretary of the Foreign Department did not then live in much splendour. His salary was only £280 a year.

It is touching to remember that here his blindness became complete. A letter dated September 28th, 1654, gives an account of the rise and progress of this sad malady. 'It is now about ten years,' he says,

---

[1] Art has depicted Cromwell and Milton together—the man of action and the man of thought; the latter listening to the apparently oratorical-like dictation of the former. We do not think Milton and his master managed things after that fashion. How the Protector gave his instructions to the great Latin Secretary we cannot presume to imagine.

'since I first perceived my sight beginning to grow weak and dim. When I sat down, my eyes gave me considerable pain. If I looked at a candle, it was surrounded by an iris. In a little time a darkness covered the left side of the left eye, which was partially clouded some years before the other intercepted the view of all things in that direction. Objects in front seemed to dwindle in size whenever I closed my right eye; this eye too for three years gradually failing. A few months previous to my total blindness, while I was perfectly stationary, everything seemed to swim backward and forward; and now thick vapours appear to settle on my forehead and temples, which weigh down my lids with an oppressive sense of drowsiness, especially in the interval between dinner and the evening. I ought not to omit mentioning that before I wholly lost my sight, as soon as I lay down in bed, and turned upon either side, brilliant flashes of light used to issue from my closed eyes; and afterwards, upon the gradual failure of my powers of vision, colours proportionably dim and faint seemed to rush out with a degree of vehemence, and a kind of inward noise. These have now faded into uniform blackness, such as ensues on the extinction of a candle, or blackness varied only and intermingled with a dimmish grey. The constant darkness, however, in which I live day and night inclines more to a whitish than a blackish tinge; and the eye in turning itself round admits, as through a narrow chink, a very small portion of light.'

How very affecting is this detail, especially the allusion to the 'narrow chink' which remained in the dark shutter folded over the windows of the eye, to admit mementoes of the precious gift he had for ever lost. But his soul bows with Christian patience to the Divine behest :—

> 'Yet I argue not
> Against Heaven's hand or will, nor bate a jot
> Of heart or hope ; but still bear up, and steer
> Right onward.'

The lustre of his dark grey eye did not fade after blindness had smitten it. His portrait brings him before us, with light brown hair parted in the middle and clustering on the shoulders, and a countenance which, till manhood was advanced, retained its youthful ruddy hue. The remembrance that his stature was of the middle height ; that he was not at all corpulent, but muscular and compact ; his gait erect and manly, bespeaking courage and dauntlessness ; places in our sight the full-length shade of that illustrious personage. Then when we add to it the little anecdote, that he wore, as was the custom of the day, a rapier by his side, we seem to have the living man, walking in at his garden gate out of St. James's Park, leaning on the hand of a servant. The loss of sight was, in a measure, compensated by the exquisite acuteness of his hearing. He judged, as blind men are wont to do, of people's appearance by their voice. 'His ears,' says Richardson, 'were now eyes to him.' No doubt, in that home next Lord Scudamore's, Milton had his organ and bass viol, and would cheer the hours of his unintermitting darkness by music, for which he had a taste by nature. Milton's voice is said to have been sweet and harmonious, and he would frequently accompany the instruments on which he played.

No longer able to guide the pen, he dictated in this same house some of his famous prose works, which, in the nineteenth century, are beginning to attract that notice and study too long denied them. His 'Defence of the People of England' was probably written in Scotland Yard; but his 'Second Defence,' his 'Treatise of Civil Power in Ecclesiastical Causes,' his 'Likeliest Means to remove Hirelings out of the Church,' his 'Present Means and Brief Delineation of a Free Commonwealth,' and some smaller pieces, were all produced in the house we are speaking of. We may add, that in this same house he lost his second wife, to whom he was so tenderly attached.

But it is time to turn eastward. Changes come, and Milton can no longer tarry near the palaces of old England. Too deeply implicated in the proceedings of the Commonwealth, he is forced to hide himself after the Restoration. And as we come near Bartholomew Close, looking out of Smithfield, we are not far from the place of his temporary concealment. Some friend guided and sheltered the blind man from the storm. Its fury past, or turned aside by the influence of some who venerated his genius and character, Milton goes to live in Holborn, near Red Lion Square, and then in Jewin Street. Probably, it was early after the Restoration, and while living in these abodes, that he was not only in darkness, but 'with dangers compassed round,' fearing assassination from some Royalist hand, sleeping ill, and restlessly. In the latter place he marries his third wife ; and there Ellwood, the Quaker, was introduced to him—the kind, patient Ellwood, who sits for hours reading Latin with a foreign accent, and sometimes little understanding what he reads, for the recreation of his now poor but illustrious friend. But highly honoured was that same Ellwood, when the great poet put into his hands a manuscript, asking his opinion of it—which proved to be the 'Paradise Lost.' That scene was a little cottage at Chalfont, in Buckinghamshire, where Milton had gone during the plague ; but in Jewin Street, probably, the great poem was nearly brought to its completion. It was the work of years. Every former strain prepared for it. Prelusive touches had there been from boyhood of rich, sweet, solemn harmony ; but in 'Paradise Lost' came out the prolonged oratorio, swelling forth from the organ of his soul in notes of bird-like sweetness, in tones of deep-pealed thunder. The history of it is probably associated with most of the previous residences of Milton, but in Jewin Street it was nearly perfected, and in our mind wakens some echo of the poet's song whenever we walk along the pavement of that most unpoetic region.

He leaves Jewin Street—for he was strangely changeful in his liking of a residence—and goes to live, we know not where, except that it was to lodge awhile in the house of Millington, the celebrated auctioneer, whom we greatly love and honour for the story told of his leading the bard by the hand when he walked about the streets.

Two doors from the corner of Milton Street, running out of Fore Street, there stood a shop kept by a confectioner, with overhanging storeys rising above it, evidently more than two hundred years old. That, and the adjoining one—both now entirely rebuilt—were originally united, and there, according to local tradition, we have another of Milton's numerous habitations. The house was mean enough, and never could have been very much better; but that circumstance throws no doubt on the tradition, as the lot of our bard after the Restoration was poor and lowly.

Then we come to his last abode in what was Artillery Walk, in Bunhill Fields, in whose vicinity, for Milton's sake alone, we love to linger. While living here, he published both his 'Paradise Lost' and his 'Paradise Regained,' as also the 'Samson Agonistes,' and other works. But we are thinking now more of the man than the author. We see him sitting before his door in a grey coat of coarse cloth, in warm, sultry weather, to enjoy the fresh air; or, walking in with Dr. Wright, an ancient clergyman from Dorsetshire, we find him in a room up one pair of stairs, hung with rusty green, sitting in an elbow chair, clothed in black, and neat enough, pale, but not cadaverous, his hands and fingers gouty and covered with chalk stones. Were he free from the pain he feels, he tells us his blindness would be tolerable. Or we listen to him, as he talks with the Laureate Dryden, who admires the 'Paradise Lost,' and asks leave to put it into a drama in rhyme. Milton, with much civility, tells him '*he will give him leave to tag his verses.*'

Milton's biographers enable us to trace his daily life. He rises early; has a chapter in the Hebrew Bible read to him; then meditates till seven; till twelve he listens to reading, in which he employs his daughters; then takes exercise, and sometimes swings in his little garden. After a frugal dinner he enjoys some musical recreation; at six he welcomes friends; takes supper at eight; and then, having smoked a pipe and drunk a glass of water, he retires to repose. That repose is sometimes broken by poetic musings, and he rouses up his daughter that he may dictate to her some lines before they are lost.

Although neglected by the great among his countrymen, illustrious foreigners search out the man whose literary fame is heard through Europe; and many who came before the Fire of London, ere they left our shores, found the house in Bread Street, with the sign of the Spread Eagle, for even then it was thought a privilege to enter Milton's birthplace. One Englishman of rank, however, is said to have visited him, but the visit was most unworthy in its motive. The Duke of York, as the story goes, expressed a wish to his brother

Charles II. to see old Milton, of whom so much was said. The king had no objection, and soon the duke was on his way to the poet's house, where, on introducing himself, a free conversation took place between these very 'discordant characters.' The duke asked Milton whether he did not consider his blindness to be a judgment inflicted on him for writing against the late king? 'If your highness thinks,' he replied, 'that the calamities which befall us here are indications of the wrath of Heaven, in what manner are we to account for the fate of the king your father? The displeasure of Heaven must, upon this supposition, have been much greater against him than against me; for I have only lost my eyes, but he lost his head.' The duke, disconcerted by the answer, went his way, and exclaimed on reaching the court: 'Brother, you are greatly to blame that you don't have that old rogue Milton hanged.' 'Why, what is the matter, James?' said the monarch; 'you seem in a heat. What! have you seen Milton?' 'Yes,' answered James, 'I have seen him.' 'Well,' said the king, 'in what condition did you find him?' 'Condition—why, he is very old, and very poor.' 'Old and poor, well; and he is blind, too, is he not?' 'Yes, blind as a beetle.' 'Why, then,' observed the merry monarch, 'you are a fool, James, to have him hanged as a punishment; to hang him will be doing him a service; it will be taking him out of his miseries. If he be old, poor, and blind, he is miserable enough: in all conscience let him live.'

But it is time to approach Milton's last resting-place. St. Giles's Church, Cripplegate, is one of the old ecclesiastical structures which escaped the Fire of London. It contains the ashes of John Foxe, the martyrologist, and John Speed, the historian: the mural tablet to the memory of the former, and the effigy which brings before us the grave face and quaint costume of the latter, adorn the right side of the chancel within the altar rails. But from these and other monuments we turn to look at the bust of Milton, placed to the left as you enter the church, on the third pillar from the east end. The spot beneath, now covered with a spacious pew, has been pretty well identified as the poet's grave. To this last earthly home he was borne on the 12th November, 1674, 'the funeral being attended,' according to Toland, ' by the author's learned and great friends in London, not without a friendly concourse of the vulgar.' Milton's funeral must indeed have been a solemn sight! One fancies it slowly winding down from Artillery Walk, through the picturesque streets of the seventeenth century. We have just visited his grave with deep emotion; and we learn it is with Milton dead as it was with Milton living, that more foreigners than Englishmen visit the church in honour of his memory.

Yet though we know so much of the dwelling-places of Milton, how little do we know of his visible presence and his social intercourse! There is a mystery about him, rendering the great poet a shade in the ghostly sense of the expression; at least so it appears to us. We can imagine honest Isaak Walton easily enough—can see him at his business—and go with him a-fishing, and, as he takes off his glove, can shake him by the hand. We are at home at once. And Richard Baxter—we can bring him before our eyes—and listen to him as a friend; and there seems nothing to prevent our opening his study door and sitting down on a chair beside him, to state some case of conscience for his judgment, or some theological difficulty for his solution. But we stand in awe of Milton. There is a magic circle round the man which it would be bold indeed to overstep. Flesh and blood he has like other mortals, but his sympathies seem to be wholly intellectual and spiritual. His inner nature penetrates his outward being, so as to shed an unearthly halo round his face and form, his walk and ways. We should not call Milton a genial man. Of no interview with him could we conceive which might leave the impression of amiableness or sociability. Was it possible for him to be domestic—to take much interest in common everyday life—to chat about the thousand things which most people find interesting now and then?[1] We are at an utter loss to fancy his conversation with his family and friends. It was not magniloquent, for he had no affectation; but surely he spake with an air of grandeur

---

[1] We do not wonder at what we read about the disappointments and misunderstandings of his married life. It must have been a rare daughter of Eve who was fit to be Mistress Milton.

which made folks feel that he and they were not walking on the same level. Not solely to intellectual preeminence do we attribute the production of this feeling —for one can fancy Shakespeare as genial enough, making his inferiors of a distant class feel themselves at home by his fireside at Stratford. Peculiar habits had from some causes, constitutional, or educational, or circumstantial, withdrawn our classic poet and republican philosopher far away from the beaten and crowded walks of human kind, and made him what Wordsworth has so truly described, a star '*which dwelt apart.*'

II.

RICHARD BAXTER.

ONE day, filled with thoughts of olden times, we went down to Whitehall—the stately-looking Whitehall—the palace of so many English kings—with that fine relic of Inigo Jones' architecture, the Banqueting House, still standing, with the memory of something far different from revelry connected with it. The edifice spread out, and other buildings rose around it; and in the street, altogether changed, there stood Holbein's gateway, with its eight medallions. People were going in and coming out, some of them with doublets of silk and collars of pointed lace, wide boots ruffled with lawn, and short mantles thrown over the shoulders, while their heads were crowned with broad-leafed Spanish beavers. There were also men in armour with leather jackets, and people of a very staid appearance with Genevan cloaks and lofty wide-brimmed hats. We fancied we saw one of them walking with a youth, about eighteen years of age, rather sickly looking, with a wonderfully intelligent face, a forehead which bespoke thought, eyes which flashed with earnestness, and a quick step which showed he was not, and never meant to be, an idler. The two were going to the lodgings of Sir Henry

Newport, Master of the Revels; and in at a side door, and up an oak staircase, they vanished. The boy was Richard Baxter, fresh from the country, who had come to seek his fortune at court, as so many did; but he had been brought up in Puritan ways of thinking; and so, as he found that at Whitehall comedies were liked better than sermons, and were even played on a Sunday afternoon, he was very glad to go home again. The youth had read a book by Dr. Sibbs, who lived, and preached, and died in Gray's Inn Lane—a book called 'The Bruised Reed;' one which old Isaak Walton so much valued that he left it to his children; and that book, in the hands of more than a human teacher, had changed his very soul.

If on Richard Baxter's first visit to London the wishes of his friends had been accomplished, instead of a Puritan theologian and a preacher of the Gospel of Christ, he had become a Cavalier, courtier, and a man of fashion, how would the course and issue of his days have varied from what they actually became; and how infinitely different would have been the eternal harvest from that which the holy husbandman has now for some two centuries been reaping in the fields of light!

Walking down the street to Westminster Abbey, we soon saw St. Margaret's Church, like a daughter sitting in her mother's shadow; a building whose painted window in the chancel, and whose historical associations clustering so thick, have been too much thrown into the shade by the architecture and stones of the older and vaster pile. We could not help thinking of Southey's anecdote of Cowper, who, late one evening, was passing through the churchyard, and saw a glimmering light which looked very mysterious, and on approaching found it to be the lantern of a grave-digger, who was just throwing up a skull; an incident which struck the tender-minded youth, and left, as he said, the best religious impression which he received while at Westminster: but the shade that was haunting us belonged to an earlier period; and entering the church, we saw him there. The place seemed very full; and the congregation was grave and very attentive. It was composed of the members of the Restored Parliament after Richard Cromwell had resigned the Protectorate. Everything indicated that the times were unsettled—that poor old England's affairs were out of joint—that the vessel of the State was driven about by storms, and wanted sadly a strong hand to hold the helm. The restoration of the king seemed pretty near, in which some saw much of hope. The preacher in St. Margaret's pulpit on that occasion was no other than the person whom we had seen at Whitehall, long since become a minister. He looked much older now, for thirty more years had rolled over him, and many cares had lined his face. He had on a Genevan gown and broad bands; and the expressive countenance, lighted up with fire as he spoke, was surmounted by a round black cap, from under which there came out thick locks of dark flowing hair. He spoke of differences, and the way to heal them, and insisted that a man could not be Protestant without being loyal. And so he was for the king's return, and pleaded for some comprehensive scheme that should unite in the Church all contending parties.

OLD ST. PAUL'S CATHEDRAL.

As we pass through St. Paul's Churchyard we are again reminded of the Puritan preacher. We recall the cathedral as it was in the year 1660; not St. Paul's with the dome, but St. Paul's with a spire; not with its Italian arcades and decorations, but with its Gothic aisles and choir, and mediæval adornments. That broad nave is a sort of public promenade and thoroughfare, where crowds of London citizens might at times be seen transacting business or seeking pleasure; but now we seem to see it filled with a congregation very grave and thoughtful—and well they may be, for Richard Baxter is delivering to them one of his characteristic discourses, not spiced with political declamation, like so many at the time of the Restoration, but full of plain, scriptural, searching truth, which makes my Lord Mayor and Aldermen, sitting there in their scarlet gowns, look very thoughtful, and causes not a few of the crowded audience to tremble and weep.

His memory haunts many other spots in London. In the street called London Wall, there stood until lately an old-fashioned edifice, known as Sion College, with its almshouses founded by Dr. Thomas White, the vicar of St. Dunstan's in the West, and its library, the munificent gift of John Simson, the rector of St. Olave's, Hart Street. It was removed to a new and handsome building on the Thames Embankment, near Blackfriars Bridge, in 1886, and it is still an occasional gathering-place for the London clergy. In Baxter's time there were famous meetings held there. 'We appointed,' says he, 'to meet from day to day at Sion College, and to consult there openly with any of our brethren that would please to join, that none might say they were excluded. Some city ministers came upon us, and some came not, and divers country ministers who were in the city came also to us; as Dr. Worth, since a bishop in Ireland; Mr. Fulwood, since archdeacon of Totnes; but Mr. Matthew Newcomen was most constant among us.'

Linked with Sion College,[1] not in local neighbourhood, but in biographical association, is the Savoy, so named from a palace built in 1245, by Peter, Earl of Savoy and Richmond. The only relic of the old palace, which was burnt down by the rebels under Wat Tyler, is the Chapel Royal of Mary le Savoy, which was the chapel of the Hospital of St. John the Baptist. The passenger going along Savoy Street, from the Strand to the Thames Embankment, can hardly fail to notice the building on the right-hand side. It is historically remarkable as the scene of the Savoy Conference, which was held there in July 1661.

The Conference was between certain Episcopalians on the one side and certain Presbyterians on the other, for the purpose of revising the Liturgy. It was a fruitless attempt at union. There Baxter went with Dr. Bates and Dr. Jacomb, and others, expecting to have a verbal discussion with the opposite party, and by mutual explanations get at harmonious action; but the plan of free talk which Baxter loved was overruled, and it was determined that he and his brethren should state in writing what they objected to and what they wanted: whereupon they set to work most diligently, the larger part of the task devolving upon Baxter, who not only

[1] Old Sion College was burnt in the Fire of London.

drew up in the main a huge paper of objections, but entirely compiled a reformed Liturgy. The poor man complained, and well he might, that *his papers were never read.* Whatever may be thought of his opinions or his papers, his motives were above suspicion. Earnestly did he desire union; and beautifully did he say, 'I thought it a cause that I could comfortably suffer for, and should as willingly be a martyr for charity as for faith.'

Baxter was one of those men who, honestly intent upon a public purpose, sacrifice to it time and toil, and suppose that those with whom they must confer are just as disinterested and sincere as themselves. But, like all such persons, he was met by some who, whatever might be their professions, were influenced by utterly different views and motives, and who were quite willing to let him read and write, and think over and digest no end of considerations *pro* and *con*, while they were letting the questions which tasked his intellect take a shape and get an answer as best they could from worldly politicians, or were themselves, by craft and intrigue, securing a settlement of the matters on their own side. Thus they attained success by a short and easy cut; while good Richard, in his simplicity, was trying to compass his end by a circuit of most conscientious and self-denying labours.

We must tarry no longer in the Savoy, but hasten off to St. Dunstan's in the West—that handsome church which stands in Fleet Street, hard by Chancery

Lane. No remains of the old building exist, but some old people can remember the clock which projected far into the highway, and the two quaint-looking figures which stood behind to strike the quarters. In that church Richard Baxter used to preach, and amazing congregations of people there were to hear the Puritan Demosthenes. Once on a time, he tells us, 'It fell out in St. Dunstan's Church, in the midst of a sermon, a little lime and dust, and perhaps a piece of a brick or two, fell down in the steeple or belfry, near the boys, so that they thought the steeple and church were falling, which put them all into so confused a haste to get away, that the noise of their feet in the galleries sounded like the falling of stones. The people crowded out of doors, the women left some of them a scarf, and some a shoe behind them, and some in the galleries cast themselves down upon those below, because they could not get down the stairs. I sat down in the pulpit, seeing and pitying their vain distemper, and, as soon as I could be heard, I entreated their silence and went on. The people were no sooner quieted and got in again, and the audience composed, but some who stood upon a wainscot bench, near the communion table, brake the bench with their weight, so that the noise renewed the fear again, and they were worse disordered than before. One old woman was heard at the church door asking forgiveness of God for not taking the first warning, and promising, if God would deliver her this once, she would take heed of coming hither again. When they were again quieted, I went on.' Bates tells us he inproved the catastrophe by saying, 'We are in the service of God to prepare ourselves, that we may be fearless at the great noise of the dissolving world, when the heavens shall pass away, and the elements melt with fervent heat.'

As we go by St. Bride's, the shadow of Baxter going in to preach, meets us there. As we walk through Milk Street—upon which, as the birthplace of Sir Thomas More, Fuller could not help perpetrating the pun, that 'he was the brightest star that ever shone in that Via Lactea'—again we are reminded of our zealous divine, for there he shone as a guiding star to Christ, and there he tells us that Mr. Ashhurst and twenty citizens desired him to preach a lecture, for which they allowed him 40*l.* per annum. The parish church of St. Anne's, Blackfriars, is no more, having never been rebuilt after the Fire of London (the church of St. Andrew by the Wardrobe serving instead): had it remained, it too would have been by association suggestive of Baxter's eloquent memory.

There is a church in Gresham Street, Cheapside, called St. Lawrence Jewry. We recollect stepping in one evening when service was being performed, and not a dozen people were scattered over the place. On its site there stood, before the Fire, a church, described by Stowe as 'fair and large,'which presented a startling contrast to the miserable desolation in service time of its architecturally pretentious successor. Baxter was asked to preach there. He tells us he had no time to study, and was 'fain to deliver a sermon which he had preached before in the country.' So immense was the crowd gathered to hear him, that though he sent the day before to secure room for Lord Braghill and the Earl of Suffolk, yet when they came there was no possibility of getting near enough to listen. So they had to go home again. The Earl of Warwick stood in the lobby, and the minister of the church was obliged to sit in the pulpit behind the preacher. 'He was fain to get up into the pulpit,' says Baxter, 'and sit behind me, and I stood between his legs.' We can imagine the congregation in that old church :—aisles, galleries, and stairs filled to overflowing—the people clustering about the windows like bees—all intent upon what the preacher was saying, as with awful earnestness he warned them against the sin of 'making light' of the Gospel and of Christ.

'Men,' said he, 'have houses and lands to look after, they have wife and children to mind, they have their body and outward estate to regard; therefore, they forget that they have a God, a Redeemer, a soul to mind. These matters of the world are still with them. They see these; but they see not God, nor Christ, nor their souls, nor everlasting glory. These things are near at hand, and therefore work naturally, and so work forcibly; but the others are thought on as a great way off, and therefore too distant to work on their affections or be at the present so much regarded by them. Their body hath life and sense; therefore, if they want meat or drink or clothes, will feel their want and tell them of it, and give them no rest till their wants be supplied, and therefore they cannot make light of their bodily necessities: but their souls in spiritual respects are dead, and therefore feel not these wants, but will let them alone in their greatest necessities, and be as quiet when they are starved and languishing to destruction as if all were well and nothing ailed them. And hereupon poor people are wholly taken up in providing for the body, as if they had nothing else to mind. They have their trades and callings to follow, and so much to do from morning to night, that they can find no time for matters of salvation. Christ would teach them, but they have no leisure to hear Him. The Bible is before them, but they cannot have time to read it. A minister is in the town with them, but they take no opportunity to go and inquire of him what they should do to be saved. And when they do hear, their hearts are so full of the world and carried away with their lower matters, that they cannot mind the things which they hear. They are so full of the thoughts, and desires, and cares of this world, that there is no room to pour into them the waters of life. The cares of the world do choke the Word and make it unfruitful. Men cannot serve two masters, God and mammon; but they will lean to the one and despise the other. He that loveth the world, the love of the Father is not in him. Men cannot choose but set light by Christ and salvation, while they set so much by anything on earth. It is that which is highly esteemed among men that is abominable in the sight of God. Oh, this is the ruin of many souls! To see how the world fills people's mouths, their hands, their houses, their hearts; and Christ hath little more than a bare title to come into their company, and to hear no discourse but about the world; to come into their houses, and to hear and see nothing but for the world, as if this world would last for ever, or would purchase them another. When I ask sometimes the ministers of the Gospel how their labours succeed, they tell me, "People continue still the same, and give themselves up wholly to the world, so that they mind not what ministers say to them nor will give any full entertainment to the Word, and all because of this deluding world."'

Now, that was preaching of a kind to rouse attention and excite inquiry, and carry home burning truths to the hearts of men; and with a beseeching voice and melting manner, such as Baxter is said to have commanded, it was just the preaching, not only to gather crowds, but to create a revival of religion and save the souls of men. Sylvester says of him, with as much force as quaintness: 'He had a moving pathos and useful acrimony in his words, neither did his expressions want that emphatical accent which the matter did require. When he did speak of weighty concerns you might find his very spirit drenched therein.'

We must walk down to the Borough, and pause by the Park Street Brewery, to remember that there stood formerly a timber edifice, where Mr. Wadsworth's congregation was accustomed to assemble. 'Just when I was kept out of Swallow Street,' says Baxter, 'his flock invited me to Southwark, where, though I refused to be their pastor, I preached many months in peace, there being no justice willing to disturb us.'

Passing through Bloomsbury Square, we are again in the footsteps of this persecuted one. There he lived in what he calls his 'pleasant and convenient house,' and there died Mistress Margaret, his wife,—of whom Howe said, in his funeral sermon for her, that she displayed 'a strangely vivid and great wit, with very sober conversation.'

Baxter was sent to gaol. We see him taken there as we pass by Clerkenwell Prison; but have far more vivid images of him and his sufferings as we visit Westminster Hall. A thousand memories gather round the former from the time when Rufus built the first edifice down to the present day; but among the crowds of the good and the evil, who, as we pace up and down beneath the oak-raftered roof, 'come like shadows, so depart,' we single out, with special honour, our great divine; and there, in what was the Court of King's Bench, we think we see the whole of the process—for trial it cannot be called—before the infamous Jeffreys, when Baxter was arraigned and sentenced for publishing his notes on the New Testament. There sits the

Chief Justice in his ermine. There are the counsel for the prosecution and the defence. There stands, in conscious rectitude, the arraigned, like Paul before Festus. We hear the miserable mockery of the Puritans from one who ought to have held even-handed the balance of justice, squeaking and snorting in pretended imitation of their tone and manner; and we catch the smart reply of Pollexfen, Baxter's counsel: 'Why, my lord, some will think it hard measure to stop these men's mouths, and not let them speak through their noses.' Then comes a torrent of abuse: 'Come, what do you say for yourself, you old knave? I'm not afraid of you for all the snivelling calves you have got about you'—looking at the people in tears. 'Does your lordship think any jury will pretend to pass a verdict upon me upon such a trial?' asks Baxter. 'I'll warrant you, Mr. Baxter,' says the man in the red robe; 'don't you trouble yourself about that.' No story more arouses our indignation than this of the doings at Westminster in 1685.

Matthew Henry visited Baxter when he was confined 'within the rules,' and found him cheerful and resigned. He says: 'I went into Southwark, to Mr. Baxter; I was to wait upon him once before, and then he was busy. I found him in pretty comfortable circumstances, though a prisoner, in a private house near the prison, attended on by his own man and maid. My good friend, Mr. S(amuel) L(awrence), went with me. He is in as good health as one can expect; and, methinks, looks better and speaks heartier than when I saw him last. The token you sent he would by no means be persuaded to accept, and was almost angry when I pressed it. From one outed as well as himself he said he did not use to receive; and I understand his need is not great. We sat with him about an hour. I was glad to find that he so much approved of my present circumstances. He said he knew not why young men might not improve as well by travelling abroad. He inquired for his Shropshire friends, and observed that of those gentlemen who were with him at Wem, he hears of none whose sons tread in their fathers' steps but Colonel Hunt's. He inquired about Mr. Macworth's and Mr. Lloyd's (of Aston) children. He gave us some good counsel to prepare for trials; and said the best preparation for them was a life of faith, and a constant course of self-denial. He thought it harder constantly to deny temptations to sensual lusts and pleasures, than to resist one single temptation to deny Christ for fear of suffering—the former requiring such constant watchfulness; however, after the former, the latter will be the easier. He said, we who are young are apt to count upon great things, but we must not look for them; and much more to this purpose. He said he thought dying by sickness usually much more painful and dreadful than dying a violent death; especially considering the extraordinary supports which those have who suffer for righteousness' sake.'

This leads us to Charterhouse Square, where once Venetian ambassadors lived in palaces. Howell says, in

1651, 'The yard hath lately been conveniently railed, and made more neat and comely.' There are still rails, but no palaces; yet have the houses an air of old-fashioned comfort and old English domesticity. Baxter died in Charterhouse Square. We have tried to ascertain whether the house is in existence, but in vain; yet we can never go near it without thinking of his calm, hopeful, joyous deathbed, thus described by his friend Sylvester:—

'I went to him, with a very worthy friend, Mr. Mather, of New England, the day before he died; and speaking some comforting words to him, he replied, "I have pain; there is no arguing against sense, but I have peace, I have peace." I told him, you are now approaching to your long-desired home; he answered, "I believe, I believe." He said to Mr. Mather, "I bless God that you have accomplished your business; the Lord prolong your life." He expressed great willingness to die; and during his sickness, when the question was asked, "How he did?" his reply was, "*Almost well.*" His joy was most remarkable when in his own apprehensions death was nearest; and his spiritual joy was at length consummated in eternal joy. 'On Monday,' says Sylvester, 'about five in the evening, Death sent his harbinger to summon him away. A great trembling and coldness extorted strong cries from him, for pity and redress from Heaven; which cries and agonies continued for some time, till at length he ceased, and lay in patient expectation of his change. Being once asked by his faithful friend and constant attendant in his weakness, Mrs. Bushel, his housekeeper, whether he knew her or not, requesting some sign of it if he did; he softly cried, "Death, death!" He now felt the benefit of his former preparations for the trying time. The last words that he spoke to me, on being informed I was come to see him, "Oh, I thank him, I thank him;" and turning his eye on me, he said, "The Lord teach you how to die."'

In Christ Church, near the communion table, we stand over his grave. There his beloved Margaret was entombed in 1681. It was the highest next the old altar or table in the chancel, on which her daughter had caused a very fair, rich, large marble stone to be laid twenty years before. The fair, rich marble stone was broken in the Fire of London. The church was in ruins when Mrs. Baxter was buried there. The present edifice was rising to its completion when, in 1691, the laborious minister of Christ was buried beside his wife.

Richard Baxter was one of the most earnest workers that the world ever saw. Many an old church in London echoed with his earnest preaching. Many an old house could bear witness to his earnest pastoral visitations. Many a quiet study—for the good man had often to change his abode, in those troublous times—saw his earnest reading, writing, watching, and praying. Many a printing-press was occupied in the production of the books he wrote; which, as we number the reprints on our shelves, and think of those which have never reached a modern edition, make us feel that it would fill any man's life with hard work to write out all those pages for the printers' hands. And many a MS. in Dr. Williams' Library, never published, affords additional evidence, as we can testify from personal examination, of Baxter's almost unparalleled industry.

To notice one memorial of Baxter of another kind. In the British Museum is preserved a large stone resembling the kidney in shape, extracted after his death, the cause of his intense sufferings. The catalogue he gives of his diseases is quite appalling. He seems to have had centred in his frail body all the ills that flesh is heir to. It is wonderful to think of his afflictions,—of what deep waters he had to wade through,—what terrible billows he breasted, and how the floods rose higher as life advanced—how the sharpest trials were the last. Richard Baxter's life would be to us an utterly hopeless mystery, did we not believe in Him who has brought life and immortality to light by the Gospel, and who, by the discipline of pain as well as of labour, prepared him for the restful services of another and a higher existence. Some are fitted for heaven by toil alone—or chiefly; others by tears alone—or chiefly. Baxter underwent both kinds of meetening for the inheritance of the saints, and in almost equal degrees. Now he is where they serve but do not suffer; where they work, but do not weep; where the cessation of pain is experienced, and the discipline of pain is ended, and the mystery of pain is fully and for ever solved.

III.
ISAAK WALTON AND HIS FRIENDS.

PERHAPS a scene of greater bustle, compressed in a space so narrow, could hardly anywhere be found, than may be daily witnessed about noon, and for some hours afterwards, in the immediate vicinity of the Temple Bar Memorial. What a host of jostling wayfarers on the pavement—like motes in a sunbeam—pressing on, as if heedless of one another's presence, exhibiting very plainly curious specimens of mental abstraction, and affording inexhaustible materials for speculation on their thoughts and schemes. How the crowd stops, swells, gurgles, at the corner of Chancery Lane,—like a dammed-up mill-stream,—while some gigantic waggon or awkward omnibus impedes the passage, and leaves eager walkers on both sides like people on the shores of a river waiting for a ferry-boat. Then, how confused is the assemblage of vehicles in the middle of Fleet Street, rattling with noisy earnestness and terrific speed, till, like a huge mass of machinery, it overdoes itself, a piece gets out of order, and the whole is stopped. And now what perplexity and impatience! Omnibuses, carts, carriages, cabs, barrows, and other indescribable things, become locked—anything but lovingly—in each other's embrace; some elegant chariot striving to get free from the arms of a brewer's dray, or some aristocratic 'Clarence' tearing itself from the rude clasp of a plebeian 'Hansom.' A little opening made, and no leaders of a forlorn hope ever more boldly rush into the breach, than do barristers with wigs, and attorneys with blue bags, and bankers' clerks with leather cases full of bills, plunge into the vacant space, and thread their way through its perilous windings.

Are there any shadows of bygone times and men departed, bringing up memorials of the solemn, romantic, picturesque, and tender, meeting us amidst *this* scene of bustle? Indeed there are. If there be no spot more strikingly expressive of the present, there is not one in London more richly and variously redolent of the past. Here we are in the midst of the old Inns of Court, which arose in the infancy of the legal profession in England, and which were in the full bloom of their quaint dramatic splendour in the reign of James I. Under the narrow gateway, nearly opposite Chancery Lane, you enter the Temple, now the home of lawyers, once the abode of knights, who, in coats of mail and cross-decked mantles, reined their steeds in gaudy procession along this thoroughfare; or bowed their knees on the pavement of the famous round church, whose architecture places us in the very midst of the thirteenth century. Yonder house, with some traces of antiquity lingering on it still, was once, as the inscription on it imports, the palace of Henry VIII.

and Cardinal Wolsey; and one sees bluff Harry and the cardinal issuing forth from long since vanished portals on their way to the setting of the city watch on Midsummer Eve.

But it is not our intention to call back the shades of knights-templars, or great lawyers, or city functionaries; nor yet to walk and talk with the spirits of the famous wits, from Ben Jonson to Addison, who frequented the house where now stands Child's Bank; nor yet to step in and look at Goldsmith, in his lodgings within Brick Court, or Johnson, at No. 1, Middle Temple Lane: that we may do some future day. Our thoughts are now fixed on one who was far removed in habit from men of the sword, gentlemen of the bar, and civic officials, but who, though neither a professed poet or philosopher, had in him some elements of both. We are thinking of old Isaak Walton, the immortal angler.

This seems hardly the place for meeting him. We associate his name with silvery rivers and green meadows, trout streams and shady banks. How distinctly does his form, in the costume of the seventeenth century, appear before us, and how smilingly does his open countenance, with flowing hair, give us friendly greeting as we ramble alongside of the Lea, near Hoddesdon! And then in Dovedale, the romantic Dovedale, as we once wandered through its rock-girt and tree-crested avenues, and sat down and watched the stream, and the floating of dead leaves we threw into the water—did we not see Isaak himself, with rod and line and basket; and, as evening drew on, and the hills became a dark blue, and a deep shade gathered over the dale, did we not seem to hear him bidding goodnight to the scene of his day's sport, saying, 'Go thy way, little Dove; thou art the prettiest of rivers, and the fullest of fish, that I ever saw'? But, after all, with the neighbourhood of Temple Bar, Isaak Walton had more to do than with either the Lea or the Dove. It was here he lived. We have no traces of his house remaining now, but we can identify the site. There lies before us an old print of part of Fleet Street, showing the end of Chancery Lane. It reminds us more of a street in old Paris, or Frankfort, or some Flemish city, than of anything to be found in the vicinity now. There is a tall narrow house of five stories at the corner, with bay windows carved and adorned in front, the edges of the stories supported by odd-looking corbels like caryatides, and the old dwelling crowned with a thatch roof. The second, a narrower strip of building, is a little modern; then comes the third, lower and broader than the first, with windows along the whole front. Here lived Isaak Walton.

Sir John Hawkins found an old deed, dated 1624, in which this house is described as abutting on a house bearing the sign of the Harrow, and as being in the joint occupation of Isaak Walton and John Mason, hosier; whence he concludes that half a shop was sufficient for the business of Walton. This makes some critical antiquaries rather angry. They consider

Isaak was a man of more worldly importance than this would indicate. He was a Hamburg merchant, say they, not needing much frontage, but letting a part of it off to a hosier, while he retained the whole dwelling-house. Be it so; it appears not unlikely that Walton was above a little shopkeeper, since he had alliances and friendship with the great and wealthy. Walton took this house, we may imagine, in consequence of his intending to get married, for in 1623 he began, he says, a happy affinity with the family of his first wife, Rachel Floud, a descendant of Archbishop Cranmer, to whom he was married in 1626.

Walton was born at Stafford, on the 9th of August, 1593, and it is conjectured that he served his apprenticeship, as a hosier, to a relative of his of the same name in Whitechapel. Shadows of the boy Walton—belonging to a time when London apprentices were still a distinct and recognized class, though less boisterous and ungovernable than they had been—may therefore flit before our eyes the next time we go into that region of butchers' shops; but it is in Fleet Street, No. 3 from Chancery Lane, that we get our first distinct view of the genial fisherman. He did not publish his 'Angler' there, nor any of his works; yet with the hosiery or Hamburg trade, we doubt not, he associated, when a young man, not only his love for the rod and line, but an inkling after old books. He not only visited Mr. Margrave, who dwelt among the booksellers in St. Paul's Churchyard—and Mr. John Stubbs, near to the

Swan, in Golden Lane, to purchase tackle—and went out on fine May mornings for a fishing excursion in the neighbourhood of Ware—and snatched a few hours on a summer day to throw in a line from London Bridge for the 'leather-mouthed' roach, which, he says, were there 'the largest and fattest in this nation,'—but he sat down many a long winter night, with his wife Rachel, conning black-letter volumes of history, divinity, and poetry. And we may well fancy that though none of his own works issued from the press while he lived in Fleet Street, there were in that old house growing up within him, some of the curious thoughts he expressed in his 'Angler,' for the book is an image of himself—just a revelation of the man Walton—as his brother-in-law Robert Floud, a frequent visitant no doubt at Fleet Street, used afterwards to tell him :—

> 'This book is so like you, and you like it,
> For harmless mirth, expression, art, and wit,
> That I protest ingenuously, 'tis true,
> I love this mirth, art, wit, the book and you.'

Most probably, too, in this very house he began to collect materials for his charming 'Life of Master Richard Hooker;' since George Cranmer, his wife's uncle, with whom, at the time we refer to, Walton must have been on intimate terms, had been one of Hooker's pupils. It requires no great stretch of imagination to see and overhear Walton and Cranmer talking about old times; the latter telling the former of the great divine, his manner of life, his learning and meekness, his devotion and charity; and the former putting down, from the lips of the latter, in the thick, cramped handwriting with which his autographs have made us familiar, facts and observations which became the germ of this invaluable piece of biography.

We are also within a few paces of another dwelling, in which the author and angler domiciled. Ten years after he came to Fleet Street he went to live a few doors up Chancery Lane; there two sons were born, and his poor wife died, in 1640, after giving birth to an infant daughter. The same year Walton published his 'Life of Dr. Donne,' prefixed to the sermons of that eloquent divine. He also is one of the *genii loci* belonging to the region, and his shadow meets us in company with his illustrious parishioner, for he was vicar of the parish of St. Dunstan, to which the house we have noticed belonged. We can see the vicar, with cropped hair, open forehead, arched eyebrows, full eyes, handsome nose and lips, thick moustache, peaked beard, and high ruffed collar, sitting in the brown oak parlour of his friend; and then we go with Walton to the Church of St. Dunstan, when Donne preached from the text, 'To God the Lord belong the issues of death.' 'Many that then saw his tears,' says Walton, 'and heard his faint and hollow voice, professed they thought the text prophetically chosen, and that Dr. Donne had preached his own funeral sermon.' The good man was well fit to die, for Walton tells us he said: ' Though of myself I have nothing to present to Him but sin and misery, yet I know He looks not upon me now as I am of myself, but as I am in my Saviour, and hath given me even at this present time some testimonies by His Holy Spirit that I am of the number of the elect; I am therefore full of inexpressible joy, and shall die in peace.' In anticipation of his death, the worthy divine did an odd thing with a pious intent, which had in it a dash of quaintness rather peculiar even in that quaint age. 'A monument being resolved on,' Walton tells us, 'Dr. Donne sent for a carver to make him in wood the figure of an urn, giving him directions for the compass and height of it, and to bring with it a board of the just height of his body. These being got, then without delay a choice painter was got, to be in readiness to draw his picture, which was taken as followeth: Several charcoal fires being first made in his large study, he brought with him into that place his winding-sheet in his hand, and having put off all his clothes, had this sheet put on him, and so tied with knots at his head and feet, and his hands so placed, as dead bodies are usually fitted to be shrouded and put into their coffin or grave. Upon this urn he thus stood, with his eyes shut, and with so much of the sheet turned inside as might show his lean, pale, and deathlike face, which was purposely turned toward the east, from whence he expected the second coming of his and our Saviour, Jesus. In this posture he was drawn at his just height, and when the picture was fully finished, he caused it to be set by his bedside, where it continued and became his hourly object till his death, and was then given to his dearest friend and executor, Dr. Henry King, then chief residentiary of St. Paul's, who caused him to be thus carved in one entire piece of white marble, as it now stands in that church.'

This strange sort of monument is preserved, with other relics of old St. Paul's, in the crypt of the present cathedral. Just after the picture was drawn as above described, Donne 'sent for several of his most considerable friends, of whom he took a solemn and deliberate farewell, commending to their considerations some sentences useful for the regulation of their lives, and then dismissed them, as good Jacob did his sons, with a spiritual benediction.' We enter the bedchamber, cold and stately, with wainscot furniture and tester bed, and there see the faithful and affectionate Walton, whose soul was formed to be an altar for the fire of friendship, reverently bending over his loved and honoured minister. He tells us of unknown mournful friends who repaired to the tomb of 'Donne, as Alexander the Great did to the grave of the famous Achilles, and strewed it with an abundance of curious and costly flowers.' We are ready to think he was himself one of the number. How beautiful the reflection he makes over the sepulchre in old St. Paul's: 'He was earnest and unwearied in the search of knowledge, with which his vigorous soul is now satisfied, and employed in a continual praise of that

God who first breathed it into his active body—that body which once was a temple of the Holy Ghost, and is now become a small quantity of Christian dust. But—' he adds, with sublime simplicity, the noble fruit of Christian faith—'I shall see it reanimated.'

Walton did not remain long in the parish after Donne had gone to heaven. His many bereavements there threw sad associations over the place. He could not read, and go a-fishing pleasantly, as he had done. His losses made him look at things in the neighbourhood through a melancholy medium, which darkly tinged all he saw; so he took leave of the place, and we lose sight of him for a while altogether. He goes off into darkness and silence, whither the antiquaries follow and look for him in vain, till years after his shadowy presence brightens upon us somewhere about Clerkenwell.

Troublous times came over England in 1640, indeed had long before come over it, but now burst into a storm. London was often in fierce commotion. King and Parliament, Parliament and royal army, agitated the citizens from Temple Bar to Whitechapel. Men plunged into political strife, felt with vehemence, and acted with energy. Out of all this the shadow of our angler seems to glide away in quest of Nature's peace and loveliness. While Cavalier and Puritan were sharpening their swords for earnest strife, 'Isaac went out to meditate in the field at the eventide.' He was no party man, and had friends whom he retained on both sides, though his sympathies were doubtless with the Royalists; and, indeed, we find him entrusted with one of the badges of the Order of the Garter—the lesser George, as it is called, which Charles II. had delivered up to a friend for safe keeping after the battle of Worcester. 'It was,' says Ashmole, a friend of Walton's, 'strangely preserved by Colonel Blague, one of that king's dispersed attendants, who resigned it for safety to the wife of Mr. Barlow, of Blarepipe House, in Staffordshire, where he took sanctuary; from whom Robert Milward, Esq., received and gave it into the hands of Mr. Isaak Walton (all loyalists). It came again into Blague's possession, then prisoner in the Tower, whence making his escape, he restored it to King Charles II.' We suppose Walton gave or sent the treasure to the captive in the Tower. The quiet man of the angle was trustworthy and unsuspected. 'He was well known,' says his friend in the Heralds' Office, 'and as well beloved of all good men.'

Walton has been vastly praised for his moderation, meekness, and quietness. He disliked 'the active Romanists,' and 'the restless Nonconformists,' and was himself 'one of the passive and peaceable Protestants' whose character he so much preferred. Now, with all our love and veneration for honest Isaak, we must think that this same peaceableness of his has been over-estimated. 'In general and most certainly,' says Dr. Arnold, 'with our country life, and our English constitutions, partaking something of the coldness of our northern climate, it is extraordinary that any should have regarded this as a rare virtue, and praised the meekness of those who being themselves well-off, and having all their own desires contented, do not trouble themselves about the evils which they do not feel, and complain of the noisy restlessness of the beggars in the street, while they are sitting at their ease in their warm and comfortable rooms. Isaak Walton might enjoy his angling undisturbed, in spite of Star Chamber, ship-money, High Commission Court, or popish ceremonies: what was the sacrifice to him of letting the public grievances take their own way, and enjoying the freshness of a May morning in the meadows on the banks of the Lea?'

Between the writer of these eloquent words and Isaak Walton, as between the subject of this present chapter and the last, as great a contrast exists as well can be. Baxter and Arnold were both earnest men—not only realizing as they did, both of them, the great spiritual truths of the Bible in relation to their own souls, but looking at them in their social aspects and bearings—and longing to see a perfected commonwealth, and a pure and comprehensive Church; and labouring to reduce their ideal visions of these things to facts, and that with the force of their whole nature, which, in each of them, was as a cloud, 'that moveth all together if it move at all.' Men of the calibre of Baxter and Arnold make our confessors and our reformers—the true heroes of our country and of Christendom—those who do the double work, each painful in its turn, of pulling down what is old and rotten, and building up what is new and strong. For the overturning of error, for the exposition and establishment of truth, of course we must not look to men of the Isaak Walton stamp. If England had had no other sons, we are afraid there would have been neither reform nor Puritanism, and the letting things alone to go and angle, or even write quaint and beautiful books like Walton's 'Angler,' and Walton's 'Lives,' would have entailed an amount of mental slavery and moral impotence on the England of this hour, which would have been a curse to every one of us. We are not blaming Walton, for he was not cut out for a reformer; his quiet neglect of the stormy questions of the day was not a vice, neither was it a virtue—not censurable, neither was it admirable—but simply the following out of a natural tendency. But if any do set up Isaak as a model for all times and for all men, then we do demur most decidedly to their unwise judgment, and have no sympathy with their narrow admiration.

Walton mentions Ashmole in the 'Compleat Angler,' and takes us down to his house at Lambeth, near London, where he shows us the antiquary's curiosities, abounding in specimens of natural history—to the heart's delight of the author, who pores over them there with unutterable interest. He enumerates the 'hog-fish, the dog-fish, the dolphin, the coney-fish, the parrot-fish, the shark, the poison-fish, the sword-fish and other *incredible* fish;' also the salamander and bird of paradise, snakes and solan geese, not forgetting the barnacles, which were said to grow on trees within shells like eggs, and then to drop off, and come out, soon to fledge and take their place with winged creatures—all of which is duly illustrated in a large woodcut in Gerard's 'Herbal.' In such recreations we can see Walton and Ashmole seeking relief from the angry storms of politics and war.

After leaving Chancery Lane, Walton married Anne Ken, half-sister of the nonjuring bishop of that name— a circumstance which links him with another of the celebrities of that age, though Ken did not perform the act which has made his memory so famous in English history till after Walton's death. The resistance of James the Second's commands by the seven bishops, who were imprisoned in the Tower, and afterwards so triumphantly acquitted, did not occur till 1687.

Walton died in 1683. In his will he devised to his son-in-law, Doctor Hawkins, and his wife, his 'title and right of, or in part of, a house and shop in Paternoster Row,' which he held by lease from the Lord Bishop of London for about fifty years to come. This lease he took in 1662 and the house was called the Cross Keys. Though he resided about that time very much with his friend Dr. Morley, then recently made Bishop of

Winchester, whose residence was in Cheyne Walk, Chelsea, yet his name certainly becomes associated with the realm of the booksellers; and we think of Isaak in Paternoster Row; as, indeed, independently of any local connection through residence or property, we could not help being reminded of him there, since his popular works bring before us the shadow of his presence, looking down upon us invitingly from the shelves of every bibliopolist's shop.

We are no lovers of angling; for, besides thinking there is cruelty in the sport, we believe we can better employ our time even in the way of recreation—though this is a daring thing to say in the presence of Walton's shade, whose portrait, lying before us as we write, seems to knit its brows while we pen the words. Yet, for all that, we love Walton's 'Angler.' There is a soft, gentle, benignant spirit pervading the whole, which irresistibly soothes us, when harassed with business and wearied with toil. We apprehend, that if we were to try to reduce to practice the fishing rules of the renowned author, we should, like Washington Irving, hook ourselves instead of the fish, and tangle our line in every tree, lose our bait, break our rod, and give up the attempt in despair, confessing that 'angling is something like poetry—a man must be born to it.' But reading his book,—not only under the green trees, but by the fireside, and even in an omnibus going home from the city at eventide—has often refreshed us like the murmur of the brooks, and the fragrance of the cowslips, and the song of the early birds he so sweetly talks of. And if, perchance, we be careful and troubled about many things, and wonder how we are to obtain what is needful in this crowded world, so full of competition, it does us good to muse upon such a passage as this : 'When I would beget content and increase confidence in the power and wisdom and providence of Almighty God, I will walk the meadows by some gliding stream, and there contemplate the lilies that take no care, and those very many other little living creatures that are not only created, but fed (man knows not how) by the goodness of the God of Nature, and therefore trust in Him.'

But much as we admire his 'Angler,' we admire, in some respects, his 'Lives' still more ; for though there are sentiments expressed and opinions indicated, with which we do not agree, we have brought before us portraitures of piety, especially in the characters of Hooker, Donne, and Herbert, which may well awaken our Christian sympathies, and stimulate us to holy imitation. But we are losing the shadow of the man among his books. We can trace him no further. In his last days he lived away from London with his son-in-law. He lies buried in Winchester Cathedral.

We come back to Fleet Street, and pass under the shadow of the Law Courts at the midnight hour. The moon is up, and little stars are opening their eyes and smiling over the city of sleepers. The streets are now still, very still, almost like the disentombed Pompeii.

A few hours have made a mighty difference. The busy, noisy, bustling crowds have disappeared and melted away in silence. So, in a few years, writer and reader will disappear, and sleep the long sleep in the land of silence, where Walton, and Donne, and Ashmole, and all the rest of that generation, have been for two centuries. We shall leave no shadow behind us, such as some of them have done. The most we can expect is that our children, perhaps our children's children, will sometimes think of us, and perchance image to themselves their ancestor from an old portrait we may leave behind. Where then will the still living and conscious spirit be? Will it be in that glorious world of which Walton used to think in the dead hour of night, as he walked in some favourite grove? 'He that at midnight, when the very labourer sleeps securely, should hear, as I have very often, the clear airs, the sweet descants, the natural rising and falling, the doubling and redoubling of her voice, might well be lifted above earth, and say: Lord, what music hast Thou provided for the saints in heaven, when Thou affordest bad men such music on earth!'

IV.

ANDREW MARVELL AND LORD WILLIAM RUSSELL.

WHEN travelling in Switzerland, and walking on the edge of some magnificent glacier—for example, creeping down the rocky ledges of the sides of Montanvert to the Mer de Glace—we have been struck, as everybody is, with the marvellous contrasts in adjacent objects; for while standing in this region of everlasting winter, touching, or almost touching, with his foot the thick-ribbed ice, the traveller can pluck a beautiful nosegay out of the rhododendrons which there grow in beds of rich pink bloom, in these borders of far-spread frost and snow. This frequently occurs to us now as an image of what we see, and of the associated thoughts which occupy our minds as we ramble about London. Poverty and wealth, vulgarity and refinement, ignorance and learning, wretchedness and joy, vice and virtue, crime and integrity, profaneness and religion, death and life, here come into close neighbourhood, and stand arrayed face to face in irreconcilable opposition, on the sides of our pathway. Illustrations of such a kind belonging to the present are yielded in abundance; in like manner, they come before us as we dwell upon the past.

Do you not sometimes pass through the region around Drury Lane and Covent Garden? It abounds in associations of profligacy. The haunts of the depraved lie there in nearest neighbourhood. Its history tells of licentious wits and abandoned rakes, from the days of the Stuarts downwards. Sad reflections come, not only as we speculate on the probable future of those who now in that vicinity pursue their career of sinful pleasure and degrading revelry, but as we think of the present state, in the invisible regions, of many who long since figured here, and have left their names imprinted in the annals of this spot in infamous notoriety.

Passing away from those miserable beings, we meet hard by, as an example of the indicated contrast, the shade of one of the most pure and incorrupt of English worthies. In Maiden Lane lived Andrew Marvell. Cast on times when bribery scarcely knew any bounds, when most men's political consciences had their price, and could be bought by the Government, if only gold enough were paid, this remarkable man was proof against all the tempting offers which were made to belie his convictions and betray his country. There he was, in that very Maiden Lane, in humble lodgings, just going to pick the remains of a bone of mutton, without a guinea in his pocket—in fact, on the point of sending to a friend to borrow one, when my Lord Treasurer Danby ascended the stairs with a message and bribe from Charles II. His lordship was Marvell's schoolfellow, and thought that it only required a little tact to win over this poor but formidable statesman. He professed to wish a renewal of their old acquaintance, and on leaving the room slipped into his hand an order on the Treasury for 1,000*l*. As the courtier was stepping into his chariot, Marvell called after him : 'My lord, I request another moment.'

They went up again to the garret, and Jack, the servant boy, was called.

'Child, what had I for dinner yesterday ? '

'Don't you remember, sir, you had the little shoulder of mutton that you ordered me to bring from a woman in the market ? '

'Very right, child. What have I for dinner to-day ? '

'Don't you know, sir, that you bid me lay by the blade-bone to broil ? '

' 'Tis so ; very right, child : go away. My lord—' turning to the Treasurer—' do you hear that ? Andrew Marvell's dinner is provided : there's your piece of paper; I want it not. I know the sort of kindness you intended. I live here to serve my constituents ; the ministry may seek men for their purpose ; I am not one.'

A memorable picture that of sublime integrity, worthy to be often looked at and thought upon. 'A good conscience is a perpetual feast,' was one of the maxims we used to write in our copybooks at school. It comes in here as an appropriate legend, to be inscribed under the historical painting which our fancy has already sketched and coloured. Marvell's conscience supplied him daily with a banquet better than Lord Danby's thousand pounds could ever have purchased. Enjoying that, he could put up with the broiled mutton-bone. Had he put away his conscience, he knew that the costly viands of Whitehall or St. James's would have been to him as the apples of Sodom—mere bloom-coloured ashes. Let every man and boy who reads these lines think of that fine scene in the Maiden Lane of the seventeenth century, the next time that any temptation whatever solicits him to sell his conscience.

It would only be carrying out into further application this principle of contrast, to look at another shadow of a bygone age whose haunt is hereabouts. Voltaire, after his release from the Bastile— where he had been imprisoned for libel—came to England and lodged in Maiden Lane, at a perruquier's, whose house exhibited the sign of the white peruke; and there, it is said, he was once borne home in triumph by an English mob, who, after obstructing him in the street, through curiosity awakened by his foreign and otherwise odd appearance, were thrown into raptures of admiration by an eloquent speech he made to them in English, on the steps of a doorway.

But we must hasten on, in spite of the interruption of a motley group of associations which crowd upon us just now—as the people did about the Frenchman—for our purpose is not to tarry in Maiden Lane and talk of Voltaire, or even Marvell: we part from the latter, however, so soon, only because the scanty records of his life furnish us with no other incidents that can be connected here by local ties. We are on our way to Lincoln's Inn Fields, and a melancholy shade there standing in the midst beckons us on.

But before we look at him, let us for a moment survey the place and give a passing thought to other memories. Here we are in what used to be called in days of yore, when London was only creeping out a little way beyond Temple Bar, the Ticket Fields. Buildings were springing up hereabouts in the time of James I., and the monarch, like his predecessors, frightened at the growth of the metropolis, tried to put a stop to the architects and bricklayers; but, in defiance of royal proclamations, they would have their way. The square, we are told by some, was planned by Sir Inigo Jones, and was designed to agree in its dimensions with the base of one of the Egyptian pyramids—a circumstance enough to lead away our unruly thoughts to the banks of the Nile, there to muse under the shadow of those wondrous works of art, of which the device in planning the square gives so distinct and gigantic an idea. In the immediate neighbourhood, on the north side, between the fields and Holborn, there ran in ancient times a range of tenements, long since exchanged for stables, and once well known by the name of Whetstone's Park—so called from the proprietor, a famous vestryman of St. Giles's in the time of Charles I. and the Protectorate. It was among the most infamous of the infamous haunts whither the thieves and reprobates and vagabonds of the days of the Stuarts were wont to repair: so that, like spots already noticed in this chapter, Lincoln's Inn Fields is edged with associations dark and revolting. But here —and it is to bring out the contrast on which we touched at the beginning that we mentioned Whetstone Park—even here, with this scene of moral abandonment in the background, stands out to view a character which will ever be regarded by his country as one of the noblest impersonations of moral heroism.

To place before us this remarkable man, and the affecting circumstances under which his name will for ever remain associated with Lincoln's Inn Fields, we will transport ourselves into the seventeenth century, and fancy ourselves standing at the end of Queen Street, on the morning of 21st July, 1683.

The trees and shrubs remaining in the neighbourhood look all the fresher for the sharp showers which fell last night. Summer skies and summer air, as if in mockery of woe, are looking down and breathing over the preparations for death, which busy workmen have been building up in the midst of the now increasingly mansion-girded square. From the windows of the surrounding houses multitudes are looking on the broad area, where a scaffold stands in deathlike loneliness. A wide space is kept around, guarded by pikemen, with bright steel caps and polished breast and back pieces, and long slender weapons, forming rows of palisades about the ghastly instruments of execution which occupy the middle. Lincoln's Inn supplies its full quota of spectators, and the wall which separates the lawyers' courts from the public square is surmounted by not a few who are eagerly watching for the tragedy at hand. Lord Russell has been accused of treason, tried at the Old Bailey, and condemned to die, and is now on his way from Newgate hither along Holborn Hill.

Unhappy but noble-minded Russell! He has long been a patriot; a true and earnest one, if not the wisest and most eloquent. Things have long been going on badly in the high places of old England. With a heartless monarch, and a licentious court, and a corrupt ministry, and a free constitution despised and trampled on, what else could be expected? To add to other troubles, the dark prospect of a popish successor to the throne, on the death of Charles, has filled all sincere Protestants with dismay—Russell among the rest. So he has been thinking much about what could be done for the rescue of English liberty from the perils which threatened it. With zeal outstripping discretion, he has suffered himself to listen to schemes for the overthrow of tyranny by force, as in the civil wars; but that he ever pledged himself to the execution of such schemes, much less that he ever entertained any purpose of compassing the death of the king, no proof whatever can be offered. A Rye House Plot indeed has been much talked of; men have been charged with meeting there to attack the king on his way to Newmarket; but it is certain that Russell, though accused of connection with it, is perfectly innocent of any such design, and has not had the least to do with the dark conspirators. On the trial, no evidence at all sufficient to convict the patriot was adduced; a great deal of it being vaguely given, and much consisting of mere hearsay. But the forms only, without the spirit, of English justice presided on the bench and guided the proceedings of the court; so that the mind of the monarch and his ministers being known to desire it, the crimination of the accused was beforehand certain, however innocent the man might be. Accordingly, Russell, feared by Charles, hated by James, and maligned by courtiers who could not understand his virtuous patriotism, has been found guilty of treason, and sentenced to perish on the block.

His condemnation occurred several days ago, since which period his friends have been using every means to save his life. Large sums of money have been offered, and other projects devised for the purpose. Even the idea of rescuing him by force has been entertained. One friend, Lord Cavendish, has offered to assist his escape, by taking his place in prison, and exchanging with him his clothes. But the only thing the noble sufferer himself has done has been to write to the king and the Duke of York, and to offer to live beyond the seas in any place which the royal pleasure might appoint, pledging himself also no more to take part in English politics. All, however, has been in vain; and, as an aggravation of his punishment, it has been proposed by the duke that Russell should die in Southampton Square, at the door of his own residence—a proposition which the king has had humanity or prudence enough to reject. While in prison, most of his time has been spent in retirement and religious meditation. He received the death-warrant with calmness, and is anticipating his departure with Christian hope. Six or seven times he has been in his chamber on this the last morning of his life engaged in prayer; and on parting with Lord Cavendish he earnestly has urged on him the importance of personal piety. Winding up his watch, he observes he has done with time, and is going to eternity. Asking what he should give the executioner, and being told ten guineas, he says with a smile, 'A pretty thing to give a fee to have my head cut off!'

But the coach, with all the array of judicial death, is now turning round the corner to Little Queen Street, and he remarks:—'I have often turned to the other hand with great comfort, but now I turn to this with greater.' A tear falls from his eye as he speaks; and while some among the crowd weep and others insult, though touched with tenderness at the commiseration of his friends, he shows no resentment at the conduct of his enemies. He is singing psalms, saying he hopes to sing better soon. He looks upon the dense multitude, observing he expects to meet a nobler assembly ere long. And now the coach enters the Fields, while the concourse moving their heads towards the spot, like tree-tops waving under the winds, watch with eager eyes the slowly advancing procession. As the broad space, so familiar to him in his young days, opens before him, and houses are seen associated with the recollection of early gaieties, not unpolluted with the vicious habits of the age, he sorrowfully exclaims: 'This has been to me a place of sinning, and God now makes it the place of my punishment.' With him in the coach are Drs. Tillotson and Burnet, his faithful attendants and spiritual advisers in the gloomy cell at Newgate. And now the sable train stops. The condemned nobleman, with his clerical friends and the sheriffs and other officers, stand at the scaffold's foot. They slowly ascend the steps, and when all are assembled on the fatal eminence the devoted one calmly paces round the black-covered platform, looking upon the crowd. He then puts into the hands of the sheriffs a long paper, verbally declaring at the same time that it has always been far from his design to plot against the king's life or government. He prays that God would preserve both, and the Protestant religion, and wishes all Protestants may love one another, and not make way for popery by their animosities. In the paper delivered, he declares that he is a member of the Church of England—that he wishes all would unite against the common enemy— that Churchmen would be less severe, and Dissenters less scrupulous—that he has been ready at all times to venture his own life for his country and his religion, but has never been moved 'to anything with relation to the king's life'—that he was earnest in the matter of the exclusion, as the best way, in his opinion, to secure both the king and the Protestant religion—that he forgives his enemies, though he thinks his sentence hard—and that killing by forms of law is the worst kind of murder.

The last moment approaches. That form, now vigorous and healthy, is in a few more instants to lie still and pale in yon black coffin. The soul now looking through those eyes uplifted to heaven in thought, is, when the beating pulse has throbbed a little more, to pierce beyond the shades which hide the eternal future, and to be with God. Reverently he kneels down to pray. Many hearts are praying fervently with his. There is a pause. Dr. Tillotson now engages in intercession for his dying friend. The sufferer unfastens the upper part of his dress, takes off his outer garment, lays bare his neck, and then places it on the block without change of countenance. He lifts up his hands, but there is no trembling. The executioner touches him with the axe to take sure aim, but he does not shrink. Faces, like the leaves of forest trees, are all around, and are looking on with trembling emotion. His friends at this moment turn aside their eyes. We do so.—It is all over. The headsman has done his duty with two strokes, and Russell's soul is gone where vindictive passion can never follow.

Thus he fell; and we feel, with Charles James Fox, that his name will be for ever dear to every Englishman. When his memory shall cease to be an object of respect and veneration, 'it requires no spirit of prophecy to foretell that English liberty will be fast approaching to its final consummation.' His deportment was what might be expected from one who knew he was suffering, not for his crimes, but his virtues. He was connected with the world by private and domestic ties; and 'the story of the last days of this excellent man's life fills the mind with such a mixture of tenderness and admiration, that I know not any scene in history that more powerfully excites our sympathy, or goes more directly to the heart.'

How grateful it is, after picturing the sad scene which Lincoln's Inn Fields exhibited in 1683, to look upon the quiet, pleasant, open square now, with its garden of trees and shrubs and flowers, covering the space set apart for the tragedy of Lord Russell's execution. As we rejoice in our present freedom, we feel as if the drops of the patriot's blood had been as precious seeds from which have grown up those liberties that now 'blossom as the rose.' Through God's blessing, the day when despotism prompted men to perilous enterprises, and then crushed them for longing after liberty, is gone by, we trust for ever.

Bloomsbury Square is not very far from Lincoln's Inn Fields. Southampton House occupied the whole north side of it. 'It was a large building,' says

Strype, 'with a spacious court before it, and a curious garden behind, which lieth open to the fields, enjoying a wholesome and pleasant air.' It was erected for Thomas Wriothesley, Earl of Southampton, whose only daughter and heir Lord Russell married. This was the never-to-be-forgotten Lady Rachel, with whom he lived in that very house, in the enjoyment of a domestic lot which rarely falls to the share of mortals. With the history just noticed fresh in our memory, we cannot help thinking of her devotion and heroism—of her sitting in the Old Bailey court under the bar where her noble husband stood a prisoner, taking notes, and assisting in his defence—of her casting herself, bathed in tears, at the feet of Charles, supplicating the life of her beloved lord—of her calm converse with him in prison when his fate was fixed —and of the scene of the last night, so touchingly described in Burnet's journal. 'At ten o'clock my lady left him. He kissed her four or five times, and she so kept her sorrows to herself, that she gave him no disturbance by their parting. After she was gone, he said: "Now the bitterness of death is past," and ran out a long discourse concerning her—how great a blessing she had been to him, and said what a misery it would have been to him, if she had not that magnanimity of spirit joined to her tenderness as never to have desired him to do a base thing for the saving of his life.'

Walking through Bloomsbury Square, with the

associations just indicated in our minds, we cannot but see the shade of the calm, heroic, gentle, saintly wife, and now widow, of the martyred lord. She passes by in her mourning weeds, her amiable countenance beclouded only with sorrow; or we see her sitting in her little closet, at her desk, in the mansion of her father, on the anniversary of the sad day in July. We see her writing: 'I know I have deserved my punishment, and will be silent under it; but yet secretly my heart mourns and cannot be comforted, because I have not the dear companion and sharer of all my joys and sorrows. I want him to talk with, to walk with, to eat and sleep with: all these things are irksome to me now; all company and meals I could avoid, if it might be. Yet all this is, that I enjoy not the world in my own way, and this same hinders my comfort. When I see my children before me, I remember the pleasure he took in them: this makes my heart shrink.' Again she says:— 'I hope this has been a sorrow I shall profit by. I shall, if God will strengthen my faith, resolve to return Him a constant praise, and make this the season to chase all secret murmurs from grieving my soul for what is past, letting it rejoice in what it should rejoice, His favour to me in the blessings I have left, which many of my betters want, and yet have lost their chiefest friends also.' Once more: 'God knows my eyes are ever ready to pour out marks of a sorrowful heart which I shall carry to the grave, that quiet bed of rest. My friendships have made all the joys and troubles of my life; and yet who would live and not love? Those who have tried the insipidness of it would, I believe, never choose it. Mr. Waller says:—

"What know we of the blest above,
But that they sing, and that they love?"

and it is enough; for if there is so charming a delight in the love and suitableness in humours to creatures, what must it be to the clarified spirits to love in the presence of God?'

Here she died in 1723, and here we must leave Lord William and the Lady Rachel, with the thought, that long since they have been re-united in that happy world reserved for all who, regenerated by the Holy Spirit, have been reconciled to God by living faith in the atonement of His Son. Their remains slumber in the beautiful old church of Chenies, Buckinghamsire, the mausoleum of the Bedford family. We shall never forget visiting that spot, one bright summer's day, and gazing on the tomb of that honoured pair whose love and sorrow have enshrined their memory in sympathizing hearts, while their heroism has exalted them to a bright place in England's history. And well, too, do we remember the broken lily sculptured in pure white marble over the grave of the first wife of Earl Russell. A touching memento that of life's crushed joys, and a monitory symbol to every reader of the frailty of all earthly good.

V.

MARGARET GODOLPHIN.

The Blagges—an ancient Suffolk family—had attained to high consideration as early as the reign of Henry VIII. One who bore the name, with the title of Sir George, was, before his knighthood, which was not conferred till the reign of Edward VI., well known at court, and enjoyed the friendship of the unfortunate Surrey and Sir Thomas Wyatt. Suspected as 'a favourer of the Gospel'—a title given to such as were on the side of the Reformation in those times of conflict—he was arrested by the leaders of the popish party, and narrowly escaped the stake through the interposition of the capricious monarch. Henry was in the habit of addressing those he liked by some humorous designation, often intensely vulgar. Saluting George Blagge, after he had just missed being burnt, with the odd *sobriquet*, '*Ah, my pig!*' —the courtier replied, 'If your majesty had not been better to me than your bishops were, your pig had been roasted ere this time.'

One of the descendants of Sir George was Colonel Thomas Blagge, of Horningsheath, in Suffolk, Groom of the Bedchamber to Charles I., and Governor of

Wallingford. He married Mary North, daughter of Sir Robert North, of Mildenhall, in the same county. Report speaks of the husband as of 'extraordinary wit and signal loyalty!' and of the wife as 'so eminent in all the virtues and perfections of her sex, that it were hard to say whether were superior, her beauty, wit, or poetry.' Stormy were the times, and sadly interrupted must have been the domestic joys of this worthy couple; especially after the death of their royal master and the establishment of the Commonwealth, when to them, as Royalists, their path must have been thorny indeed, and the sky of the future all dark.

Three years after the execution of Charles, Mary Blagge, on the 2nd of August, folded in her arms a babe—the fruit of her sorrow, the flower of her hope. She and the colonel gave the girl the name of Margaret, and brought her up with care. 'Her extraordinary discernment soon advanced to a great and early sense of religion,' which proved her safeguard against the dangers to which she was early exposed; for while yet a child, before her seventh year, she was taken, by the old Duchess of Richmond, into France, and consigned to the care of the Countess of Guildford, a bigoted papist, who tried to persuade the child to go to mass; but she, then so intelligent and religiously disposed, refused to comply, though rudely treated, and menaced by the countess, as Margaret in after life used to relate to her friends, with many 'pretty circumstances.' But she did not stay long in France. On her return to England she lived with her much-loved mother. In 1665 came the raging pestilence, like Death on the pale horse, striking terror into the hearts of the Londoners; when Mrs. Blagge, in common with thousands more, hastened from the infected city to the fresh air and the sequestered scenes of the country.

The depression of the Royalists had at this time come to an end; Charles had been restored, and Whitehall was once again a scene of Cavalier pomp and courtly revelries. As a mark of favour to a family that had suffered in the civil wars, the Duchess of York offered to Mrs. Blagge to take Margaret, now only twelve years old, to place her at court, and make her one of her maids of honour. The proposal, so flattering in a worldly point of view, was accepted, and the young lady soon found herself in a 'surprising change of air and a perilous climate.'

'A perilous climate' indeed, for the atmosphere was loaded with the pestilence of vice. It would pollute our pages to enter into the details of profligacy and intrigue which filled to overflowing the court of the second Charles. Taste, elegance, and wit might throw a veil of fascination over the habits indulged, and screen from general observation a portion of their deformity; but the intrinsic evil of licentiousness will and must remain, however it may wear a fashionable disguise. 'The manners of Chesterfield' may be united with 'the morals of Rochefoucault;' but whatever some may have smartly said to the contrary, vice can lose nothing of its guilt, though it should part with all its grossness. Margaret, after the pure example and moral instructions of her mother, was shocked at what she saw and heard at court; and the marvel is how such a mother could have trusted one she so much loved in such a furnace of temptation. But there was that in the young girl's heart which kept her amidst the fires. Not long had Margaret Blagge been a maid of honour, when she lost both her mother and her mistress. Among her papers she thus records the bereaving stroke, exhibiting, in instructive contrast, the different manner in which it fell on the sufferers.

'My mother dead; at first surprised and very unwilling; she was afterwards resigned; prayed much, had holy things read to her, delighted in heavenly discourse, desired to be dissolved and be with Christ, ended her life cheerfully and without pain, left her family in order, and was much lamented.'—'The D—— dead; a princess honoured in power, had much wit, much money, much esteem;—none remembered her after one week, none sorry for her, she was tost and flung about, and every one did what they would with that stately carcase. What is this world, what is greatness, what to be esteemed or thought a wit? We shall all be stripped without sense or remembrance. But God, if we serve Him in our health, will give us patience in our sickness.' Perhaps this twofold stroke of death tended to increase that habitual seriousness which so remarkably distinguished Margaret Blagge, for, as she often said, she loved to be in the house of mourning.

'She had not been above two years at court, before her virtue, beauty, and wit made her to be looked upon as a little miracle; and, indeed, there were some addresses made to her of the greatest persons—not from the attractions of affected charms, for she was ever, at that sprightful and free age, severely careful how she might give the least liberty, which the gallants there do usually assume, of talking with less reserve; nor did this eclipse her pretty humour, which was cheerful and easy amongst those she thought worthy her conversation.' Having been promoted to the station of a maid of honour to the queen, the moral perils of her position became still more imminent, but her watchfulness was proportionably great. 'Be sure never to talk to the king,' she says in her diary; 'when they speak filthily, though I be laughed at, look grave, remembering that of Micah, there will come a time when the Lord will bind up His jewels. Before I speak, Lord, assist me; when I pray, Lord, hear me; when I am praised, God humble me; may everything I see instruct me; Lord, cleanse my hands, let my feet tread Thy paths!'

Providence had in reserve for Margaret two friends, with whom the rest of her history is bound up; and the attachment she felt for them was, no doubt, among the subsidiary means employed by the Divine Keeper of that young soul for the strengthening of her virtue, the growth of her piety, and the establishment of her peace.

The first of these friends—one who became to her a kind of moral and spiritual mentor—was the well-known John Evelyn, of Wotton, to whose pleasant and easy pen we are indebted for what we know of her history and character. Minding his books and his garden—a circle, he used to say, 'big enough for him'—he never sought acquaintanceships at court; and when he heard some distinguished persons speaking of Margaret Blagge, he 'fancied her some airy thing that had more wit than discretion.' But making a visit to Whitehall with Mrs. Evelyn, he fell in with the youthful maid of honour, and one day dined in her apartments, when he 'admired her temperance, and took especial notice that however wide or indifferent the subject of their discourse was amongst the rest, she would always divert it to some religious conclusion, and so temper and season her replies, as showed a gracious heart, and that she had a mind wholly taken up with heavenly thoughts.' A sincere friendship arose between the Whitehall lady and the Wotton sage, which was ratified by a quaint solemnity, illustrative of the character of the parties far more than the fashion of the times. After a formal solicitation that he would look upon her thenceforth as his child, she took a sheet of paper, upon which Evelyn had been carelessly sketching something in the shape of an altar, and wrote these words:—'Be this a symbol of inviolable friendship: Margaret Blagge, 16th October, 1672;' and underneath, 'For my brother E——.' There was something of romance in the daughter-like attachment which this girl of twenty formed for the amiable Evelyn; but it was indulged for the guidance of her affairs, the increase of her wisdom, and the ripening of her piety. 'The most consummate friendships,' said he, his heart glowing while he wrote, 'are the products of religion and the love of God;' and such, beyond doubt, was the origin of the mutual affection between him and Margaret Godolphin.

The quick-sighted Evelyn soon discovered that there was another who held a different place in her heart from that which he had been chosen to occupy; so, after he had rallied her on the subject, Margaret one day sat down in her chamber at Whitehall, and wrote a confidential epistle, communicating to him tidings of the attachment she had formed for one to whom she was subsequently united. That his tastes were in unison with her own may be gathered from her own account: 'At first we thought of living always together, and that we should be happy. But at last he was sent abroad by his Majesty and fell sick, which gave me great trouble. I allowed more time for prayer than before I had ever done, and, I thank God, found infinite pleasure in it, and I thought less of foolish things that used to take up my time. Being thus changed myself, and liking it so well, I earnestly begged of God that He would impart the same satisfaction to him I loved. 'Tis done, my friend, 'tis done; and from my soul I am thankful; and though I believe he loves me passionately, *yet I am not where I was;* my place is filled up with Him who is all in all.' She then goes on to say that they were determined not to precipitate their marriage; indeed, she indicates some inclination to a perpetual single life, from a mistaken notion that thereby she could more effectually serve God than in a married condition.

Never at home amidst the gaieties of Whitehall, to say nothing of the immorality which there prevailed, Margaret felt, after seven years' continuance in the place, that she could no longer endure to remain amidst its scenes, and therefore earnestly sought, and at length with difficulty obtained, permission from their Majesties to retire from court. It was on a Sunday night, Evelyn tells us, after most of the company were departed, that he waited on her down to her chamber, where she was no sooner entered, but, falling on her knees, she blessed God as for a signal deliverance; 'she was come,' she said, 'out of Egypt, and was now in the way to the Land of Promise.' Tears trickled down her cheeks, 'like the dew of flowers, making a lovely grief,' as she parted with one of the court ladies who had a spirit kindred to her own; but the feelings which predominated in her bosom were more like those of one fleeing from the City of Destruction.

Her new place of abode was Berkeley House, a

mansion which stood on the site of the present town residence of the Duke of Devonshire in Piccadilly. There she found a home with Lady Berkeley, and a pleasant chamber with a library, and quietude and retirement, and, what she specially sought, time for meditation and prayer. She was, however, exposed to occasional interruptions from the visits of distinguished personages, and this, owing to her increased love of seclusion, induced her to contemplate a removal into the country. The desire of celibacy at this time returned with increased force; and it is plain, from her whole story, that there was a strong infusion of asceticism in her piety; an element alien from the religion of Christ, which, while it enjoins self-denial, cherishes the social instincts and domestic charities of our nature, purifying and crowning them with Divine benedictions. Evelyn had, in this respect, more sober and scriptural notions of Christianity; and he availed himself of his influence over his young friend, to persuade her to renounce those erroneous views of a spiritual life into which she had been betrayed. And he succeeded. She indeed withdrew herself from the amusements of the world of fashion; she burst through the entanglements which continued to surround her, even after she ceased to be a maid of honour; she was prepared to give up all for Christ; but she was brought to see that union with a person whose religious sentiments and feelings were in harmony with her own, would tend rather to promote than to retard the progress of piety.

Accordingly, she was married privately in the Temple Church, on the 16th of May; but in a letter written shortly after, she showed what was still the main bent and purpose of her mind. 'I have this day,' she says to Evelyn, 'thought your thoughts, wished I dare say your wishes, which were that I might every day sit looser and looser to the things of this world; discerning, as every day I do, the folly and vanity of it; how short all its pleasures, how trifling all its recreations, how false most of its friendships, how transitory everything in it; and on the contrary, how sweet the service of God, how delightful the meditating on His Word, how pleasant the conversation of the faithful, and, above all, how charming prayer, how glorious our hopes, how gracious our God is to all His children, how gentle His corrections, and how frequently, by the invitations of His Spirit, He calls us from our low designs to those great and noble ones of serving Him and attaining eternal happiness.'

The person to whom she was married, and to whom she had been attached before she became acquainted with Evelyn, was Sidney Godolphin, before his death created Earl of Godolphin.

Berkeley House was the first scene of her wedded life. Sweetly 'she lived in retirement all the winter,' till the return of Lord Berkeley from Paris obliged her to remove, when she repaired to 'a pretty habitation which had been built and accommodated for her in Scotland Yard.' A burst of grateful joy went up to her Heavenly

Father when she found herself settled in her new abode. 'When I this day consider my happiness, in having so perfect health of body, cheerfulness of mind, no disturbance from without nor grief within, my time my own, my house quiet, sweet, and pretty, all manner of conveniences for serving God in public and private; how happy in my friends, husband, relations, servants, credit, and none to wait or attend on but my dear and beloved God, from whom I receive all this; what a melting joy ran through me at the thoughts of all these mercies, and how did I think myself obliged to go to the foot of my Redeemer, and acknowledge my own unworthiness of His favour.'

Margaret Godolphin was exemplary as a wife, even as Margaret Blagge had been exemplary in her unmarried estate. Where the religion of Christ dwells in the heart, its developments are beautifully adapted to the circumstances of individual life, and the calls of relative duty; like some luxuriant plant which winds, curls, and throws out its tendrils and leaves, in directions indicated by the position in which it is placed. With ease she instructed her servants, sedulously maintaining the forms of domestic religion, and breathing, in her whole intercourse with them, its kind, considerate and benignant spirit; while, with the Christian dignity and condescension of the mistress, were blended, in all her conduct towards him she most loved on earth, the devotion, tenderness, and sympathy of the wife. She had learned the beautiful lesson, that pure and undefiled religion (that is, religion in its outward service, its external form) 'before God and the Father is this, to visit the fatherless and widows in their affliction, and to keep himself unspotted from the world.' In addition to the practical expression of religion in indifference to the world, she cultivated its practical expression in activities for the good of others; passing from the kingly palace, or the mansions of the noble, to the cottages of the humble and the hovels of the indigent; and visiting and releasing prisoners, of whom Evelyn says he could produce 'a list of above thirty, restrained for debts in several prisons, which she paid and compounded for at once.' Nor did she omit alms-*deeds*, while abounding in alms-*gifts*. She was like Dorcas, who was full of good works; like Priscilla, who instructed many more perfectly in the ways of God; like Mary, who bestowed much labour. She was a servant of the Church, a succourer of the saints, a helper in Christ Jesus, and ready to lay down her life for the Gospel.

One joy was wanting to crown her wedded bliss, and anxiously she longed for it; not with the impatience, but almost with the intensity, of Rachel. 'She took home to her a poor orphan girl, whom she tended, instructed, and cherished with the tenderness of a natural mother.' Providence at length crowned her hopes. She anticipated the event with confidence in the Divine power and mercy, but withal with a dash of melancholy and a foreboding that 'she should not outlive the happiness she had so long wished for.' A son was born on Tuesday, the 3rd of September, 1678. All went on well for a few days. On the following Saturday, Evelyn received from Mr. Godolphin an alarming note. Dangerous symptoms appeared. All that medical skill could accomplish in those days, and under her circumstances, was done; but in vain. She lingered till Monday, September 9th, when she departed, in the 25th year of her age. She lies buried in Breage Church, Cornwall, where her tomb reminds one of the pillar of Rachel's grave.

Such is the simple story of Margaret Godolphin, as told by John Evelyn. It is a quaint but beautiful account of practical piety, with some traits indicating a want of fuller light and richer knowledge. We must never forget that genuine piety springs from a simple reliance upon the Son of God, and from the indwelling of the Spirit of grace, the Fountain of truth, holiness, and love. While noticing, in the object of our sketch, imperfections arising from the want of clearer views on some points, brightly does the star of this godly woman gleam amid the darkness that envelops the court of one of England's most degraded monarchs.

VI.

JOSEPH ADDISON.

Few places are so suggestive as public schools. What thick-coming fancies we have, when perchance only for two minutes we pause by the iron railings in front of Christ's Hospital, Newgate Street, to look at the boys in yellow and blue, and listen to their light-hearted shouts—shouts which cruelly stab some hearts with recollections of like gladness now for ever gone! We speculate upon what those merry roisterers may become in future days—what positions they may fill in the State—what eminence may await that timid-looking little fellow who leans so thoughtfully against the corner column of the arcade—and what a downward destiny may come to that beautiful lad, with ruddy cheeks and golden locks, the life of yonder group, who evidently regard him as their Magnus Apollo. And those two youths, with their arms fondly thrown over each other's shoulders talking so very earnestly—how divergent may be their paths, or how symbolical of future friendship may be their present attitude! Then, with fancies about the future, there come remembrances of the past, as we walk into the old schoolroom, with its desks so profusely covered with penknife carvings, and its walls so closely studded with inscriptions, great and small. We decipher here and there, amidst gigantic capitals which tell of those forgotten, tiny letters forming the names of those who will never be forgotten.

We have mentioned Christ's Hospital, but our purpose is to take the reader to another old school in London, not far distant—that which belongs to the Charterhouse; and if it were not that we are now in search of a celebrity belonging to the eighteenth century, we might tarry to talk of a boy educated there who from his sedate and thoughtful ways gained the *sobriquet* of Old Phlos—the same who won for himself immortal renown in the Indian war, whose name will be remembered by a distant posterity as the great Sir Henry Havelock.

But we mean to go back more than a century and a half, that we may meet with a boy who studied then, and, as we look on the lad, to connect with it the thought of the man he was to be. Indeed, several shades among the most illustrious of which our country boasts meet us there in boyish stature. There is Isaac Barrow, noted among his playmates as a famous pugilist, but in fact an embryo mathematician and divine. And there is one whose pastime is not so unapt a type of the future; three times every morning, most methodically, by his father's command, does he run round the green: it is Master John Wesley, the

OLD CHARTERHOUSE, FROM THE GREEN.

son of the Epworth rector. Between the periods in which Barrow fought and Wesley ran, Master Joseph Addison and Master Richard Steele were then at school; and we can fancy these two early friends walking about, like the Bluecoat boys just sketched, little dreaming of the subsequent union of their names in connection with the history of periodical literature and elegant letters. It is the shade of Joseph Addison that we come to visit. His future career, in connexion with his genial boyhood, we wish to trace; and from the precincts of the Charterhouse we propose to start on a short tour to some of his London haunts, where again we shall find him in company with Richard Steele.

But before we go, one word about the Charterhouse. It was originally a monastic foundation. A wealthy citizen, Thomas Sutton by name, richly endowed it at the end of the sixteenth century, both as a hospital and a school; and every year on December 12th, the anniversary of his death, his name used to be celebrated by the pensioners, who met in the Old Court Room and sang the following ditty:—

> 'Then blessed be the memory
> Of good old Thomas Sutton,
> Who gave us lodging, learning,
> And he gave us beef and mutton.'

Thomas Sutton, by the way, is most worthy of being had in remembrance and imitation by the wealthy of this world, if we are to believe what Fuller tells us of his retiring into his garden, and being overheard in prayer, exclaiming: 'Lord, Thou hast given me a large and liberal estate: give me also a heart to make use thereof.' Under a sense of responsibility to the Giver of all good, Sutton has left an enduring monument of his liberal care for his fellow-creatures in the two extremes of age. Old men, after the rough storms of life, here put into harbour awhile, before stepping on the infinite and eternal shore; and boys, ere they battled with the tempest, used to find the Charterhouse[1] a dockyard where the vessel was prepared for coming voyages. Snug were the dormitories, spacious the halls, and liberal the allowance made to the former, while the latter were provided with a good education and every reasonable comfort. The architecture is of different kinds, exhibiting a series of examples extending through the sixteenth and part of the seventeenth century, and as we pass round the quadrangle and along the corridor, it is easy to fancy ourselves transferred to the reign of James I. or Henry VIII. It is one of those recesses in the heart of Old London, into which the contemplative may dive, and, forgetting the crowds and conflicts of passing times, indulge in a quietude which he may improve for his intellectual pleasure and his spiritual advantage.

But to return to Joseph Addison, who used to sleep in one of those rooms, and to say his lessons in the old school. We catch the next glimpse of him down

[1] The school is now at Godalming.

Fulham way. Faulkner, the historian of Fulham, who wrote in 1811, describes at the eastern extremity of the parish, situated by a small creek running to the Thames, a building called Sandford Manor House, formerly of some note from having been the residence of the notorious Nell Gwynn. 'The mansion is of venerable appearance; and immediately in front are four walnut-trees, affording an agreeable shade, that are said to have been planted by royal hands; and the fruit is esteemed of a peculiarly fine quality.' According to the authority just quoted, Addison was residing in this house in the year 1708. He had, in 1693, left Oxford, whither he went from the Charter-house; he had, from 1699 to 1702, pursued his travels on the Continent, of which his 'Dialogue on Medals' and his 'Cato' are mementoes; he had passed two years in retirement, and then devoted himself to political business; and at the time to which we now refer had reached the office of Under Secretary of State. Two letters, stated by Mr. Faulkner to have been written from Sandford Manor House, are interesting memorials of the state of the neighbourhood round about Fulham then, and of the intense relish for rural scenes and pleasures, and the minute observation of natural objects, which always distinguished the author of the *Spectator*. The letters are addressed to the young Earl of Warwick, to whom he subsequently became stepfather. He has been represented as the youthful nobleman's tutor, but it would appear that he never sustained such a relation. In the first letter, he gives a particular account of a curious bird's-nest found near the house, about which his neighbours were divided in opinion, some taking it for a nest of skylarks, some of canary birds, but he judging the inmates to be tomtits. In the second letter he says: 'I can't forbear being troublesome to your lordship while I am in your neighbourhood. The business of this is to invite you to a concert of music which I have found on a tree in a neighbouring wood. It begins precisely at six in the evening, and consists of a blackbird, a thrush, a robin redbreast, and a bullfinch. There is a lark that by way of overture sings and mounts till she is almost out of hearing, and afterwards falls down leisurely, and drops to the ground, as soon as she has ended her song. The whole is concluded by a nightingale, that has a much better voice than Mrs. Tofts, and something of Italian manners in its diversions. If your lordship will honour me with your company, I will promise to entertain you with much better music and more agreeable scenes than you ever met with at the opera, and will conclude with a charming description of a nightingale out of our friend Virgil:

> "So close in poplar shades her children gone,
> The mother nightingale laments alone,
> Whose nest some prying churl had found, and thence
> By stealth conveyed the unfeathered innocents;
> But she supplies the night with mournful strains,
> And melancholy music fills the plains."'

The letter places our elegant essayist distinctly before us, on a bright May evening, with upturned ear, beneath some lofty elm or oak, charmed with the beautiful oratorio of the birds in the wood at Fulham. One sees in every line the simple unaffected tastes of the man— so much more charmed with the grove than the opera, so decidedly preferring the nightingale to Mrs. Tofts; nor can we fail to recognize the amiable and benevolent feelings which prompted Addison to strive after reclaiming the youth of vitiated predilections, by the inspiration of a love for purer pleasures.

But the lover of Nature had a wonderfully keen eye for the observation of men and manners, of which every volume of the *Spectator* abounds in examples. As a companion sketch to the one just given, of Addison listening to the birds in a wood, we may draw from the *Spectator* one representing him as he listens with equal interest, but of another kind, to the stir and bustle of the Royal Exchange:—'I have often been pleased to hear disputes adjusted between an inhabitant of Japan and an alderman of London, or to see a subject of the Great Mogul entering into a league with one of the Czar of Muscovy. I am infinitely delighted in mixing with these several ministers of commerce as they are distinguished by their different walks and different languages: sometimes I am jostled among a body of Armenians, sometimes I am lost in a crowd of Jews, and sometimes make one in a group of Dutchmen. I am a Dane, Swede, or Frenchman, at different times;

or rather, fancy myself like the old philosopher, who upon being asked what countryman he was, replied that he was a citizen of the world.' We can see him in the old Exchange, as we remember it before the last fire, looking with a keen eye from under that flowing wig and cocked hat of his, upon British and foreign merchants. He himself paints a bit of background for his own portrait, where he says :—' When I have been upon the 'Change, I have often fancied one of our old kings standing in person where he is represented in effigy, and looking down upon the wealthy concourse of people with which that place is every day filled.' The old effigies are restored as we listen to the *Spectator's* reflections, and we muse on the shade of the man who, perhaps rudely pushed aside by some burly citizen, full of the consciousness of being a millionaire, is about by his quiet pen to immortalize the whole scene, though he alone of all the group will remain capable of being individualized by posterity.

In 1710 Addison was living in St. James's Place. He had lodgings there, and, according to Pope, the essayist's old schoolfellow and literary coadjutor, Steele, together with Budgell, Phillipps, Carey, Davenant, and Colonel Brett, used to drop in and take breakfast with him. The *Tatler* and the *Spectator* had then been recently established, and were exciting no small interest in all reading circles, royalty even looking out for the new number to be served up with the provisions of the breakfast table. The new number of the periodical, fresh from the press, and lying before them, would of course be the subject of conversation among the wits who met in St. James's Place, to enjoy Addison's hospitality, including, as the party did, some who were contributors; nor would they be so regardless of the number sold as not to touch at times on that point. It is rather curious in these days of large circulation for such productions, to be told by Dr. Johnson, relative to the *Tatler* and the *Spectator*:—'I once heard it observed that the sale may be calculated by the product of the tax, related in the last number to produce more than twenty pounds a week, and therefore stated at one and twenty pounds, or three pounds ten shillings a day; this, at a halfpenny a paper, will give 1,680 for the daily number.' The doctor speaks of this as no great sale; and intimates that the circulation of the *Spectator* at the time of its periodical issue, was likely to grow less if, as Swift says was the case, the public were wearied by incessant allusions to 'the *fair* sex.'

Following the shade of Addison, we are plunged into the midst of the fashionable society of the metropolis, both literary and political. In those days, taverns were to them what West End clubs are to the same classes now. Between the Temple gates and Temple Bar was a famous place of this description, bearing the hideous name of The Devil's Tavern. Child's Bank adjoins the site on which it stood. Ben Jonson and the wits of his day had made it their *rendezvous*. His 'Leges Convivales' were written for the regulation of their proceedings, and the Latin law of *Insipida poemata nulla recitantur* (Insipid poems are not to be repeated) is supposed to mean that the rare Ben Jonson considered his own productions would certainly be otherwise, and that he ought to have the business of recitation pretty much to himself. In 1710 we meet with our great essayist in this tavern with the ugly appellation. He is in the midst of political excitement; for a general election is raging throughout the land, full of all sorts of excesses, such as Hogarth afterwards delineated in one of his admirable pictures. 'I dined to-day—' (Oct. 12) Swift tells us in a letter to Stella— ' with Dr. Garth and Mr. Addison, at the Devil Tavern, near Temple Bar : and it is well I dine every day, else I should be longer making out my letters ; for we are yet in a very dull state, only inquiring every day after new elections, where the Tories carry it among the new members six to one. Mr. Addison's election has passed easy and undisputed, and I believe if he had a mind to be chosen king he would hardly be refused.'

So Addison was then in the zenith of popularity ; and though a Whig, when Whigs were at a discount, could hold up his head aloft among Tory rivals. The pictorial scene of Addison, Garth, and Swift, in an oak parlour, round a table covered with smoking viands, is prosaic and conceivable enough ; but some may think there must have been rare discourse between such a trio—wonderful scintillations, brisk repartees, keen satire, shrewd remarks : only experience teaches that such men in private are often commonplace, like other people—that the learned do not always appear so very learned, or wits so very witty. In a snug little party of intimate friends, Addison was likely to be at ease and communicative. Pope tells us his conversation had a charm in it he had never found in any other man's; but before strangers he was stiff and silent. Chesterfield declared him the most timorous and awkward man he ever saw, and Addison himself was conscious enough of the difference between the power he had over his pen and his tongue. He used to say of his mental resources, that though 'he could draw bills for a thousand pounds, he had not a guinea in his pocket.' Johnson thinks Chesterfield's testimony must be qualified; perhaps so. But though Addison succeeded so well in the world, it does not follow that he was not very timorous and awkward; for high reputation won by literature may cover a good deal of that, and much that is attractive and lovable may be even visibly beneath the surface.

Addison's haunts, we are sorry to notice, lay very much among taverns; and though there is no doubt he there picked up a good deal of that practical wisdom which runs throughout his essays, he could hardly fail to contract habits injurious to his character and welfare. Though it is not known that he was ever intoxicated, he often transgressed the bounds of moderation—a fact we dare not conceal, but which we record with deep sorrow, furnishing as he does one of a large collection of examples showing that the most refined intellectual taste is no sufficient check against temptations to the excessive indulgence of the appetites. Whatever might appear to the contrary in his writings, there must have been in Addison a weakness of moral and religious principle as applied to the deportment of his life; but we hope that in his last days, after religion had more than ever occupied his pen, its influence more powerfully touched his heart, producing contrition for the past and reformation for the future.

The house that Addison most frequented was Button's, on the south side of Russell Street, Covent Garden. The landlord, whose name it bore, had been a servant in the family of the Countess of Warwick, and had taken the house under Addison's express patronage. It was in 1712 that the place was opened, just as the fame of the poet was established by the publication of 'Cato.' A lion's head and paws, serving as a letter-box for the reception of literary communications, was placed in front of the building, and the editor of the *Guardian* says:—'Whatever the lion swallows, I shall digest for the use of the public.' 'He is indeed a proper emblem of knowledge and action, being all head and paws.' 'Addison usually studied all the morning, then met his party at Button's, dined there, and stayed five or six hours, and sometimes far into the night.'

A glimpse of the relations between Addison and Pope is given in the following extract from the latter:

'There had been a coldness between me and Mr. Addison for some time, and we had not been in company together for a good while anywhere but at Button's Coffee House, where I used to see him almost every day. On his meeting me there one day in particular, he took me aside and said he should be glad to dine with me at such a tavern, if I would stay till those people (Budgell and Phillipps) were gone.'

Of a visit by Addison to St. James's Coffee House, St. James's Street, now swept away, we have a graphic sketch from his own pen, full of easy description and delicate satire—characteristics of a style in which he has few rivals :—'I called at the St. James's, where I found the whole outward room in a buzz of politics. The speculations were but very indifferent towards the door, but grew finer as you advanced towards the upper end of the room, and were so much improved by a knot of theorists who sat in the inner room, within the steams of the coffee-pot, that I heard the whole Spanish monarchy disposed of, and all the line of Bourbon provided for, in less than a quarter of an hour.' Addison also was a member of the Kit-Kat Club, which met at an obscure house in Shire Lane. Into the archæological question of the origin of its title we cannot enter; some deriving it from Christopher Kat, a pastry-cook, and some from the name given to certain pies of great celebrity. Whencesoever the appellation came, it is still preserved to denote portraits of a certain size, from the circumstance of pictures so painted by Sir Godfrey Kneller having been hung up round the clubroom.

Addison's parliamentary career is quite a mystery. He was for some time a representative, and actually rose to be one of the principal Secretaries of State, under the Stanhope Ministry, in the reign of George I., yet his name never figures in debate : and though he held high office, the historian of England finds scarcely any occasion for introducing him, except to record his appointment and resignation. He could not speak : so we have to picture him on the Ministerial Bench in Old St. Stephen's in the days of the first George, among the curly wigs and court suits that crowded the House of Commons, listening to the orations of others, and well weighing their arguments, and inwardly cogitating replies, but all the while remaining silent—a hard case indeed for a Secretary of State, and for his fellow-senators, too. Nor did the pen, so fluent with the *Spectator*, seem made for official documents ; for we are informed that his fastidiousness about style so embarrassed him, when called to prepare an urgent despatch, that he was compelled to resign the task into the hands of one of his subordinates in office. In literary composition, we are informed by Steele, that Addison, when he had 'made his plan for what he designed to write, would walk about a room, and dictate it into language, with as much freedom and ease as anyone could write it down, and attend to the coherence and grammar of what he dictated.' His difficulty about despatches, and his inability to speak in Parliament, would of themselves have speedily necessitated his retirement from public life; but ill health occurred as an additional reason, and brought Addison's official career to an end in 1718. Steele, whom we saw as his playmate in the Charterhouse School, had been through life the intimate friend of Addison; but the closing days of the latter were beclouded by the disruption of this friendship, and by a violent controversy between them about a bill for the limitation of the peerage. 'Truly,' says the best of books, 'a brother offended is harder to be won than a strong city, and their contentions are like the bars of a castle.'

In 1716, Addison had married the Dowager Countess of Warwick, and thereby became occupant of Holland House, Kensington, the ancestral abode of that lady.

In the old coaching-days, the traveller to the west of England, as he passed through Kensington on a bright summer morning, was sure to turn with admiration and pleasure to look on the fine green elm trees which line the border of the park next the road; and through the openings under and between the branches he would catch glimpses of the quaint arcades, gables, towers, turrets, roofs, and chimney-tops, which compose this lordly habitation, erected in the reign of the first James. Since that kind of traffic has been drained off by railways, fewer strangers see the most interesting specimen of old architecture to the west of London. Considerable changes have been wrought in its appearance, not, indeed, at all altering its outlines or even details, but rather restoring the freshness of its original beauty; while the new terrace raised in front of the house, with its bright brick walls, stone balustrades, and huge white garden vases full of geraniums, greatly adds to the attractiveness of the picture, especially as seen on a clear summer's afternoon, when a morning's shower has given richer tints and warmer life to grass and trees, plants and shrubs. There is a vast deal connected with the edifice upon which we are here tempted for a while to dwell; but the associations of Holland House, save as they belong to Addison, must be omitted. With the long gallery, or library, which forms the west wing, tradition links his name in by no means honourable conjunction. 'I have heard,' says Faulkner, 'that Addison had a table with a bottle of wine placed at each end, and when in the fervour of composition, was in the habit of pacing this narrow gallery between glass and glass.' He adds, 'Fancy may trace the exquisite good humour which enlivens his paper to the mirth inspired by wine; but there is too much sober good sense in all his lucubrations, even when he indulges most in pleasantry, to allow us to give implicit credence to a tradition invented probably as an excuse for intemperance by such as can empty two bottles of wine, but never produce a *Spectator* or a *Freeholder.*'

This is a charitable surmise, and may be true; but if Addison—even beyond some of his companions in an age not distinguished for sobriety in polite circles—indulged occasionally in potations beyond the limits of temperance, probably it was the result of domestic unhappiness; for it is well known that his marriage with the countess was by no means felicitous. His home had no charms. Princely apartments, magnificent furniture, tasteful ornaments, pictures, and statuary, could not compensate for the want of domestic harmony and peace. So he wandered from scenes embittered by sad associations, in quest of social pleasures such as had too often led him astray.

It was within a chamber in Holland House that there occurred the scene, so often noticed, of Addison's farewell to the young Earl of Warwick. Having sent for him, he grasped his hand, and softly said: 'See in what peace a Christian can die.' Well-founded indeed is that peace which rests on 'the hope set before us in the Gospel;' when whatever of sin and folly there has been in life becomes the subject of sincere repentance.

Addison sleeps in Westminster Abbey, having been honoured to lie in state in the Jerusalem Chamber. Tickel mourned over his death in an elegy, of which Johnson said, that 'a more sublime or more elegant funeral poem is not to be found in the English language.' The description he gives of the poet's obsequies places us beside the procession as it slowly paces down the aisle to lay Addison in his last earthly home ; and with these lines we bid him farewell :—

> 'Can I forget the dismal night that gave
> My soul's best part for ever to the grave?
> How silent did his old companions tread,
> By midnight lamps, the mansions of the dead,
> Through breathing statues, then unheeded things,
> Through rows of warriors and through walks of kings!
> What awe did the slow solemn knell inspire,
> The pealing organ and the pausing choir,
> The duties by the lawn-robed prelate paid,
> And the last words, that dust to dust conveyed.
> While speechless o'er thy closing grave we bend,
> Accept these tears, thou dear departed friend.'

VII.
SIR ISAAC NEWTON.

THE present Somerset House is sometimes confounded with its predecessor, the 'large and goodly house' described by John Stowe, and built by the bold and proud Protector of that name, who swayed the destinies of England during the nominal reign of Edward VI.—the amiable boy-king. That princely abode—connected with the memory of its founder; of Henrietta, the queen of Charles I., to whom it was assigned by her royal husband; of Oliver Cromwell, who there lay in state; and of Monk, Duke of Albemarle, to whom a similar honour was paid within its walls—was demolished pursuant to an Act of Parliament passed in 1775. The present pile of buildings, which so many thousand Londoners pass without notice, but which the stranger pauses to look upon as a noteworthy edifice, was reared upon the site of the old one, in accordance with plans which had been formed by Sir William Chambers, a distinguished architect of that day. The building is not without grandeur in its general design and proportions, or without beauty in its particular and minute details; but a far greater interest belongs to the place as derived from its manifold associations.

'When I first came to this building,' an old clerk in the Audit Office told Mr. Cunningham, who records the fact in his interesting 'Handbook of London,' 'I was in the habit of seeing for many mornings a thin spare naval officer, with only one arm, enter the vestibule at a smart step and make direct for the Admiralty, over the rough round stones of the quadrangle, instead of taking, what others generally took and continue to take, the smooth pavement at the sides. His thin frail figure shook at every step, and I often wondered why he chose so rough a footway; but I ceased to wonder when I heard that the thin frail officer was no other than Lord Nelson, who always took the nearest way to the place he wanted to go to.' It was indeed the manner of the man; and within that slim frame there beat a lion's heart, allied to a quickness of perception, a power of calculating probabilities, a calmness of reflection, and a mastery of will, before whose united influence fleets under his command sailed on to victory, and adverse armaments fled or struck in disorder and defeat. He heeded not the roughness of his way, was blind to difficulties, and would not recognize the word 'impossible,' but steered right on by the most direct route to the accomplishment of his designs.

We are not, however, in quest of warlike associations, though having lighted on this notable one we would not pass it by unnoticed: our search is rather after those who have won more enduring triumphs than were ever gained on field or flood. 'The results of intellectual labour or scientific genius,' says Sir H. Davy, 'are permanent, and incapable of being lost. Monarchs change their plans, governments their objects, a fleet or an army effect their object, and then pass away; but a piece of steel touched by the magnet preserves its character for ever, and secures to man the dominion of the trackless ocean.' The illustrious man who penned this profound sentence will long be remembered in connection with that part of the building appropriated to the Royal Society from 1780 to 1857, when it removed to Burlington House. It is to the left as you enter within the elegant vestibule, crowned with its keystone masques of river deities. Through that doorway often passed the inventor of the safety-lamp, and within the rooms devoted to the learned conclave of which he was president there were frequently disclosed the results of his extraordinary discoveries. Watt, and Wollaston, and other great names, recur to us as we turn aside from the dense throng of wayfarers who crowd all day along the pavement, to muse in the portico on past times, and to meditate on the humanizing influences of the studies pursued by those of whom the building will, as long as it remains, be the magnificent memorial.

But it is beyond our design to dwell upon the numerous reminiscences of the biography of science revived by the sight of these smoke-stained walls, in Burlington House, Piccadilly. We are concerned only with the shade of Sir Isaac Newton, which rises before us, portly but not tall, his locks silvery but abundant, with eyes sparkling and piercing. His figure and face as they are presented to us seem to awaken grateful homage as we reflect on his character and history. Wonderful humility blends with intellectual greatness. To other men he seems a spirit of higher rank, having superhuman faculties of mental vision, wont to soar into regions which the vulture's eye hath never seen: to himself he seems but a little boy, playing with shells by the seaside. Others were taken up with what Newton did: he himself was thinking of what remained undiscovered. So it is ever with genius—the broader the range of view, the wider the horizon of mystery. He who understands more than others, is conscious beyond others of what cannot be understood.

Let us enter the apartment devoted to meetings of the Royal Society. There hang three portraits of the great philosopher; one, as it ought to be, suspended over the president's chair, to indicate, we may suppose, that Newton is ever to be regarded as the presiding genius over the researches and deliberations of British science. Still more lively mementoes of him are preserved among the Royal Society's treasures. There is a solar dial made by the boy Isaac, when, instead of studying his grammar and scanning Virgil and Horace, he was busy making windmills and waterclocks. In fancy, we see him going along the road to Grantham on a market-day, with the old servant whom his mother sent to take care of him, and then stopping by the wayside to watch the motions of a waterwheel, reflecting upon the mechanical principles involved in the simplest contrivances. It is pleasant, with our knowledge of what he afterwards became, to sit down on the green bank by the river-side, and to speculate upon the ignorance of the old servant who accompanied him, and of the farmers they saluted by the way, as to the illustrious destiny which awaited the widow's son who lived in the manor house of Woolsthorpe. The reflecting telescope, preserved along with the dial, was made by Newton in his thirtieth year, and reminds us of the deep mathematical studies he was then pursuing at Cambridge. The autograph MS. of the 'Principia,' also kept here, gives increased vividness to the picture of this extraordinary person in his study, solving mysterious problems, and suggesting others still more mysterious: and then the lock of silvery hair, the last of the Newtonian relics belonging to the Society, comes in as a finishing touch to fancy's picture, like one more stroke of the pencil, which, when a portrait is just complete, gives life and expression to the whole.

After all, it must be remembered that in Newton's time the Royal Society met elsewhere. The gatherings out of which it arose were first in Oxford during the Commonwealth, and then subsequently at Gresham College, London. There it continued after Charles II. gave the philosophers a charter and the body was completely formed, which happened in 1664. Isaac

Newton became a member in January, 1674, when he was excused the customary payment of a shilling a week, 'on account of his low circumstances, as he represented.' The old Gresham College was long since swept away. It stood in Old Broad Street, on the ground now occupied by business premises; so, in following the shades of the departed, we pause in the busy thoroughfare, and under the guidance of archæological research, call to mind the old quadrilateral range of buildings, a storey high, with attics above, enclosing an open square, refreshed by rows of trees; the whole in the Flemish style, and having a very sober and quiet look—and there we see the shadow of Isaac, a young man of thirty-two, passing along the court to ascend the steps. If he was awhile a pecuniary debtor to the slender amount of a shilling a week, certainly he soon laid the Society under obligations of another description, to an incalculable extent, by his great discoveries, which were acknowledged, so far as conferring honour could be an acknowledgment, in 1703, by his election to the presidential chair.

We have an account, by a foreign member of the Society, of the appearance of the room and the assembled philosophers, about ten years after Newton's admission. The sketch he gives is very graphic, and is no doubt a truthful picture of the scene presented in Gresham College, Basinghall Street, after Newton had attained the presidency. 'The room,' says Sorbière, historiographer to the French king, 'where the Society meets is large and wainscoted: there is a large table before the chimney, with seven or eight chairs covered with green cloth about it, and two rows of wooden and matted benches to lean on, the first being higher than the others, in form like an amphitheatre. The president and council are elective; they mind no precedency in the Society, but the president sits at the middle of the table in an elbow chair, with his back to the chimney. The secretary sits at the end of the table on his left hand, and they have each of them pen, ink, and paper before them. I saw nobody sit in the chairs; I think they are reserved for persons of great quality, or those who have occasion to draw near the president. All the other members take their places as they think fit, and without ceremony; and if any one comes in after the Society is fixed, nobody stirs, but he takes a place presently where he can find it, so that no interruption may be given to him that speaks. The president has a little wooden mace in his hand, with which he strikes the table when he would command silence: they address their discourse to him bareheaded till he makes a sign for them to put on their hats; and there is a relation given in a few words of what is thought proper to be said concerning the experiments proposed by the secretary. There is nobody here eager to speak that makes a long harangue, or intent upon saying all he knows: he is never interrupted that speaks, and differences of opinion cause no manner of resentment, nor as much as a disobliging way of speech; there is nothing seemed to me to be more civil, respectful,' and better managed than this meeting; and if there be any private discourses held between any while a member is speaking, they only whisper, and the least sign from the president causes a sudden stop, though they have not told their mind out. I took special notice of this conduct in a body consisting of so many persons and of such different nations.'

This Teniers-like painting of the old room, with its learned occupants, gives a very clear idea of the scene when Newton attended as a simple member; and it only requires us to put him in the chair, with the wooden mace in his hand, to have the picture of the Royal Society under his presidency, till the year 1710, when the meetings were removed to another place. It was Crane Court, Fleet Street, whither the illustrious institute emigrated, and there our great English philosopher continued to preside till his death in 1727. On its site is a modern but picturesque turreted redbrick building.

Crane Court, then, is another of the nooks, beside a noisy bustling street in the great metropolis, where a contemplative mind may escape the turmoil of the present and enter the shadowy regions of the past; and in this instance it is to commune not with one great genius only, but with a number of kindred spirits, who in his wake were pushing their barks over the broad pacific ocean of Nature's mysteries. Charles II. used to laugh at Boyle's weighing the air, and thoughtless persons may fancy that the hours spent, during the last century, in Crane Court, by English philosophers, were for the most part spent in learned trifling; but no one acquainted with the connection between science and the useful arts will fail to see how much the physical comforts of the present generation have been increased by the labours of those illustrious men; while every man, who has not made his mind a slave to mere utilitarian pursuits, will recognize the value of knowledge for its own sake, the high value of its influence on the human faculties, and the incalculable importance of an ever-brightening and enlarging perception of the wonders of God's glorious universe. It was in 1780 that the Royal Society removed to Somerset House, where the Crown had just assigned to its use the apartments which it occupied until 1857.

This great man was elected by the University of Cambridge, in 1688, to serve for them in Parliament; and in 1695 he became Warden of the Mint, with a salary of between 500*l.* and 600*l.* He was promoted to the Mastership in 1699, after which his salary was from 1,200*l.* to 1,500*l.* There could be no excuse now, on the score of scanty means, for not paying the shilling a week. Newton grew rich, and died worth 32,000*l.* For some years before he obtained the Wardenship he resided at Cambridge, though of course frequently visiting town on political and scientific business. During one of these visits we find him dating a letter from 'the Bull in Shoreditch;' a letter, by the way, painful to read, as it indicates that he was at the time labouring under nervousness to an extent that painfully affected his mind. He was thought by some to be positively *insane*, but the affection does not seem to have gone so far as to justify the application of that term.

After his appointment to office under Government, he came to live in London, and for some time Jermyn Street was the place of his abode. It was while living there that the rupture began between him and Flamsteed. They had been intimate friends; but a coolness arose from some unexplained cause in 1696. Flamsteed had supplied Newton with lunar observations, and had mentioned the fact to his acquaintance, perhaps with some little vanity. The more renowned philosopher, on this account, rather querulously rebuked his fellow-labourer, and in the year 1704 very serious differences appeared between them. Flamsteed's catalogue of stars, a most valuable contribution to the cause of science, was placed in the hands of Newton and others for examination, in consequence of Prince George of Denmark having offered to bear the expense of printing it. According to the *ex parte* statement of Flamsteed, he received from this committee a good deal of vexatious treatment, after which they demanded that a copy of the catalogue, which Flamsteed still held in his possession, should be given up to them. This demand was complied with under protest; the catalogue being sealed up, with the understanding that so it should remain until the industrious student and observer should be able to complete it. In 1710 Flamsteed found the seal had been broken, and that the work was going through the press; a circumstance which greatly enraged him, he being by no means one of the meekest of men. Violent recriminations between the two illustrious astronomers immediately ensued, into the details of which we have neither time nor inclination to enter. We cannot acquit Newton of all blame in this affair. The breaking of the seal looks like an offence, and so far as he participated in it can scarcely be regarded otherwise than as leaving some shade (we cannot determine the depth of its hue) on the memory of our great philosopher. Still his eminent virtues, which Sir D. Brewster has so laboriously illustrated and so eloquently eulogized, shine with a radiance too brilliant to be much obscured by this instance of culpability. Yet our reverence for no man's memory can justify us in shutting our eyes to his faults, and we should always feel that historical justice demands impartiality in the judgment of every question, however it may implicate the fame of distinguished individuals. But an end to this. Our ramble into Jermyn Street, in the endeavour to trace out the footsteps of the philosopher, has involved us in allusions of a painful nature, though it leaves us still among the admirers of his character as well as of his discoveries.

From 1710 till two years before his death, Sir Isaac lived in St. Martin's Street, Leicester Square. Next door to the chapel where Toplady used to preach, there stands an old house now covered with white stucco. It has seen in its time, like a number of other London dwellings, a good many changes. Here once dwelt the Envoy of Denmark, then Sir Isaac Newton, next Paul Dominique, after that Dr. Burney. Who besides may have lived here we cannot tell; but it has now reached the fag-end of its history, and the formerly aristocratic residence is let out in separate floors, and partly turned into a printing office. Reverence for the great astronomer led us lately to pay a visit to the place. We found the rooms somewhat altered, but no doubt the staircase remains as it was in the days of Newton. The part of the house most intimately associated with his name is the little observatory perched on the roof. We were permitted to ascend into that spot, to see it profaned by its present use, for there we found a shoemaker busy at his work. Yet, on second thoughts, a shoemaker's humble employment is no profanation of an astronomer's study, for shoemakers have a mission in this world as well as astronomers. They are fellow-workers in the great hive of human industry. Mutual helpers are they too. For if the stargazer instructs the shoemaker, the shoemaker makes shoes for the stargazer. We thought, as we stood in that little airy nest, looking at our humble friend, and thinking of the great philosopher, how Providence binds all ranks together by ties of inter-dependence, and how wrong it is for the hand to say to the foot, 'I have no need of thee.' A glass cupola probably crowned the observatory in Newton's time, and evidently there was a window in each of the four walls. So here he looked out on the London of nearly a century and a half ago, hardly less crowded and smoky about the neighbourhood than now. Overhead, where Newton turned his eyes with most interest, we know it was just the same—the same beautiful stars shining out on a cold winter's night, the same planets sailing along the same blue ocean, the same moon throwing its light over the same blue fields. What observations, keen and searching—what calculations, intricate and profound—what speculations, far-reaching and sublime—must there have been, when one of the most gifted of mortals from that spot looked out upon the heavens, and in thought went forth on voyages of discovery into the most distant regions of the universe! At the calm, still hour of midnight—Sirius watching over the city of sleepers—Jupiter carrying his brilliant lamp along his ancient pathway—every one of the luminaries in the place appointed by Him who calleth them all by their names—there stands the silvery-headed man with his reflecting telescope, occupied with thoughts which we common mortals in vain endeavour to conjecture.

We must journey now further westward, as far as Kensington, then a place of great repute for invalids, and also distinguished by the residence of the monarch George I., at the old palace there. Newton was well known at court. On one occasion, the king, when congratulated upon reigning over two kingdoms, replied:—'Rather congratulate me on having such a subject in one as Newton, and such a subject in the other as Leibnitz.' And Caroline, wife of the Prince of Wales, afterwards George II., loved to converse with the man who filled Europe with his fame. Declining health and the infirmities of years led Newton, in 1725, to seek an abode at Kensington. 'It was Sunday night,' says his nephew, Mr. Conduit, 'the 7th March, 1724-5: at Kensington, with Sir Isaac Newton, in his lodgings, just after he was come out of a fit of the gout, which he had had in both of his feet for the first time, in the eighty-third year of his age; he was better after it, and had his health clearer, and memory stronger, than I had known him then for some years.' A year after, we have another notice. 'April 15th, 1726: I passed the whole day with Sir Isaac Newton at his lodgings, Orbell's Buildings, Kensington, which was the last time I saw him. He told me that he was born on Christmas Day, 1642.' The house still remains, occuping a retired corner in the old suburbs, with new squares and terraces springing up all around it. It is situated in Bullingham Place; and retaining still its mansion-like aspect, with a large quiet garden and tall shady trees, it carries us back to the last days of Sir Isaac; and looking in through the gate, we picture the feeble man of eighty-four, in his garden chair, sitting on the grass-plot on a sunny afternoon, musing on subjects more sacred than the stars; for Newton was not a mere philosopher, but also a student of revelation. In that house he died, on Monday the 20th March, having on the previous Saturday been able to read the newspaper, and hold a long discourse with Dr. Mead.

One more visit, and we complete our pilgrimages to spots where we meet the shade of the great Sir Isaac. In the Jerusalem Chamber, at Westminster, where the scene of the polemical assembly convened there in 1644 flits before us, we behold the coffin of our philosopher placed in state, and then see it borne away—dukes and nobles counting it an honour to support the pall —to its last earthly resting-place under the pavement of the Abbey. There, shades of the departed thickly throng around us: crowds of the illustrious meet us in those venerable aisles: but no one is more illustrious than he whom we now leave among them. We may apply to him, with a little alteration, the beautiful words employed, with another reference, by a favourite author in describing Westminster Abbey:—'Well may the world cherish his renown; for it has been purchased, not by deeds of violence and blood, but by diligent dispensation of knowledge. Well may posterity be grateful to his memory; for he has left it an inheritance, not of empty names and sounding actions, but whole treasuries of science, bright gems of speculation, and golden views of wisdom.'

VIII.

ISAAC WATTS.

Abney Park is a place associated with melancholy thoughts in the minds of ever-growing numbers, within and around the great metropolis. They remember a mournful visit there, when the funeral procession went slowly winding up the cemetery paths—and hillock after hillock, and stone after stone, solemnly glided past the carriage window—and the little chapel was entered—and the last service was performed—and finally the sorrowing group was circled round the grave, to leave there, till the resurrection of the just, the ashes of the dead. Many a precious deposit has been laid within the chambers of earth and stone which hollow out the under-soil of that great burial-ground, and names are celebrated there on slab and monument which time will not soon let die. A cenotaph monument and statue to the memory of the man whose history we are trying to note down rises in Abney Park conspicuously above other mementoes of the departed, connecting the place with his honoured name, and exciting the visitor to recollections of his works and virtues. The figure of Watts, long since dead, is meant to remind us of his association with the place for so long a time when living.

ABNEY HOUSE.

A hundred and fifty years ago, on the site of Abney Park, there stood a mansion, which was the happy home of Sir Thomas Abney and his family. We have an indistinct remembrance of it, just before it was pulled down, as we happened to glance at it in our rambles through the quiet street of Stoke Newington, with its old brick front, its old brick wall, and its old iron gate, all redolent of the times of William III. and Queen Anne. There it was in all its prime during those eventful reigns—full of quaint and somewhat cumbrous furniture—and compassed about, in the garden portion of the territory, with noble trees and primly cut shrubs, and box-bordered beds of tulips and roses, and sundry old-fashioned flowers, cultured according to the most approved taste of Dutch gardening. Sir Thomas Abney was Lord Mayor of London in 1700; and we fancy we see his lordship with the appendages and satellites of his state, starting from Newington to the City to enter on his office, and, being a devout and pious man, resolving by God's help not to let the cares and pleasures of his new station draw him away from the exercises of faith and prayer; for it is stated that during his mayoralty he would suffer no engagement to interfere with the regular performance of family devotion. In the house of Sir Thomas, Isaac Watts found a home for nearly half the period of his long life, and hence our large allusion to the place and its worthy master. Not only so, but before Dr. Watts became the inmate of Sir Thomas Abney's mansion, he abode for a while under the roof of Sir John Hartopp, who also resided at Stoke Newington, and there he performed the office of tutor to the good knight's son.

The parish church has many monuments and memorials of the family, and among the rest this curious entry, relative to the wife of Sir John: '1711, Dame Elizabeth Hartopp was buried in woollen, the 26th day of November, according to an Act of Parliament made on that behalf: attested before Mr. Gostling, Minor Canon of St. Paul's, London.' And again, relative to another member of the family: 'My lady Hartopp was buried in a velvet coffin, September 22, 1730, in the church.' The Dame Elizabeth who was buried in woollen was the mother of the boy entrusted to the charge of Dr. Watts, and what is more important, she was daughter of General Fleetwood, who married Bridget, one of Oliver Cromwell's children.

Dame Hartopp has been sometimes regarded as the offspring of Bridget, and consequently as the Protector's granddaughter; and if that view of her lineage were correct, then the youth to whom Watts became tutor would be no other than a great-grandson of the strong-willed man who, without a crown, swayed a sceptre over three old kingdoms. But Noble, in his 'Memoirs of the Protectoral House,' shows, as we think satisfactorily, that Elizabeth, who was married to Sir John Hartopp, was a daughter of Fleetwood by his first wife, Frances Smith. Still the Hartopps would be intimately connected with the Cromwells, the family traditions of the latter would be familiar to the former, and stories of Oliver and his son-in-law would often be told in the dining-hall and the gardens of Sir John at Newington.

Isaac Watts had begun to preach while living with the Hartopps. In his twenty-fourth year he delivered his first sermon. He was soon invited to assist Dr. Chauncey in Mark Lane, where the church assembled of which Sir John Hartopp was member. Afterwards, on the retirement of the old pastor, Watts was invited to undertake the charge, and he was ordained March 18th, 1702. But ill health, which made him reluctant to accept the office, interfered very often with his discharge of the duties. He suffered violent illness, and had to go to Tunbridge Wells to recruit his strength. In 1712 nervous disease had so grown upon him that he was compelled totally to suspend his public labours.

For four years Watts was obliged to abandon the exercise of his ministry, and Mr. Price became his assistant at Bury Street, whither the congregation had removed from Mark Lane. Sir Thomas Abney was a member, and he and his amiable and excellent lady were devoted friends to the poet and divine. Watts being lonely—a bachelor in the midst of his sad affliction—the Abneys thought a pleasant, quiet retreat at Stoke Newington would at least relieve his sorrows. So they invited him to come and stay with them. He did so. One day, long afterwards, the Countess of

Huntingdon called upon the invalid :—' Madam,' said he, 'your ladyship is come to see me on a very remarkable day.' 'Why so remarkable?' she asked. 'This day thirty years I came hither to the house of my good friend Sir Thomas Abney, intending to spend but one single week under his friendly roof, and I have extended my visit to the length of exactly thirty years.' 'Sir,' added Lady Abney, in words which contained infinitely more than mere compliment, 'what you have termed a long thirty years' visit, I consider as the shortest visit my family ever received.'

Stoke Newington, under the roof of the Abneys, thus became Watts's home. Here, and at Theobalds, that famous spot in the days of Elizabeth and James I.—where Sir Thomas Abney had a favourite summer retreat—the nervous poetical philosopher spent many a happy day when his malady left bright intervals of thought and affection. 'Here he enjoyed the uninterrupted demonstrations of the truest friendship. Here, without any care of his own, he had everything which could contribute to the enjoyment of life and favour the unwearied pursuit of his studies. Here he dwelt in a family which, for piety, order, harmony, and every virtue, was a house of God. Here he had the privilege of a country recess, the fragrant bower, the spreading lawn, the flowery garden, and other advantages, to soothe his mind and aid his restoration to health, to yield him, whenever he chose them, the most grateful intervals from his laborious studies, and enable him to return to them with redoubled vigour and delight.

Watts was chaplain. And morning and evening he led the devotions of the household, and on Sunday night preached to the family. Two discourses delivered at Theobalds are inserted in the first volume of his sermons, under the title of 'Appearance before God;' and we can picture the thoughtful conductor of the service, with pale face and bent figure, but with piercing eye and distinct though feeble voice, slowly and impressively unfolding his subject, to the great delight of Sir Thomas and his lady, and the circle of family and visitors; while coachmen and footmen and other servants are sitting round the spacious hall, not inattentive to the reverend man whose gentle ways have won their heart, and inspired sympathy and love.

Theobalds often saw Watts hard at work with his books and his studies, his treatises on philosophy, his sermons and his hymns. There, too, he would walk and muse, rambling through the lanes, sitting in the garden, or loitering in the churchyard, where he has left the traces of his muse on the gravestones. One night he was watching from a western window the sun as it went down. There was a dial over the casement, and the last rays were lingering on it, when he took out his ready pencil and wrote:—

> 'Little sun upon the ceiling,
> Ever moving, ever stealing
>   Moments, minutes, hours away;
> May no shade forbid thy shining,
> While the heavenly sun declining
>   Calls us to improve the day.'

A little incident is also recorded which gives a pleasant glimpse of the retired life spent at Newington and Theobalds, showing how Watts was intent on his Father's business. 'A gentlewoman now living, who is an ornament to her sex, told me,' says Dr. Gibbons, ' that in younger life, when on a visit at Lady Abney's, she was taken somewhat ill, and was left in the house (the rest of the family being gone abroad) with only the doctor; and the good man improved the occasion to enter into discourse with her, and gave her most excellent advice, of which she has a pleasing remembrance to the present day.'

Watts had the pastor's and the preacher's heart, though his delicate constitution and impaired health unfitted him for much public labour. We see him watching by the deathbeds of Abney and Hartopp, and we hear him preach funeral sermons for both these worthies. They had been men of rank and celebrity; and Watts loved to think of their service on earth as a preparation for heaven. So he beautifully said: 'In the world of spirits made perfect, David and Moses dwell; both of them were trained up in feeding the flocks of their fathers in the wilderness, to feed and to rule the nation of Israel, the chosen flock of God; and may we not suppose them also trained up in the arts of holy government on earth, to be the chiefs of some blessed army, some sacred tribes in heaven? They were directors of the forms of worship in the Church below under Divine inspiration; and might not that fit them to become leaders of some celestial assembly, when a multitude of the sons of God above come at stated seasons to present themselves before the throne? We know for certain that there are gradations of rank and authority among the angels, that excel in strength, thrones and dominions, principalities and powers; and the same may be predicated of glorious saints, not merely upon the ground of analogy, but upon the Scripture testimony that assigns to the possessor of ten talents rule over ten cities, and of five talents over five cities.'

We can follow Watts also to the dying chamber of the Reverend Samuel Rosewell, as we listen to his account of that holy man's departure, given one Sunday morning to the congregation at Bury Street.

'Come, my friends,' says he, 'come into the chamber of a dying Christian; come, approach his pillow, and hear his holy language: " I am going up to heaven, and I long to be gone—to be where my Saviour is. Why are His chariot wheels so long in coming? I hope I am a sincere Christian, but the meanest and the most unworthy. I know I am a great sinner, but did not Christ come to save the chief of sinners? I have trusted in Him, and I have strong consolation. I love God; I love Christ. I desire to love Him more, to be more like Him, and to serve Him in heaven without sin. Dear brother, I shall see you at the right hand of Christ. There I shall see our friends who are gone a little before [alluding to Sir T. Abney]. I go to my God and to your God—to my Saviour, and to your Saviour."'

Watts's health improved in 1722, and he preached regularly and often; but, though an able minister of the New Testament, delivering sermons instructive and edifying, it does not appear that his forte lay in the work of the pulpit so much as in the work of the press. The great Master of all meant that Watts should chiefly benefit mankind by his writings. The grand instrument of his service was the pen. Thus 'he served his generation according to the will of God;' and we cannot but see the hand of Providence in the arrangement which brought him into the family of the Abneys for that long visit, which stands unrivalled in the annals of hospitality, since by such means extraordinary facilities were afforded for literary occupation; leisure was supplied, while stimulus was not withdrawn. Fully do we concur in the view taken of Dr. Watts's vocation, and of the value of his labours, as given in the following passage from the *North British Review* :—

'As far as his own instincts and the circumstances of the times could indicate, Dr. Watts's calling was the improvement of Christian literature. In the previous century, Bishop Hall had published the banns between letters and religion, and in his pungent "Characters" and entertaining "Epistles" he had laboured to press into the service of the sanctuary the shrewd observation of Theophrastus and the varied intelligence and vivacity of Pliny. But the example had not been followed. Notwithstanding the unprecedented amount of theological authorship with which the intervening age had overflowed, little or nothing had been done to propitiate men of taste to evangelical religion; and although, as regarded the older generation, who had listened to Baxter and Owen, this was of minor moment, it greatly concerned their successors. Pious matrons in the country, and God-fearing merchants in the city, felt a famine of the Word; and whilst, in the meetings they frequented, they sighed for the sop and the savour to which they had been accustomed in their youth, their sons and daughters were reading Pope and Addison throughout the week, and in the selfsame meetings to which they were dragged by their pious seniors on the Sabbaths they were yawning at the prolixity of the sermon, or tittering at the grotesque similes of the preacher. Nor on the Sunday evening in the parlour at home was the matter greatly mended. It would have been well for the young people if they had read the good books which their parents recommended, or sung the psalms of which these never wearied; but, after yesterday's *Spectator*, Owen on

Perseverance was heavy reading, and even the best disposed youth could hardly convince himself that Sternhold was sublimer than Dryden. Dr. Watts felt the *desideratum*. The whole course of his studies had prepared him for supplying it, and there was nothing to which he was more inclined by the entire bent of his genius. And, now, in the good providence of God, he enjoyed the opportunity, and the rest of his life was mainly spent in advancing the cause of Christian culture, through the medium of an attractive authorship.'

Among lives barren of incident though fruitful in interest, that of Dr. Watts is particularly so. Almost always living in seclusion, for long periods an invalid, finding his chief stimulus and recreation in study and the companionship of a few select friends, what very remarkable events could occur in his history? Passing from Stoke Newington to Theobalds, or down to Tunbridge Wells or Southampton, there you have Watts's travels. Preaching at Bury Street, with more or less irregularity in consequence of ill health, or hearing Mr. Price, his assistant, delivering a charity sermon on some rare occasions; paying pastoral visits now and then; and discharging the duties connected with certain trusts, of which he had in part the administration: there you have Watts's public life. Reading, writing, thinking, making books and despatching letters: there you have Watts's main occupation, the business and the burden, and we believe the pleasure too, of his most useful days.

His study in Sir Thomas Abney's house at Stoke Newington was the local centre of his existence. From it he at times diverged, only to return to it again with a deeper feeling of home attachment. So let us step into that favoured retreat, as it appeared before it was pulled down to make room for the cemetery which now occupies the site. We pass the stately elms which shadow the Manor House, and enter the hall of the hospitable abode. Wait for a moment here, in what is called the painted room. It is moulded in gilt, with panels enclosing pictures, the subjects taken from the poems of Ovid. But in the window shutters are some strange contrasts with these heathen embellishments; for there, contributed, we are told, by Watts's pencil (the poet being an artist too), are emblems of grief and death, mingled with the arms of Gunston and Abney, and intended doubtless to honour their memory. There are other sketches, too, in this apartment by him who is the *genius loci*—heads of Democritus, Heraclitus, Aristotle, and Alexander, executed with taste and skill.

But now let us approach the doctor's study. Here are some lines from Horace, hung up in a frame outside the door, denouncing the faithless friend. Within, the shelves are loaded with a goodly array of books—poetical, philosophical, historical, theological, and critical. Where there are no shelves, there are prints of noted persons, chiefly divines. A lofty panel covers the fireplace, with inscriptions from Horace on either side: the one where the portraits are numerous indicating that the space is filled up by shades of the departed; the other, where they are fewer, soliciting additions to the illustrious group. The classical fancifulness of all this indicates the scholar and the poet; but the avocations of the worthy occupant of this literary retreat indicate those noble purposes, those high Christian aims, of which all else in his character and habits were ornamental adjuncts.

There he sits at his writing-table, enveloped in a scholarly robe, small in figure, and sickly in complexion; the forehead not so broad and high as we might expect, limited somewhat by the wig that crowns and borders it; the features large and marked, the eyes clear and burning. On his table lie MSS. full of facts and speculations which he is moulding into form, and will ere long publish as 'Philosophical Essays,' and 'A Scheme of Ontology.' He has just been writing a letter to Mr. Coward, the founder of a trust for the education of ministers and the promotion of evangelical religion, of which Dr. Watts is a trustee. Dr. Doddridge is tutor of an academy largely supported out of the funds. Here is a letter from him, which fills the now famed hymn-writer with the purest and richest joy and thankfulness:—' On Wednesday last I was preaching in a barn to a pretty large assembly of plain country-people at a village a few miles off. After a sermon from Hebrews vi. 12, we sang one of your hymns (which, if I remember right, was the 140th of the second book), and in that part of the worship I had the satisfaction to observe tears in the eyes of several of the auditory; and after the service was over, some of them told me that they were not able to sing, so deeply were their minds affected with it; and the clerk in particular told me he could hardly utter the words of it. These were most of them poor people, who work for their living. On the mention of your name, I found they had read several of your books with great delight, and that your hymns and psalms were almost their daily entertainment. And when one of the company said, "What if Mr. Watts should come down to Northampton?" another replied, with a remarkable warmth, "The very sight of him would be like an ordinance to me."'

Watts and Doddridge—the former an old man, the latter a comparatively young one—grew into one another's hearts most remarkably during the last dozen years or so of life—the younger not long surviving his ministerial friend and father. 'The Rise and Progress of Religion in the Soul' was a work projected by Dr. Watts, but from growing infirmities unexecuted by him, and committed to the charge of Doddridge. He says, in 1743: 'I am hard at work on my book on the "Rise and Progress of Religion," which Dr. Watts is impatient to see and I am eager to finish, lest he should slip away to heaven before it is done.'

Watts wrote to Doddridge in the following year: 'I long to have your "Rise and Progress of Religion" appear in the world. I wish my health had been so far established that I could have read over every line with the attention it merits; but I am not ashamed, with what I have read, to recommend it as the best treatise on practical religion which is to be found in our language; and I pray God that it may be extensively beneficial.' Again says he: 'Since you were pleased to read me some chapters of the "Rise and Progress," I am the more zealous for its speedy conclusion and publication, and beg you would not suffer any other matters to divert your attention, since I question whether you can do anything more necessary.'

December 14th, he writes as follows:—'I thank you that your heart is so much set upon the book I recommended you to undertake. I long for it, as I hope it will be a book of great usefulness, and shall be glad to see the first appearance of it; and hope that by that time I shall be able to read a little more. I thank God I was in the pulpit last Lord's day, though for only thirty-two minutes, which almost overset me, so that my capacities of that kind still run exceedingly low: may they be increased through your prayers, if God please to hear and answer them!'

'February 24th, 1743.—That day on which I sent my last letter to you, I was seized with something of a paralytic disorder, which, though it soon went off, has left various disorders behind it, so that I was confined to my chamber till this day.'

Some of the latter days of Dr. Watts were sadly beclouded by mental depression. At times his nervousness was very great, though stories of it told by anxious friends, or by those who delighted in idle gossip, were grossly exaggerated. Certain speculations on theological points—especially the mysterious subject of the Trinity, deviating from the orthodox line, yet by no means such as to render his faith in the clearly revealed facts and doctrines of the Gospel at all questionable—had raised in some minds suspicions injurious to Dr. Watts's theological character; a dishonour to his name, which certain of his injudicious admirers sought to remove by circulating the report that he was labouring under mental aberration, and not responsible for his opinions. It appears, however, from the testimony of those who knew him best, that though dejected and absent, loving loneliness and silence, losing interest in things and persons once most dear, enfeebled in action—in short, unfitted for work—he was never in a state that could with propriety be termed, in the customary meaning of it, one of mental derangement. Besides physical and nervous debility, he was oppressed by certain family trials. He had unworthy relatives, who from selfishness and spite assailed his character; a circumstance which, as it never affected his general reputation, may here be left in the oblivion it deserves, except as it may be noticed with a passing glance among the tribulations of this eminent servant of God. Doddridge makes allusion to Watts's depression and absence of mind, and mentions a visit in which he was greatly pained by his friend's appearance and manner. Yet we have on record an account of an interview between the two divines, not long before the death of the elder, which would seem to indicate gleams of cheerfulness.

The Rev. Samuel Lavington, of Bideford, a man of congenial spirit, and one who ever venerated the memory of both, happened to be present, in the freshness of his youth, listening with intense delight to the interesting colloquy of men so famous in Israel; and he was wont to relate, in advanced life, when talking of the days of 'auld lang syne,' the story of this parting scene. They supped at Mrs. Abney's house, at Stoke Newington, in company with Dr. Gibbons. Much cheerful conversation passed between them; and the poet pleasantly related to the company how he had been imposed upon by certain persons who had tasted of his bounty, and now, after the death of some of his pensioners, the relatives actually continued, in the names of the deceased, as if they had been living, to claim and receive his accustomed gratuities. The narrative, one would imagine, did not fail to divert the amiable Doddridge, who had himself so often, in various ways, been victimized by designing knaves; and if he did not on the occasion crown the stories of his friend with similar ones relating to himself, we could almost answer for it that this was not because he was unable. Supper over, the venerable bard, oppressed by his infirmities, rose from his chair to retire to his chamber, when Doddridge rose and followed him to the door, in an attitude expressive of ardent attachment and veneration, stretching out his arms as if (to use Mr. Lavington's language, who, when he told the story, suited the action to the words) Elisha was endeavouring to catch the mantle of the ascending prophet.

This little incident was related to us in writing by the Rev. Mr. Rooker, of Tavistock and Plymouth, who also mentioned a pleasant circumstance communicated to him by a friend of the Abney family; namely, that Dr. Watts was greatly beloved by the domestics, and that they were wont to put themselves in the way of the venerable sojourner under their mistress's roof, that they might receive marks of approval and kindness. His amiableness must have been very great, and it attached to him a circle of friends, many of whom had been drawn into that sphere by the brightness of his literary reputation and the beneficial perusal of his works. Persons of high rank and distinction were of the number—members of aristocratic houses and officers of State. We read of the Right Honourable Mr. Onslow, Speaker of the House of Commons, going in his coach to

Newington, taking with him some of Watts's ministerial friends, to have converse with the saintlike man, before his translation to a world where all are saints. They had a hallowed interview, and after the death of Dr. Watts, the Speaker, in conversation with Dr. Gibbons, said that in him he saw a man of God, adding, 'My soul where his now is!'[1]

Nervous depression generally produces either a low state of spiritual sensibility, or intense spiritual sorrow, bordering on, if not reaching to, despair. But Watts retained throughout his malady an interest in the Gospel, and a good hope through grace. He was ever a man full of faith and of the Holy Ghost. 'I never could discover,' says Dr. Gibbons, 'though I was frequently with him, the least shadow of a doubt as to his future everlasting happiness, or anything that looked like an unwillingness to die. How have I known him recite, with self-application, those words, "Ye have need of patience, that after ye have done the will of God, ye may receive the promise!" And how have I heard him, upon leaving the family after supper, and withdrawing to rest, declare with the sweetest composure that if his Master were to say to him he had no more work for him to do, he should be glad to be dismissed that night! He discoursed much of his dependence upon the atoning sacrifice of Christ; and his trust in God, through the Mediator, remained unshaken to the last. "I should be glad," he said, "to read more, yet not

---

[1] Milner's 'Life and Times of Watts.'

in order to be confirmed more in the truth of the Christian religion, or in the truth of its promises; for I believe them enough to venture an eternity on them."

'When he was almost worn out by his infirmities, he observed, in conversation with a friend, that he remembered an aged minister used to say that the most learned and knowing Christians, when they come to die, have only the same plain promises of the Gospel for their support as the common and unlearned; "and so," said he, "I find it. It is the plain promises that do not require much labour and pains to understand them; for I can do nothing now but look into my Bible for some promise to support me, and live upon that."'

Dr. Gibbons, in one of his visits, found him exceedingly weak and low, the lamp of life very feebly glimmering in its last decay; but he was still in the perfect possession of his understanding. He said, in answer to the question whether he had any pain, that he had none; and in reply to inquiries about his soul, that all was comfortable, confessing that to be a great mercy. Dr. Stennett informs us that his discourse was most heavenly; that he particularly spoke of his dependence on Christ, declaring that to part with Christ was to part with all hope.

He had a faithful and loving attendant, of the name of Parker, who piously noted down his master's dying sayings. 'I would be waiting to see what God will do with me. It is good to say, as Mr. Baxter, "What, when, and where God pleases." If God should raise me up again, I may finish some of my papers, or God can make use of me to save a soul, and that will be worth living for. If God has no more service for me to do, through grace I am ready. It is a great mercy to me that I have no manner of fear or dread of death. I could, if God please, lay my head back, and die without terror this afternoon or night. My chief supports are from my view of eternal things, and the interest I have in them. I trust all my sins are pardoned, through the blood of Christ. I have no fear of dying: it would be my greatest comfort to lie down and sleep, and wake no more.'

The faithful servant wrote, on the 24th of November, to Mr. Enoch Watts of Southampton, as the life of his brother was now fast ebbing away: 'I said to him this morning that he had taught us how to live, and was now teaching us how to die, by his patience and composure; for he has been remarkably in this frame for several days past. He replied, "Yes." I told him I hoped he experienced the comfort of these words, "I will never leave thee, nor forsake thee." He answered, "I do." The ease of body and calmness of mind which he enjoys is a great mercy to him and to us. His sick chamber has nothing terrifying in it.' On the 26th the looked-for announcement was despatched to Southampton: 'At length the fatal news is come. The spirit of the good man, my dear master, took its flight from the body to worlds unseen and joys unknown, yesterday in the afternoon, without a struggle or a groan. My Lady Abney and Miss Abney are supported as well as we can reasonably expect. It is a house of mourning and tears. For I have told you before how that we all attended upon him and served him from a principle of love and esteem. May God forgive us all, that we have improved no more by him while we enjoyed him!'

Dr. Watts was buried in Bunhill Fields on the 5th of December, 1748, his funeral being attended, at his own desire, by two Independent ministers, two Presbyterian, and two Baptist.

Dr. Watts was as far removed from sectarianism as a man could be. The spirit of his works and life has awakened deep and lasting sympathy in the souls of multitudes; and, without noting other proofs of the esteem in which his name is held by all parties, we may mention that when a meeting was held in his native town of Southampton to determine on a monument to his memory, the chair was occupied by a dignitary of the Establishment, and a numerous body of clergymen vied with each other in doing honour to the most distinguished hymnologist of Christendom.

To use the words of an article in the *North British Review*, from which we have before made a quotation: 'Without concealing the peculiar doctrines of the Gospel, without losing the fervour of his personal devotion, he gained for that Gospel the homage of genius and intelligence; and, like the King of Israel, he touched his harp so skilfully that many who hardly understood the words were melted by the tune. Without surrendering his right of private judgment, without abjuring his love of natural and artistic beauty, he showed his preference for moral excellence, his intense conviction of "the truth as it is in Jesus." And now, in his well-arranged and tasteful study, decorated by his own pencil, a lute and a telescope on the same table with his Bible, he seems to stand before us, a treatise on logic in one hand, and a volume of "hymns and spiritual songs" in the other, asserting the harmony of faith and reason, and pleading for religion and refinement in firm and stable union. And as far as the approval of the Most High can be gathered from events, or from its reflection in the conscience of mankind, the Master has said, "Well done, good and faithful servant." Without trimming, without temporizing, he was "quiet," and without bustle; without boasting or parade, he did "his own business," the work that God had given him. And now no Church repudiates him: Nonconformity cannot monopolize him. His eulogium is pronounced by Samuel Johnson and Robert Southey, as well as Josiah Conder; and whilst his monument looks down on Dissenting graves in Abney Park, his effigy reposes beneath the consecrated roof of Westminster Abbey and, which is far better, next Lord's day, the Name which is above every name will be sung in fanes where princes worship and prelates minister, as well as in barns where mechanics pray and ragged scholars say Amen, in words for which all alike must thank his hallowed genius; and it will only be some curious student of hymnology who will recollect that Isaac Watts is the Asaph of each choir, the leader of each company.'

IX.

OLIVER GOLDSMITH.

Perhaps no face in London a hundred and odd years ago, is now so familiar to the reader, as that of Oliver Goldsmith. Not that portraits of him are more numerous than of some other distinguished men among his contemporaries; but there is that in the character of the man's features and countenance which, once seen, is not soon forgotten. He was just the person to strike the attention of people as he walked along the streets, and to furnish a study for every peripatetic physiognomist he met with. The broad cheeks, large forehead, thick lips, round nose, dark brow, and bright eyes of the poet, formed a visage unusually plain, approaching to the positively ugly, and which was saved from being altogether so only by the expression it wore of unusual good nature. But his portraits, in general, give no idea of his dress. A sort of student's robe envelops his shoulders, according to the idea of Goldsmith in our boyhood, received from the picture of him prefixed to his 'History of England,' and other books. A very differently attired personage, however, was the real Oliver, as commonly seen by the Londoners more than a century since. No man ever so delighted in velvet and gold lace. His 'bloom-coloured coat' figures in all his biographies, together with the story of the wag who met him marching along the Strand with bagwig and sword, and exclaimed, 'Look at that fly with a long pin stuck through it.'

Poor Goldsmith! Vanity and good nature lay obviously enough on the surface of his character; the latter, in spite of the former, ever saving him from contempt, but seldom from derision. He was a creature of the most generous impulses, and would give away his last shilling; but beneficence with him was the result of an unreasoning instinct, rather than of thoughtful and conscientious principle. Such generosity as Goldsmith often displayed may lie close beside a fondly cherished selfishness. It involves not the self-denial which grows out of a calm strong will, cultured by moral convictions and religious faith. True goodness is ever associated with more or less of strength. Weakness is not the companion of virtue. Tried by Christianity—the only sound standard of judgment which in such cases we can recognize—characters like Goldsmith must bring down censure, while they awaken sorrow. The deficiency, or rather absence, of principle throughout his life, deprives it altogether of the aspect of a battle with the world and sin, as every good man's life must be. 'It has been questioned,' remarks one of his biographers, whether he really had any religious feeling.' We should not raise the question. Religious feeling no doubt he had; though even that does not seem to have been intense. But of religious *faith*, which is another thing—by which we mean the realization of Divine truths, especially those revealed in the Gospel—we have, alas! no evidence in his works or memoirs. We can admire his delicate genius and appreciate his generous acts; but we feel it our duty, and we discharge it with pain, to indicate some moral and religious deficiencies.

As Goldsmith was a poet, historian, and even philosopher, intimately connected with London in the old time, we should be chargeable with a great omission if we did not notice him among the shades of the departed ones. Indeed, we feel it nothing less than a tribute of gratitude here to inscribe his name, and portray the scenes with which he was associated; for how much do we owe of instruction and pleasure to his lively prose and beautifully simple verse! He was one of the companions of our childhood, fondly cherished, and as an author we love him still; though matured understanding and reflection lead us to speak discriminatingly of his character as a man.

We find Goldsmith in London for the first time, wandering about the streets on a miserable February night, with only a few halfpence in his pocket. Disappointing his friends' expectations, he had been leading a very unsettled and vagrant sort of life, and had just arrived in the metropolis from his Continental journeyings, in which his flute had been his chief resource and best friend. 'The clock had just struck two: what a gloom hangs all around! no sound is heard but of the chiming clock, or the distant watchdog! How few appear in those streets which but a few hours ago were crowded! But who are those who make the streets their couch, and find a short repose from wretchedness at the doors or the opulent? They are strangers, wanderers, and orphans, whose circumstances are too humble to expect redress, and whose distresses are too great even for pity. Some are without the covering even of rags, and others emaciated with disease: the world has disclaimed them, society turns its back upon their distress, and has given them up to nakedness and hunger. Those poor shivering females have seen happier days, and been flattered into beauty. They are now turned out to meet the severity of winter; perhaps now lying at the doors of their betrayers, they sue to wretches whose hearts are insensible, or debauchees who may curse but not relieve them.' So wrote Goldsmith years afterwards, and doubtless, in this graphic sketch, we have a picture of what he saw on the night in question. Houseless wanderers there are still at such an hour—people who, to use a significant expression, have only the key of the street; but better times have come since Goldsmith's days, and the friendly lodging-house, which his kind heart for the sake of others would have well approved, and, we fancy, would have led him to advocate with a ready pen, now throws open its door to give shelter and welcome, with the hallowing influence of an evening prayer, to many a miserable stranger who, through vice, crime, or misfortune, has made shipwreck of home.

We next catch a wavering glimpse of our friend the poet in a chemist's shop near Fish Street Hill, where he assists in the laboratory; and then we find him practising medicine for himself, in a small way, somewhere in Bankside, Southwark. His strong passion for dress exhibits itself in the second-hand suit of green and gold, which makes him a rather conspicuous personage in the thoroughfares of the Borough; while a want of neatness, or of money to pay the washerwoman, is clearly betrayed in his shirt and neckcloth, now of a fortnight's wear. But contentment or pride provided a covering for his poverty, and he told a friend that 'he was practising physic and doing very well.' The green suit was afterwards changed for a black one, with a patch on the left breast, which he ingeniously concealed by holding up his cocked hat when he was conversing with his patients. A polite person once sought to relieve him from this apparent incumbrance, 'which only made him press it more devoutly to his heart.'

· Tired of practice, or disappointed of success, he soon exchanged the phial for the ferule, and prescriptions for spelling-books. Goldsmith came out in the character of a schoolmaster's assistant at Peckham, a kind of employment to which he had been used before; and at the table of Dr. Milner—for so the master of the school was named—he became acquainted with Smollett, who first directed him to literature as a means of subsistence, by employing him as a contributor to the *Monthly Review*. Subsequently, physic and literature were combined to eke out a maintenance, and, in the double capacity of doctor and author, he presents himself to our notice in a wretched lodging by Salisbury Square, Fleet Street. Here we have a peep into the life of a poor literary man of the eighteenth century, to which parallels are numerous enough in the nineteenth. Leaving his lodgings, he kept his appointments at some house of call; the Temple Exchange Coffee House, Temple Bar, was his most favoured resort. There, indeed, was his ostensible abode; and the people who saw him by day had little idea of the forlorn lodging where he spent his nights.

We must now visit a spot with which his name is more distinctly associated than with any of those we have thus hastily mentioned. Modern improvements have wrought marvellous changes in what used to be Fleet Market. The market is gone, or rather transferred out of sight to the neighbouring shambles, where it bears the name of Farringdon. The prison has totally vanished. The crowded scenes of trade, and vice, and infamy, which covered the broad space now known as Farringdon Street, have passed away; but until recently there still remained a memento of Goldsmith's times—an outlet not far from the south end, on the right hand, which led up through a miserable street of rag and bone shops, adorned with hideous black dolls in white frocks, to a steep flight of steps, conducting us to a place, bearing the very inappropriate name of Green Arbour Court. Once, perhaps, the miserable tenements were respectable dwelling-houses. At the upper end, in a house which was pulled down in 1834, Goldsmith was living when he wrote his 'Enquiry into the State of Polite Learning in Europe.'

The spot is intimately connected with its once remarkable and illustrious tenant, from the anecdotes of him while residing there preserved by his biographers. Here it was that Percy, the author of the 'Reliques,' called upon Goldsmith, and found him in a dirty room, with one chair, which he politely relinquished for the use of his visitor, while he sat himself down on the window seat during the interview. As the conversation proceeded, a gentle tap was heard at the door, and a ragged child came in, who dropped a courtesy, and then delivered the following message, much, no doubt, to the poet's chagrin : 'Mamma sends her compliments, and begs the favour of you to lend her a potful of coals'—a favour, no doubt, which mamma had often conferred on her neighbour. And here, too, occurred the generous but improvident transaction so often told respecting the author and his landlady. It was Christmas Day, and Goldsmith was smarting under his recent rejection at the College of Surgeons, where he had failed at his examination, when the poor woman entered his room with a heart-rending tale. Her husband had just been carried off to prison for debt. The man of literature had no money in his pocket, not enough to buy a Christmas dinner; but there hung a new suit of clothes, which in his eyes must have been precious indeed. The gratification of the instinctive emotions of pity was to be preferred to the gratification of his vanity, at least for a while, and therefore he sent off to the pawnbroker's and raised enough to pay the poor man's debt, and get him out of gaol. By the way, Griffiths, the publisher, had become surety to the tailor for these clothes, and had also lent Goldsmith books to be reviewed. The clothes gone, and no money left, he was tempted to raise money on the books too; so that, when the publisher, wanted them back, they were not to be obtained. This double failure roused the ire of Griffiths, and he wrote a letter to the author which pierced his heart. Poor man! he had not learned the lesson that we must be just before we are generous, and that there is little commendable in the generosity which prompts us to give away what is not our own.

Some interesting reminiscences of the poet while living in Green Arbour Court are preserved by Washington Irving. 'An old woman,' he says, 'was still living, in 1820, who was a relative of the identical landlady whom Goldsmith had relieved by the money received from the pawnbroker. She was a child about seven years of age at the time that the poet rented his apartment of her relative, and used frequently to be at the house in Green Arbour Court. She was drawn there, in a great measure, by the good-humoured kindness of Goldsmith, who was always exceedingly fond of the society of children. He used to assemble those of the family in his room, give them cakes and sweetmeats, and set them dancing to the sound of his flute. He was very friendly to those around him, and cultivated a kind of intimacy with a watchmaker in the court, who possessed much native wit and humour. He passed most of the day, however, in his room, and only went out in the evenings. His days were, no doubt, devoted to the drudgery of the pen, and it would appear that he occasionally found the booksellers urgent taskmasters. On one occasion, a visitor was shown up to his room, and immediately their voices were heard in high altercation, and the key was turned within the lock. The landlady, at first, was disposed to go to the assistance of her lodger, but a calm succeeding, she forbore to interfere. Late in the evening the door was unlocked, a supper ordered by the visitor from a neighbouring tavern, and Goldsmith and his intrusive guest finished the evening in great good-humour. It was probably his old taskmaster Griffiths, whose press might have been waiting, and who found no other mode of getting a stipulated task from Goldsmith than by locking him in, and staying by him till it was finished.'

The scene now shifts to Wine Office Court, Fleet

Street, and there we follow our poet. He now resided with an acquaintance or relative of Newberry, a famous publisher of books for children. He wrote much for that kindly person, and found probably a better patron and paymaster than Mr. Griffiths—for Goldsmith's circumstances were in a decidedly improved condition after he left Green Arbour Court; yet for his former landlady he seems to have retained a benevolent regard, as we are informed 'that he often supplied her with food from his own table, and visited her frequently, with the sole purpose to be kind to her.' A debating club, called the Robin Hood, used to meet in those days somewhere near Temple Bar; and there, at the conventions of the men of wit and letters, with others who had pretensions to neither, Goldsmith made his appearance. He was introduced for the first time by an Irish acquaintance of the name of Derry. It happened that the chair was that evening occupied by a baker, who seemed mightily elated with an idea of his own importance. 'This,' said Goldsmith, 'must be the Lord Chancellor at least.' 'No, no,' replied his companion, 'he is only *master of the rolls!*'

There is a building in Islington closely connected with Oliver Goldsmith. Here, again, we have to note the ravages of picturesque relics carried on by the steady march of utilitarian improvement. There lies before us an engraving of Canonbury House as it was eighty years ago, with a large piece of water flowing in front, with green-bordered banks, and a line of rustic paling. Squares and streets have risen up in close contiguity to this ancient edifice, and changed the face and fashion of the whole vicinity, blotting out all its rustic accompaniments and destroying its country views. But the old watch-tower remains, built in with modern dwellings. The bricks are black with age, the door retains an antique look, and the little windows speak of times long gone by. Some writers relate that Goldsmith resided here. Sir John Hawkins, his biographer, states that Newberry, the publisher, had apartments in the house; and that the poet there concealed himself from his creditors. It is probable that it was only an occasional and temporary abode; but it has linked itself with his name, by the report that in one of the rooms, still preserved, Goldsmith wrote his 'Deserted Village.'

Washington Irving describes the room as a relic of the original style of the castle, with panelled ornaments and Gothic windows. Our attempt to verify his description was fruitless, as the inhabitant of the classic dwelling would not admit us to the interior sensible, no doubt, of the annoyance attendant upon allowing it to remain a show-house, when what Irving relates in the person of his hero, in the 'Tales of a Traveller,' would often occur. 'In the midst of a vein of thought, or a moment of literary inspiration, I was interrupted, and all my ideas put to flight, by my intolerable landlady tapping at the door, and asking me if I would "just please to let a lady and a gentleman come in and take a look at Mr. Goldsmith's room."' Perhaps the distinguished American is here actually giving his own experience, and we are to add him to the celebrities of Canonbury Tower—a man who, for delicacy of genius, is not unlike the poet he celebrates.

Hone, in his 'Everyday Book,' gives a further account of the room, of which, from want of personal inspection, we are glad to avail ourselves. The occupant in his time was but one generation removed from a relative who lived there when Goldsmith was a lodger. She affirmed that he wrote his 'Deserted Village' in the oak room on the first floor, and slept on a large press bedstead placed in the eastern corner. From this room, Mr. Hone informs us, 'two small ones for sleeping in have since been separated, by the removal of the panelled oak wainscoting from the north-east wall, and the cutting of two doors through it, with a partition between them: and since Goldsmith was here the window on the south side has been broken through.' We are not certain whether it was while tarrying in Islington that Goldsmith wrote that pleasant 'History of England,' the most pleasant of our old school-books, though, by the way, not always conveying just views of our country's heroes and vicissitudes: at any rate the work is connected with Islington. He used to read Hume, Rapin, Carte, and Kennet in a morning, and having made a few notes, would ramble out into the fields round this neighbourhood, and then return to a temperate dinner and cheerful evening, writing off before he went to bed what had arranged itself in his mind from his morning studies. The headquarters of the poet seem still to have been in Wine Office Court, and there it was that Johnson found him, driven to extremities by his landlady's application for rent, and relieved him from difficulty, by taking a MS. Goldsmith had just written, and selling it to a publisher for 60*l*. It was no other than the famous 'Vicar of Wakefield.' 'I brought Goldsmith the money,' says the old king of critics, 'and he discharged his rent, not without rating his landlady in a high tone for having used him so ill.'

The scene changes. We must walk to the Temple, to chambers on the library staircase, and there we find the poet 'a kind of inmate with Jeff, the butler of the society.' The apartments appear to have been of a very humble sort ; but then there were the Temple Gardens and the River Thames at hand, which, in the estimation of such a man as Goldsmith, must have made up for many deficiencies. His biography takes us, during his abode there, to a very different place under very amusing circumstances, which we cannot do better than relate in his own words : 'Having received an invitation to wait upon the Duke of Northumberland,' he says, 'I dressed myself in the best manner I could, and after studying some compliments I thought necessary on such an occasion, proceeded to Northumberland House, and acquainted the servants that I had particular business with the duke. They showed me into an antechamber, where, after waiting some time, a gentleman very elegantly dressed made his appearance. Taking him for the duke, I delivered all the fine things I had composed in order to compliment him on the honour he had done me: when, to my great astonishment, he told me I had mistaken him for his master, who would see me immediately. At that instant the duke came into the apartment, and I was so confounded on the occasion, that I wanted words barely sufficient to express the sense I entertained of the duke's politeness, and went away exceedingly chagrined at the blunder I had committed.' Poor bashful man, by no means learned in the ways of this world! Sir John Hawkins, a man of a different stamp, who gives a further account of the interview between the author and the duke, blames the former for a want of dexterity in pushing his own interests. Northumberland was just going to Ireland as Lord Lieutenant, and he told Goldsmith he should be glad to do him a kindness. The visitor, much more from generosity than from confusion, commended his brother, a poor clergyman, to his grace's patronage: but sought nothing for himself.

Goldsmith gets 500*l.* for his 'Goodnatured Man,' and forthwith his domicile bears witness to his altered fortune. 'Jeff the butler's rooms' are exchanged for the second floor of No. 2, Brick Court, Temple, overlooking the pleasant garden on the river bank. The spendthrift gives 400*l.* for the lease, and squanders the rest upon splendid carpets and furniture, a suite of ' Tyrian bloom, satin-grain ' and another ' lined with silk and furnished with gold buttons.' He invites Johnson, Reynolds, Percy, and Bickerstaff to gay entertainments; and it is amusing to learn that the occupant of the ground floor is no other than the great lawyer Blackstone, who in his erudite studies, out of which grow his far-famed 'Commentaries on the Laws of England,' sadly complains of the racket made overhead by Neighbour Goldsmith's company. There they are positively playing at blind man's buff! Did Johnson join? The lexicographer upstairs, lumbering about like a big boy: the jurist below, poring over his mouldy books, and grumbling at the levity and noise of such a roister—we have here a curious pair of pictures in our literary history! Goldsmith, like a true poet, loved the country, and often made what he called a shoemaker's holiday. A few friends were invited to a good breakfast on a summer's morning, after which they went off to Blackheath, Wandsworth, or some other suburban village, to revel together among green trees and yellow fields, and to drink in the delicious liquid air floating under the blue skies. We fancy the poet, with dusty feet, and with a large nosegay stuck in his bosom, coming back at night, through the crowded street, to his sombre lodgings in Brick Court; his memory lighted up with pleasant images which haunt him in his dreams, and come forth with helpful ministration when the next day he sits down to write an essay or a lay. Besides other works, Goldsmith wrote his 'History of Rome' in the Temple. Among 'the wits, lawyers, and legal students' who associated with Goldsmith in his half-cloistered retreat, was Judge Day, of the Irish Bench, who often would talk of the poet's kindness to him and Grattan. 'I was just arrived from college,' said he, 'full freighted with academic gleanings; and our author did not disdain to receive from me some opinions and thoughts towards his Greek and Roman histories. Being then a young man, I felt much flattered by the notice of so celebrated a person. He took great delight in the conversation of Grattan, whose brilliancy in the morning of life furnished full earnest of the unrivalled splendour which swelled his meridian; and finding us dwelling together in Essex Court, near himself, where he frequently visited my immortal friend, his warm heart became naturally prepossessed towards the associate of one whom he so much admired.' The judge goes on, as Irving tells us, to give a picture of Goldsmith's social habits: he frequented much the Grecian Coffee House, then the favourite resort of Irish and Lancashire Templars; he delighted in collecting his friends around him at evening parties in his chambers, where he entertained them with a cordial and unostentatious hospitality.

Several London taverns are associated with Goldsmith, and among the rest, one in Dean Street, memorable for a conversation between Goldsmith and Johnson, which supplied some wit often imitated since. The sage philosopher was discussing some kidneys with immense satisfaction, observing as he swallowed the savoury morsels: 'These are pretty little things; but a man must eat a great many of them before he is filled.' 'Ay; but how many of them,' asked the merry poet, with affected simplicity, 'would reach to the moon?' 'To the moon! Ah, sir, that I fear exceeds your calculation.' 'Not at all, sir; I think I could tell.' 'Pray then, sir, let me hear.' 'Why, sir, one; if it were long enough.' Johnson growled for a time at finding himself caught in such a trite schoolboy trap. 'Well, sir,' he said at length, 'I have deserved it. I should not have provoked so foolish an answer by so foolish a question.'

Ranelagh Gardens, then the resort of the fashionable, offered strong attractions to the pleasure-loving Goldsmith; and doubtless often when reflecting on his visits, he felt how true were Johnson's words in one of his grave moods: 'Alas, sir, these are only struggles for happiness! When I first entered Ranelagh, it gave an expansion and gay sensation to my mind, such as I never experienced anywhere else. But as Xerxes wept when he viewed his immense army, and considered that not one of that great multitude would be alive a hundred years afterwards, so it went to my heart to consider that there was not one in all that brilliant circle that was not afraid to go home and think.'

At last, Goldsmith had to go home and die. He expired in his room at the Temple, on the 4th of April, 1774, in his forty-sixth year. Poor women, whom he had generously relieved, stood sobbing outside the door in which lay the poet's corpse: but we cannot forget that there were others who mourned his removal for a very different reason. 'Of poor Goldsmith,' said Johnson, in a letter to Boswell, 'there is little to be told more than the papers have made public. He died of a fever, made, I am afraid, more violent by uneasiness of mind. His debts began to be heavy, and all his resources were exhausted. Sir Joshua Reynolds is of opinion that he owed no less than two thousand pounds.' He was buried in the ground of the Temple Church; and as we think of the poet's dust so near us, when we are passing along Fleet Street, there come mingled with his memory solemn thoughts of the high ends of human life which he so sadly missed, or rather never seemed to aim at. We cannot write poems or essays like him whose shade we have just met, and to whose genius we do honour; but, with very humble talents, we may serve our generation according to the will of God. Neither literary nor any other form of worldly fame may guard our grave and write our epitaph: but a better immortality awaits us if we be numbered among those whom God counts righteous through faith in His Son.

> 'Only the actions of the just
> Smell sweet, and blossom in the dust.'

X.

SIR JOSHUA REYNOLDS.

THE history of English art presents a remarkable contrast to the history of English literature. Upon the dawn of the revival of letters, our Chaucer rose in resplendent beauty to vie with the Italian Boccaccio. The age of Camoens and Tasso was also the age of Spenser, Shakespeare, and Jonson. While Molière, Corneille, and Racine were writing their comedies, Bacon was laying the foundations of true philosophy, Milton was creating his grand epics, and Dryden was pouring out his 'full resounding' lines. But where, during that period, were the masters of British Art? There must indeed have been within our shores men of architectural genius to rear the magnificent edifices of the later mediæval age, the remains of which ever awaken admiration, even in uncultivated minds; but, after the decline and fall of the spirit of Gothic architecture, no man appeared in England worthy of being esteemed a master in the art of building, till Sir Christopher Wren began to cultivate a taste for Italian forms and methods of construction. But he shines in his own department in solitary grandeur. Sculpture suffered a worse fate. With the exception of some beautiful mediæval statues by unknown hands, which still adorn our cathedrals, no English work of merit proceeded from the chisel though long centuries. No English name of note appears in the annals of statuary before the eighteenth century. Painting, so far as native talent is concerned, was scarcely better. George Jamieson, the Scottish Vandyke, as he is called, who commenced his career in Edinburgh in 1628, in a measure rescues the northern part of our isle from the imputation of utter sterility of artistic taste and skill; but no painter of indigenous growth appeared on this side the Tweed worthy of being ranked with him, till a much later period. The names and works of Holbein, Rubens, Vandyke, Lely, and Sir Godfrey Kneller, if we may associate such unequal names and works, became successively celebrated enough in England, during the sixteenth and seventeenth centuries; but these were all foreign. No native artist of commanding power appeared till the following century. It is singular that the eighteenth century, the age of a perfect bathos in architecture, and during the latter half by no means pre-eminent in literature, should have witnessed the rise of English sculpture and painting.

Leicester Fields, as they were once called, and the region round about, contained the nursery of the latter beautiful art; and the facts just dotted down very naturally occur to us, as we walk through that bustling neighbourhood, so very unpicturesque and inartistic in appearance. Hogarth—who in so striking and original a manner depicted the manners of his age, performing with his pencil what Chaucer accomplished with his pen, and leading the way in English painting, as the other did in English poetry—resided on the east side of the square. It bore the sign of the Golden Head, cut by the whimsical artist himself out of pieces of cork, and then glued together. A story is told by Cole, in his curious collection of scraps, illustrative alike of the painter and the times in which he lived. 'When I sat to Hogarth, the custom of giving vails to servants was not discontinued. On taking leave of the painter at the door, I offered his servant a small gratuity, but the man very politely refused it, telling me it would be as much as the loss of his place if his master knew it. This was so uncommon and liberal, in a man of Hogarth's profession at that time of day, that it struck me, as nothing of the kind had happened to me before.'

But the shade of another name pertaining to the history of the same art—less original, perhaps, but in some respects more illustrious—meets us in the commencement of his career not far from Leicester Fields, and then fixes itself within a house which still exists on the west side. To some reminiscences of that distinguished man, preserved by admiring biographers, this chapter is devoted.

In Great Queen Street there are two houses, now numbered 55 and 56, which were originally one.

There, in the year 1740, lived Thomas Hudson, at that time a painter of great note; and there, in the October of that year, was Joshua Reynolds placed under him, as a pupil for instruction in an art for which he had already given unequivocal proofs of a distinguished taste. We see the shade of the youth, destined to become so illustrious a man, of middling stature, florid complexion, regular but rather blunt features, a calm intelligent eye, pleasing aspect, and graceful, easy manners. Industry is one of his leading characteristics, and he works hard in copying the drawings of Guercino; and so skilfully are these copies executed, that many mistake and preserve them as originals. In this method of instruction, adopted by Hudson, we detect his own want of a scientific acquaintance with the principles of his art, and recognize one reason why his pupil was ever deficient in the knowledge of the anatomy of form—a serious drawback on an artist's power; but at the same time Reynolds found in it, no doubt, a discipline highly favourable to the culture of a correct eye, a free hand, and an easy touch —attainments in which he has had few equals. The instructor soon became jealous of the pupil; and the latter had to quit Great Queen Street, and remove for a while to lodge with his uncle in the Temple, whence he speedily repaired to Devonshire, his native county. In these movements we cannot follow him; much less can we accompany him to Italy, where he spent some time in studying, with critical acumen and most refined taste, the works of the most celebrated masters. To his career in London we must confine ourselves; and this, so far as our knowledge of him extends, will keep us chiefly in the neighbourhood already indicated.

Before, however, we pass over his connection with Hudson, we may relate a curious circumstance mentioned by Northcote, as illustrative of the low state of art as cultivated by the master under whom Reynolds received his first lessons, and of the mechanical habits of his early career. Hudson, to get over the critical difficulty of well-disposing the hands in a portrait, used to tuck one in the waistcoat, and hide the other by putting a hat under his arm. Reynolds caught the trick, and so natural did it come to him, that it is positively stated, when he was requested to paint some one with a hat on, he took care to put a hat under the arm too. Nor can we forget another story connected with Reynolds's youthful days under Hudson's tutorship. He was once sent by his master to an auction, where he observed a great bustle by the door. He soon heard the name of Mr. Pope whispered. Everybody drew back as the poet entered, and formed a line on each side, all being eager to shake hands with him as he passed. Reynolds was behind; but as he was reaching under another person's arm to catch the coveted honour, Pope immediately accepted the grasp of the young artist, little thinking of the future importance of the hand he then received in his own. Amidst that crowd of departed shadows, it is interesting to notice two illustrious ones brought by accident into contiguity; and it is also curious to see how great was the popularity of the bard, and how easily the multitude obtained his friendly notice.

At the end of the year 1752, we find Reynolds established as an artist in a house in St. Martin's Lane, about opposite to May's Buildings; his youngest sister Fanny being installed as housekeeper. 'He found at first such opposition as genius is commonly doomed to meet with, and does not always overcome. The boldness of his attempts, the freedom of his conceptions, and the brilliancy of his colouring, were considered as innovations upon the established and orthodox system of portrait manufacture. The artists raised their voices first; and of these, Hudson, who had just returned from Rome, was loudest.' The originality of Reynolds's efforts, however, could not fail to attract public attention, which was speedily followed by public favour. A picture of a Turkish boy brought to his studio numerous visitors, and greatly served to promote and increase his fame. Reynolds now painted heads for ten guineas, half-length for twenty, and whole length for forty. The rich were smitten with such a desire to have themselves represented in the new and tasteful style of the popular painter, that they soon added increasing wealth to his increasing celebrity, and enabled him to remove to a much more handsome and expensive place of abode. He took a large house on the north side of Newport Street, No. 5.

'There,' says Northcote, 'the desire of perpetuating the form of self-complacency crowded his sitting-room with women who wished to be transmitted as angels, and with men who wanted to appear as heroes and philosophers.' His work so increased that he had to employ assistants, and to raise his terms to twelve, twenty-four, and forty-eight guineas, which were the prices his late master, Hudson, received. Afterwards they became fifteen, thirty, and sixty guineas; and before leaving the house in Newport Street they had so risen as to begin with twenty. Dr. Johnson related that he had heard the artist confess, at this time, that he received six sitters a day, and found it necessary to keep a list of those who were waiting for vacancies to occur. The lexicographer's intimacy with the great painter commenced soon after his return from Italy, and we find them often in company with each other in Newport Street. Opposite to the artist there lived the daughters of Admiral Cotterell, whom Johnson visited, and there it was that Reynolds first met him. An amusing anecdote is told of them as they were one evening together at the house of these ladies. The Duchess of Argyle and another lady of rank came in, and engrossed conversation with the Misses Cotterell —an offence sure to rouse the ire of the great critic; so, to mortify the pride of these aristocratic dames, by giving them to suppose that they were in very humble company, he said to Reynolds, loud enough to be heard by all in the room: 'How much do you think you and

I could get a week, if we were to work as hard as we could?'

Johnson took about an equal fancy to Reynolds and his sister, saying of the former: 'There goes a man whom property cannot spoil;' and of the latter, 'that he never saw any one but her who could bear the application of a microscope to the mind.' No doubt the lady greatly supported her influence with the eccentric philosopher by sedulously accommodating herself to his *penchant* for tea; and the story of his parody of Percy's Ballads, addressed to Miss Reynolds, has been often told:

> 'Oh hear it then, my Renny dear,
> Nor hear it with a frown,
> You cannot make the tea so fast
> But I can gulp it down.'

St. Martin's Lane and Newport Street only prepared for the still palmier days and brighter splendour of Leicester Square. Thither Reynolds removed in 1760, there to enjoy for the rest of life such a tide of prosperity as rarely rolls its treasures at the feet of genius. The building, now No. 47, occupied by Messrs. Puttick & Simpson, auctioneers, whose sale-room was the painter's studio, is the house in which he took up his permanent and final abode. Here we can easily picture Reynolds in his glory. He is an early riser, but does not breakfast till nine. At ten begins the chief business of his art. Step into his studio. It is of octagonal form, twenty feet long and sixteen broad. The window is high and small, above nine feet from the ground, and not more than half the common size. And there, raised eighteen inches from the floor, stands the chair for his sitters—the famous chair often occupied by beauty, rank, and fashion, but above all by genius; by the author of the 'Rambler;' by the bard who sung the 'Deserted Village;' the chair immortalized in the painting of the Tragic Muse, not less celebrated than the chair of Pindar in the Temple of Delphi. Reynolds is busy examining designs and touching uncompleted portraits till eleven, from which time till four he is engaged with sitters. Dr. Beattie enters, well known as a champion for reason and religion against the fallacies of David Hume. Reynolds is engaged on a fine portrait of the Scotch philosopher and divine, with two figures beside him representing Truth and Falsehood. The easel is just by the little window. There stands the artist looking at his subject, and holding a pallet, not on his thumb, but by means of a large handle. Then turning to the canvas, he lays on with a pencil of nineteen inches those colours which glow with so much richness and radiance.

The hours of toil over, Reynolds takes a ride in his carriage, which, as it draws up at the door, you might mistake for the Lord Mayor's coach, so elaborately are the panels adorned with allegorical paintings. Richly decorated vehicles are not uncommon, but this is decidedly in advance of the fashion. 'It is too showy,' says Miss Reynolds. 'What! would you have one like an apothecary's carriage?' asks her brother, showing that a love of display is one of his weaknesses, and that he has a rather vulgar notion of the attributes of dignity pertaining to his profession. The coachman, however, delights in his master's taste, for people pay him to get a sight of the carriage. At dinner, Sir Joshua is surrounded by the *élite* of intelligence and talent, who, while they share in an elegantly furnished repast, are as much gratified by the conversation of their host. There is Johnson in his drab attire, and Percy in clerical costume, and Burke and Garrick in the fashion of the day ; while Goldsmith appears in a fashion of his own, exhibiting with much satisfaction his 'plum-coloured coat.' Reynolds added to the taste of an artist the habits of a gentleman, and tended greatly, by the purity of his conversation and the virtue of his character, to discourage and repress, as far as his influence extended, those social excesses which were usual in his days, especially the earlier ones, among all classes.

Reynolds was now a great man, caressed by the mighty, and served by the humble; admired by the cultivated, and wondered at by the vulgar. What Pope had been, he became ; and it is curious to learn that the youth who was so anxious to come in contact with the illustrious poet rose to be the object of a similar kind of reverence and homage. Northcote, himself a devotee to the art of painting, and fired with all the enthusiasm of genius and ambition, when a young man attended a public meeting where Reynolds

A PARTY AT THE HOUSE OF SIR JOSHUA REYNOLDS.

was present, when he got as near to him as he could from the pressure of the people, ' to touch *the skirt of his coat ;*' which he accomplished, he says, ' with great satisfaction of mind.'

But the full prosperity of Reynolds's mature life never induced him to relax in diligent application to the duties of his calling. With all the freshness and fire of a gifted mind he associated the painstaking of the humblest labourer. It was with him a favourite maxim that, without pre-eminent industry, nothing of marked excellence can be produced. He had no faith in mere genius. So much did he extol the efforts and recommend the cultivation of intense and earnest study, that many thought he did not sufficiently recognize the difference between one mind and another, arising from the fact of varied original endowments. Of the capacities and powers with which Providence had endued him we can form no other than a very lofty estimate, but doubtless it was careful culture which developed them in so much beauty and perfection. It might be said of him, almost literally, ' that he passed no day without a line.' He was hardly ever absent from his painting-room ; and he used to say, when for a short space he had been visiting his friends, that he returned home like one who had been without his natural food ; and that, if he made a visit for three days, it required three days more on his return, before he could recover his usual train of thinking. Diligence of the nature which distinguished the life of Reynolds is commendable within limits, especially in association with another and higher kind of diligence: but it would appear, at least through the larger portion of his history, that artistic diligence in his case was carried to an extreme, which entirely absorbed his soul, and left no place for incomparably more momentous subjects. Pleasure does not seem to have been supreme with him, nor wealth, nor even fame; but the culture of his faculties, the elevation and ennobling of his taste.

Had he been merely an intellectual and social being, that might have been consistent. But he had a spiritual nature, which brought him into moral and everlasting relations to the Divine Being; he had a nature needing Divine renewal, and standing in need of purification from sinful stains. Now the practical conduct of his life looked very much as if he ignored this. His intense love of art rendered him unmindful of the great duties of religion. It is very melancholy to be informed that he was accustomed to say, 'The man will never make a painter who looks for the Sunday with pleasure as an idle day.' His habit of painting on that day explains what he meant. Johnson knew the mournful failing of his friend, and the deep and fatal sinfulness involved in it, when, as he was on his dying bed, he begged him 'to read the Scriptures carefully, and to abstain from using his pencil on the Sabbath.' To these requests Sir Joshua gave a willing assent, and is said to have faithfully observed them. So writes his biographer. We trust the artist *did* take the dying moralist's advice; we are sure that he would paint the better for it. Examples of the past and present show that Reynolds was mistaken about the need of painting *every* day. Religion—deep, earnest religion—that which takes in the whole Gospel, and which penetrates the depths of the soul—that which transforms the man and brings him into fellowship with the infinite and glorious mind of Christ—that which makes the Sabbath a delight, and gives sacredness to every portion of time by exhibiting it as a talent from the Giver of all good, to be devoted to His glory—is not only in harmony with the profession of the artist, and with all the diversified employments of social life, but it improves, exalts, and dignifies them. All genius is a Divine gift, while between that and *inspiration*, properly so called, a very bold and decided distinction is to be drawn; the former no less than the latter is a sovereign bestowment from the Father of lights. Men of genius have in many cases recognized this, and felt that in acknowledging dependence upon the Almighty for intellectual endowments, they were only doing what that fact required, when they sought from the same source the sanctification of their powers through the gracious bestowment of the Holy Spirit. Piety elevates genius, gives it a celestial glow, throws round it a saintly halo, as every one of sanctity and taste must feel who has studied the exquisite pictures of Fra Angelico at Florence, of whom it is said he never painted without prayer.

✓ In our next chapter, upon Johnson, we shall refer to the Literary Club. He and Sir Joshua Reynolds shared in the honour of founding it, and, with Burke and Goldsmith, formed the brightest stars in that constellation of intelligence, wit, and genius. Sir John Hawkins tells us, that the celebrated Mrs. Montague invited the members to dine at her house for two successive years, possibly blending, with a curiosity to hear their conversation, a desire to intermingle with it the charms of her own. She, it is said, gave the first occasion for distinguishing the society by the appellation of 'literary'—an honour, it is pretended, which they were too modest to assume. It must have been a rare intellectual treat, whatever it was in other respects, to mingle in this party of *savants*, when their conversational powers would no doubt be wound up to the hightest pitch by the presence and the stimulating talk of that eloquent and eccentric lady.

Sir Joshua, in 1770, became a member of another association, which dined together on stated days at the British Coffee House, Cockspur Street. At some occasional parties of a similar kind we also meet him; one, especially memorable, at the St. James's Coffee House, from the circumstance of the individuals present taking it into their heads to compose extempore epitaphs on each other. Poor Goldsmith came in for cutting jokes, as he often did; and this suggested his well-known poem, entitled 'Retaliation,' in which he thus hits off the character of Reynolds, who, it must be remembered, was deaf—an infirmity which he diminished by the aid of a trumpet:—

> 'Here Reynolds is laid; and to tell you my mind,
> He has not left a wiser or better behind;
> His pencil was striking, resistless, and grand;
> His manners were gentle, complying, and bland;
> Still born to improve us in every part,
> His pencil our faces, his manners our heart.
> To coxcombs averse, yet most civilly steering;
> When they judged without skill, he was still hard of hearing;
> When they talked of their Raphaels, Corregios, and stuff,
> He shifted his trumpet and only took snuff.'

In a former chapter we visited Somerset House, to meet the shade of one of the princes of British science: to the same place we now repair as we follow the shade of one of the princes of British art. The building so intimately connected with the Royal Society is also united by a bond as close to the Royal Academy. Newton was an early president of the one; Reynolds was the first president of the other. The Academy was instituted in 1768. It was opened on the 2nd of January, 1769, when the president delivered a Discourse, and was soon afterwards knighted by George III. The beautiful composition then read was followed by others, which have secured for the author a literary as well as an artistic reputation. Sir Joshua's success has long since been decided in both capacities; and 'students in art have reason to be grateful for the feeling by which the author of the Discourses was influenced in composing them, and to rejoice that the talents of their great projector were so admirably adapted to the task which he assigned himself.' As we peruse the Discourses we seem to sit on one of the benches in the venerable and spacious room at the top of the building devoted to the Society's use, in the midst of a learned and polite assembly, with whom, as the aristocracy of talent, the aristocracy of rank loved to mingle; while all were eager to catch the tasteful instructions which flowed from the lips of the accomplished president. We call to mind the story that, one evening, a certain earl was present, who at the close of the lecture went up to Reynolds, and observed: 'Sir Joshua, you read your Discourse in so low a tone that I could not distinguish one word you said.' 'That,' replied the president, with a modesty instinct with wit, 'that was to my advantage.' And then the annual banquets on St. George's Day, graced by the presence of royalty, distinguished foreigners, and other persons of renown—what ovations they proved in honour of him who had done so much, by pen and pencil, to advance the interests of the Academy! One sees him, in 1786, supported by the Prince of Wales and the Duke of Orleans, the latter sitting under his own lifelike picture by Reynolds's hands; and three years later comes the still more grateful scene, when Burke sent up to Reynolds the following note: 'This end of the table, in which, as there are many admirers of art, there are many friends of yours, wish to drink an English tradesman who patronizes the art better than the grand monarque, "Alderman Boydell, the commercial Mæcenas."' The toast was proposed by the president, and drunk with loud applause.

Four years later, on the 10th of December, Reynolds delivered in the same place the last of his Discourses, closing that beautiful production with the memorable sentence which pointed to the man whose works through life he had loved to study: 'I should desire that the last words which I should pronounce in this Academy, and from this place, might be the name of *Michael Angelo.*'

Growing infirmities led to his final resignation; and a failure of sight put an end to those artistic pursuits which he had followed from his youth with so much ardour. The house in Leicester Square acquires a touching interest from a little incident connected with his last days. He was glad to amuse himself during his melancholy affliction, 'and part of his attention was bestowed upon a little tame bird which, like the favourite spider of the prisoner in the Bastile, served to pass away a lonely hour. But this proved also a fleeting pleasure; for one summer's morning, the window of the chamber being by accident left open, the little favourite took flight, and was irrecoverably lost, although its master wandered for hours in the square before the house, in the fruitless hope of reclaiming it.' A symbol of a moral sentiment lies in that simple story: so do the cherished joys of earth in many a case take wing, leaving those who have lost them to wander after them in vain.

(Sir Joshua Reynolds, after suffering much from nervous disease, died in Leicester Square, February 23rd, 1792, aged sixty-nine. He had a public funeral. The remains were removed to Somerset House, and from thence the procession moved to the Cathedral of St. Paul: it included forty-two mourning coaches and forty-nine private carriages, and the pall was borne by three dukes, two marquises, and five other noblemen. The funeral train was met by the Lord Mayor and Sheriffs at Somerset Place, whilst vast multitudes lined the way to gaze upon the pageant; shops being shut, and people vying with each other to show homage to departed genius. He was interred in a crypt beneath the dome, where the ashes of other distinguished painters have still found their place of repose: Lawrence, Barry, Opie, West, Fuseli, and Turner. Nelson and Collingwood sleep within the same subterranean enclosure, to which Wellington is conveyed, reminding us of the truth, not less affecting than familiar, that neither skill in art nor prowess in arms can protect the sons of men from the stroke of the last enemy.

XI.

DR. SAMUEL JOHNSON.

'My first journey to London!' There are few of the country-born inhabitants of the great city who do not look back to that event with peculiar interest. How busy imagination used to be in the days of their boyhood with this object of their hope. How the old grey metropolis, painted in fancy hues, used to loom before the eye, and excite eager longings for the day when the grand expedition was to be made. With feelings bordering on envy, the lad on his way to school before breakfast, as the summer sun smiled so cheerfully on the front of the provincial inn, looked up to the passengers on the roof of the London day-coach, and paused to witness the busy preparations of the red-coated driver and guard, and followed with his eye the well-laden vehicle rattling along the stones and whirling round the corner, and caught the echo of the merry horn, becoming fainter and fainter till it died away. And when, perchance, some young schoolfellow had been to spend his holidays in the mother-city, with what curiosity was he welcomed on his return, and how eagerly did listening groups gather round him to receive his wonderful stories! When the period arrived for one's own personal adventure in this way, how broken was the sleep the night before! What dreams we had, all in glorious confusion! Nor was there any fear of lying too late that morning. With what joy did we spring into the place booked some time before, and all day long how we did wonder about what we were to see! and did we not stretch our neck to catch a glimpse of every object in advance, as the coach neared Whitechapel?

To how many has the first journey to London been really an epoch in their history! The legendary tale of Whittington dreaming of London streets being paved with gold, and finding out at last that for him they might be said to be so, has found almost a counterpart in the actual experience of not a few, who have in succeeding centuries occupied his seat of honour and worn the civic chain. Arrival in the metropolis, too, has often proved the first step out of obscurity into fame. Minds full of genius have found it a battle-ground on which—not, however, till after much hard fighting—they have won the laurels of renown. As in the biography of commerce the struggles of young men in pursuit of wealth, during the first few years of their London life, would afford materials full of interest and instruction, so are illustrations and lessons supplied by the opening chapters of a metropolitan career in the history of aspirants after literary fame.

We often think of Johnson's first visit to London.

He was twenty-eight years of age, and came up in search of fortune in a double sense. He wanted a livelihood; but literary ambition was coupled with the humbler desire. He and Garrick travelled from Lichfield together. They liked to talk of it afterwards, and would paint the picture of their poverty at the time in the very darkest colours, as men who rise are often wont to do. 'We rode and tied,' said the tragedian. 'I came to London with twopence-halfpenny in my pocket,' said the great lexicographer and critic. 'What do you say?' his companion inquired. 'Why, yes,' he rejoined, 'I came with twopence-halfpenny in my pocket, and thou, Davy, with three-halfpence in thine.' Johnson certainly was very badly off. His school at Lichfield had failed; and literature now was his only resource. It is ever, as Sir Walter Scott said, 'a good walking-stick, but a bad crutch;' and it was so then even more than now, for readers were a limited class, and the book trade far from flourishing. 'You had better buy a porter's knot,' observed Wilcox, the publisher, to the newly arrived competitor in the race of authorship, as he looked on his large frame and vigorous limbs. For some time, as far as a maintenance was concerned, Johnson could hardly have been in greater straits had he taken the man's advice. Even seven years after his first arrival, he was at times in such indigence that he could not pay for a lodging, and he and his friend Savage wandered whole nights about the streets. On one occasion they walked till morning round St. James's Square, not at all, however, depressed by their situation; as, according to Johnson's own account, 'they were in high spirits, and brimful of patriotism, and for several hours inveighed against the minister, and resolved they would stand by their country.'

The first place in which Johnson lived on reaching London was a garret in the house of a Mr. Morris, staymaker, in Exeter Street, adjoining Catharine Street, in the Strand. Frequently fourpence-halfpenny a day was all that he spent on his support, for he was rigidly honest, and would not get into debt without the means of payment; thus forming a noble exception to the too general practice of his brother adventurers in the book-making craft. When now and then a little more cash diminished the need of extreme privation, he gave himself a treat after the following fashion. 'I dined very well for eightpence, with very good company, at the Pine Apple, in New Street, just by. Several of them had travelled. They expected to meet every day, but did not know one another's names. It used to cost the rest a shilling, for they drank wine; but I had a cut of meat for sixpence, and bread for a penny, and gave the waiter a penny; so that I was quite well served, nay, better than the rest, for they gave the waiter nothing.' Johnson's life just then was a cold and comfortless one, but he had a friend in a Mr. Hervey, of whom he ever spoke with gratitude and affection. Beautiful is it to notice, amidst Johnson's stern and rugged nature, fountains of feeling such as gush up in his well-known words : ' If you call a dog *Hervey*, I shall love him.' Johnson also resided in Bow Street, Covent Garden, and in Castle Street, Oxford Market ; but his early London history is better associated with another locality.

There is a quiet spot at Clerkenwell which we are very fond of visiting. It is adorned with an archæological relic of rare interest, one of the few which time and circumstances have spared. The picture of it still lingers on the brown cover of the *Gentleman's Magazine*. We allude to St. John's Gate, through which, in days of yore, crusading knights, of the order of that name, often passed upon their high-mettled steeds; but known in Johnson's day and since for other associations. There lived, in the first half of the eighteenth century, the famous Mr. Cave, an enterprising publisher, who originated the periodical just mentioned, calling himself, in his editorial capacity, Sylvanus Urban. Johnson admired this primitive leader in a walk of literature since crowded by a host of followers. To St. John's Gate he soon made his way, and beheld the edifice ' with reverence,' as he expressly informed Mr. Boswell ; an expression which the biographer interpreted in allusion to the miscellany, whereas later annotators, who have been as busy with Johnson's works and life as their ancient predecessors were with Homer, inform us there can be no doubt the reference is to the edifice itself, with its chivalrous memories. We find Johnson writing to Mr. Cave, 'from Greenwich, next door to the Golden Heart, Church Street.' Afterwards he became a contributor to the magazine, and arranged with Cave for the publication of his early works. There he would often go with MSS. in his pocket to talk over literary and business matters with his new friend, and hence we can distinctly connect the shade of this great author, in his twenty-ninth year, with the gateway and the street adjoining. As we linger about it, we fancy we see him in shabby clothes, emerging from the little doorway under the shady arch, with that feeling of honest independence which Johnson of all men loved to cherish; a feeling which proceeded from having done his arduous work and received his scanty pay, while there were no demands upon him beyond what his slender means could fully meet.

The dictionary was commenced in 1747. While it was going forward, Boswell tells us that Johnson lived part of the time in Holborn, and part in Gough Square, Fleet Street. Here we are allowed to enter his retirement and see him at work. Up in a garret, No. 17, on the north-west corner of the square, we discover him, with six amanuenses, employed in the compilation of his *magnum opus*. There he is with piles of books, looking for passages fitted to illustrate his definitions, and marking them in the margin with a blacklead pencil, inscribing also the letters of the word under which they were to be introduced. The books are then handed over to his assistants, who copy the sentences on slips of paper, and arrange them in the order prescribed by the learned compiler. The preparation of those huge quarto volumes is tremendous drudgery, and occupies him for eight years, during which time he reaps but small profit, owing to the great expense necessarily incurred. Gough Square was the scene of other labours. There he wrote the 'Rambler' and 'Idler;' and we are informed by Miss Reynolds, that, while employed upon the latter, he was so indigent that he dressed like a beggar, and lived as such. She tells us he wanted even a chair to sit on, particularly in his study, where a gentleman, who frequently visited him, whilst writing his 'Idler,' constantly found him at his desk, sitting on a chair with three legs; and on rising from it he remarked that Dr. Johnson never forgot its defect, but would either hold it in his hand, or place it with great composure against some support, taking no notice of its imperfection to his visitor. It is humiliating to think that a man who could and did work as he was wont to do—who penned in six-and-thirty hours the life of Savage—should have been so pressed and crushed by the narrowness of his pecuniary circumstances.

Nor was his poverty the only affliction which befell him in Gough Square. It was there that he lost his wife, for whom, though they do not seem to have led a very harmonious life together, he cherished a strong affection. Her death threw him into a paroxysm of agony, heightened probably by his hypochondriac temperament. Mrs. Piozzi states that Johnson's negro servant, Francis, ran in the middle of the night to Westminster, to fetch Dr. Taylor to see his master, who was all but wild with excess of sorrow, and scarcely knew him when he arrived. 'After some minutes, however, the doctor proposed their going to prayer, as the only rational method of calming the disorder this misfortune had occassioned in both their spirits.' He preserved her wedding-ring as long as he lived, with affectionate care, in a little round wooden box, in the inside of which he pasted a slip of paper with the words : 'Eheu, Eliz. Johnson, nupta Jul. 9, 1736; mortua, eheu! Mart. 17, 1752.' It was also while living in Gough Square that his mother died at Lichfield; another circumstance which awakened in his breast poignant sorrow, while it also led to the composition of the celebrated tale of 'Rasselas'— a work which he sold for a sum sufficing to pay her funeral expenses and some little debts that remained at the time of her death. This instance of filial affection and reverence reflects honour on the man who was so remarkable for his rough demeanour and apparent want of feeling. These redeeming traits, like myrtles growing among rocks, impart much beauty to a character which would otherwise be harsh and uninviting.

In 1762 Johnson had a pension of 300*l.* a year settled upon him by the king, after which the need of labour for his support was considerably diminished, and his comforts were greatly increased. He soon afterwards removed to No. 1, Inner Temple Lane, near the Bar. It was there that Boswell visited him immediately upon the formation of that acquaintance which ripened into so fast and firm a friendship. 'He received me,' he says, 'very courteously; but it must be confessed that his apartment and furniture, and morning dress, were sufficiently uncouth. His brown suit of clothes looked very rusty; he had on a little old shrivelled unpowdered wig, which was too small for his head; his shirt-neck, and knees of his breeches were loose; his black worsted stockings ill drawn up, and he had a pair of unbuckled shoes by way of slippers.' The man who was destined to be Johnson's biographer domiciled himself hard by, in Farrer's Buildings, that he might be near the object of his almost idolatrous admiration. Poor Bozzy! he writes as if he thought posterity would smile at his excessive reverence for his hero—an anticipation verified beyond what he conceived; but, notwithstanding, he persevered, with a sort of self-sacrifice, in doing honour to his hero. While giving abundant proofs of his own weakness, he has made succeeding generations his debtors for the minute and graphic portrait he spent so much of his life in painting. One pictures him becoming, as far as possible, himself Johnsonian—and such was the fact—imitating the Great Mogul of the literary world in his slouching air, constant restlessness, and negligent attire. His clothes were too large, his wig undressed, nor could he sit still in his chair; points of resemblance to the great original which were certainly within the reach of very limited powers to attain. He would sit with mute attention to hear his oracle in conversation, while his eyes goggled with earnestness, and his ear leaned on the doctor's shoulder, and his mouth dropped open to catch every stray word, and his memory was burdened, one would think almost beyond endurance, to carry home the treasures of an evening's colloquy, and deposit all safe in a notebook for the volumes of that life the publication of which was to form the climacteric of the author's existence. And how patiently would he endure the rudest treatment from his idol! submitting to him as a servant, obeying him as a child, and cowering down under the fearful explosions: 'What do you do there, sir? Go to the table, sir. What are you thinking of, sir? Why do you get up before the cloth is removed? Come back to your place, sir—running about in the middle of meals!'

Tuesday, July 19th, 1763, is specially marked in Boswell's diary. 'Mr. Levett,' he writes, 'this day showed me Dr. Johnson's library, which was contained in two garrets over his chambers, where Lintot, son of the celebrated bookseller of that name, had formerly his warehouse. I found a number of good books, but very dusty, and in great confusion. The floor was strewed with manuscript leaves in Johnson's own handwriting, which I beheld with a degree of veneration, supposing they might contain portions of the "Rambler" or of "Rasselas." I observed an apparatus for chemical experiments, of which Johnson was all his life very fond. The place seemed to be very favourable for retirement and meditation. Johnson told me that he went up thither without mentioning it to his servant, when he wanted to study secure from interruption; for he would not allow his servant to say he was not at home when he really was.') 'A servant's strict regard for truth,' said he, 'must be weakened by such a practice. A philosopher may know that it is merely a form of denial; but few servants are such nice distinguishers. If I accustom a servant to tell a lie for *me*, have I not reason to apprehend that he will tell many lies for *himself?*' The dingy lane of the Inner Temple suited Johnson's taste very well, as he had no love for rural scenery, and would even ridicule the sentimentalism of green fields and babbling brooks: quite content was he with such verdure as he could show his friend in what he called his 'walk'—a long, narrow, paved court in the neighbourhood, overshadowed by some trees, where he was wont to ramble after tea.

Under date 1766, Boswell informs us: 'I returned to London in February, and found Dr. Johnson in a good house in Johnson's Court, Fleet Street, in which he had accommodated Mrs. Williams with an apartment on the ground floor, while Mr. Levett occupied his post in the garret; his faithful Francis was still attending him.' These were three persons well known to the readers of Johnson's life, indeed, essential features in his domestic picture. Mrs. Williams was a blind Welsh lady, an admirer of the critic, who entertained a high regard for her talents and accomplishments, mingled with sterling and practical sympathy for her reverses. 'I see her now,' says Miss Hawkins, 'a pale, shrunken old lady, dressed in scarlet, made in the handsome French fashion of the time, with a lace cap with two stiffened projecting wings on the temples, and a black laced hood over it.' Robert Levett was a very humble practitioner in the medical profession, to whom Johnson took a great fancy, and declared that without him he should be dissatisfied, though attended by the whole College of Physicians. His practice was large, but his fees were small; so that, though his patients were scattered all over London, from Houndsditch to Marylebone, he was still in a measure dependent on Johnson, whom he constantly attended through the tedious ceremony of his late breakfast. Though grotesque in appearance, stiff and formal in manners, and taciturn in company, Levett ever commanded the respect of his patron, who knew well how to penetrate through the surface of character, and get at the sweetness lying at the core, if any happened to be there. Francis was a negro who waited on the doctor with great fidelity. For this servant he always manifested a great concern, and finally by will bequeathed to him a handsome maintenance.

These were by no means Johnson's only hangers-on.

While he kept his family in Fleet Street upon a settled allowance, he had numerous dependants out of doors, who, as he said, 'did not like to see him latterly unless he brought 'em money.' Hence he would assist them not only out of his own purse, but by contributions obtained from friends; and this, he would add, 'is one of the thousand reasons which ought to restrain a man from drony solitude and useless retirement.' We are accustomed to think of Johnson only in connection with literature: it is very beautiful, in addition, to recognize him in the character of a philanthropist, bringing upon him the blessing of them that were ready to perish, and making the widow's heart to sing for joy. The healing of wounded hearts, and the assuagement of smarting sorrows, attract less attention than the prizes won in the *stadium* of scholarship, or than the bays which adorn the brows of genius; and yet we all know there are records kept of the former (when performed from right motives) in a world where the latter distinctions are overlooked as things of nought. Johnson's intellectual efforts deny imitation, but his quiet benevolence is within the reach of every one.

The *penetralia* of Johnson's domestic retirement few were permitted to enter, the tavern and club-room being the place where the literary world found access to their great oracle; but, as was fitting, Boswell was admitted to its mysteries, and he has left on record an account of dining in Johnson's Court, written in a way that indicates how rare and distinguished was the privilege. 'April 11th, being Easter Sunday, after having attended divine service at St. Paul's, I repaired to Dr. Johnson's. I had gratified my curiosity much in dining with Jean Jacques Rousseau, while he lived in the wilds of Neufchâtel: I had as great a curiosity to dine with Dr. Samuel Johnson, in the dusty recess of a court in Fleet Street. I supposed we should scarcely have knives and forks, and only some strange, uncouth, ill-dressed dish; but I found everything in very good order. We had no other company than Mrs. Williams, and a young woman whom I did not know. As a dinner here was considered a singular phenomenon, and as I was frequently interrogated on the subject, my readers may perhaps be desirous to know our bill of fare. Foote, I remember, in allusion to Francis the negro, was willing to suppose that our repast was black broth; but the fact was, that we had very good soup, a boiled leg of lamb and spinach, a veal pie, and a rice pudding.' Whether there were plums and sugar in the pie he does not say; but it is most likely there were, as these were, with Johnson, favourite ingredients in that dish.

It may be added that the privilege of dining with the philosopher was preceded by the opportunity of breakfasting with him on the Good Friday before, when Boswell tells us they had tea and hot cross buns; Dr. Levett, as Frank called him, presiding at table. 'He carried me with him,' Boswell goes on to inform us, 'to the Church of St. Clement Danes, where he had his seat, and his behaviour was, as I had imagined to myself, solemnly devout. I never shall forget the tremulous earnestness with which he pronounced the awful petition in the Litany: "In the hour of death, and in the day of judgment, Good Lord deliver us."' The seat which he occupied in the north gallery, near the pulpit, is still pointed out,[1] and there one sees his shadow under circumstances which recall some of the most solemn moments of his earthly existence; for never does the soul so assert its immortality, and come so consciously near to the edge of the invisible realms, as when truly engaged in the worship of God, and earnestly hearing and reflecting upon the momentous truths of the Gospel. We know no associations more affecting than those which take this form. Here listened and worshipped a distinguished mind that is now gone into the world of awful wonder, which then awakened curiosity and solicitude. Here he thought of those realms of being into which he has been long since introduced; here he dwelt upon his relationship to that glorious Being in whose presence he has appeared; here he speculated with fear and trembling on what would be his present condition and employments. What a change has the revelation of the secrets of eternity produced in his experience!

Johnson's fame was widely spread. He came to be one of the greatest notabilities of his day. Many

[1] A brass plate has been affixed to it, intimating that there Johnson sat.

of the great revered him, and on one occasion royalty commanded an interview. It took place in the royal library of Buckingham House; a full report of it is preserved, which previous to publication was perused and approved by the king himself. A long conversation occurred on divers literary topics, Johnson feeling himself a monarch in that domain, and the sovereign fully acknowledging his authority there. Thorough manliness marked the interview on both sides, and did credit to both parties. A remark which Johnson made about a royal compliment which he received is very amusing. He said he thought he had written too much. 'I should have thought so, too,' said the king, 'if you had not written so well.' 'No man,' said the flattered author, ' could have paid a handsomer compliment; it was fit for a king to pay. It was decisive.' When asked whether he made a reply, he observed, 'No, sir: when the king had said it, it was to be so. It was not for me to bandy civilities with my sovereign.' The monarch was George III., and it is not a little curious that Johnson should have been also in the presence of two personages so far removed from each other in point of time as Queen Anne and George IV. He was taken to the former to be touched for the scrofula; that superstitious practice, though on the decline, having not quite died out, for two hundred persons were touched when he was. Being asked if he remembered the queen, he said he had 'a confused but somehow a sort of solemn recollection of a lady in diamonds, and a long black hood'—one of the most picturesque views of her

DR. JOHNSON'S HOUSE IN BOLT-COURT.

majesty, by the way, we ever remember having seen. George IV., when a little boy, was introduced to Johnson, who took the opportunity of asking him what books he was reading, and in particular inquired as to his knowledge of the Holy Scriptures. The prince, in his answers, gave him great satisfaction; and as to the last said, 'that part of his daily exercises was to read Ostervald'—no doubt the popular catechism and abridgment of sacred history.

Another change in Johnson's residence took place in 1776; but we still find him in his favourite Fleet Street. His new abode was in Bolt Court, No. 8. Boswell, on coming to London in the month of March that year, sought out his friend, and on discovering his removal, wrote down in his journal as follows: 'I felt a foolish regret that he had left a court which bore his name; but it was not foolish to be affected with some tenderness of regard for a place in which I had seen him a great deal, from whence I had often issued a better and a happier man than when I went in, and which had often appeared to my imagination, while I trod its pavement in the solemn darkness of night, to be sacred to his wisdom and piety.' We fully appreciate the biographer's reverence for the old court, and cannot help ourselves regarding it still with feelings akin to his, although the place is now greatly changed. But Bolt Court, as his abode for the rest of his life, and the place where he died, comes in for a larger share of veneration, while round it there cling the richest recollections of its famous inhabitant. The house is gone, and the little garden has disappeared, 'which he took delight in watering;' but prints of the spot are preserved, and we can still see the three circular steps leading up to the door, with the flat projection over the doorway, and the long row of windows in the roof, and the shrubs adorning the leads of a lower room, in advance of the adjoining residence. A tavern and a printing-office now occupy the chief portion of this little nook in one of London's vast thoroughfares; but the name of Johnson inscribed on the entrance is ever associated with the locality, and though many doubtless pass it by with other thoughts, we cannot suppose that we alone are wont now and then to turn into the little retired avenue and dream of other days.

Why, there he is! with poor blind Mrs. Williams coming up the court; and on reaching the steps he whirls and twists about with strange gesticulations, and then, with a sudden spring, strides over the threshold, as if engaged in gymnastic exercises, or performing a feat for a wager; the blind lady groping about to find the entrance, while her friend continues his odd movements on his way to his own room. He makes it an object of anxious care to go in and out by a certain number of steps from a particular point, and to commence the operation always with the same foot; right and left being trained to a particular order in this exercise; and sometimes he will even count his steps with great earnestness, lest there should be an error in the important process.

Up comes Sir Joshua Reynolds's coach, and out

steps Miss Hannah More, who is shown into the little parlour, where she sits down on a chair, thinking it to be the doctor's, hoping to catch from it some spark of his genius, when he enters with formal politeness and laughs at the lady for her mistake, the seat she has selected being one he never occupies. They talk away, in the wainscoted old room upon divers literary matters, while the printer's errand boy stands impatient on the stairs, waiting for proof. The interview over, and Hannah much delighted with her reception (for the doctor likes her), she is handed by him to the coach, which, amidst a crowd of vehicles, now stands some eight or ten doors from Bolt Court, and then he exhibits such strange gesticulations that a crowd of people gather round, equally surprised and diverted.

We follow him back to his room, and watch him after he has done writing—as he muses in his chair, making sundry kinds of indescribable noises, or, as he talks to Bozzy, shaking all over, rubbing his knees, and puffing at the end of one of his sonorous sentences, like a whale rising to the surface of the water for a gasp of breath after some long deep plunge. Boswell gone, and all quiet, Johnson thinks of the necessities of his household, particularly of one member—an old cat, now very infirm and sick, Hodge by name, which is fond of oysters; and to spare Francis the negro the degradation of waiting on a four-footed creature, Johnson actually trudges forth himself to an oyster shop to bring home the desired delicacy for the feline inmate.

Gleams of humanity and kindness, often very strange, are ever and anon shining out from among the dark clouds of wrath and rudeness that roll over the spirit of this eccentric man.

Johnson walking along the street by himself was a notable spectacle; not only for a peculiar solemnity of deportment and measured step, which we fancy would have reminded us of his style of composition, as if he were beating time to his own sentences; but for a practice which is thus described: 'Upon every post, as he passed, he deliberately laid his hand; but missing one of them, when he had got at some distance, he seemed suddenly to recollect himself, and immediately returning back, carefully performed the accustomed ceremony, and resumed his former course, not omitting one till he gained the crossing.'

Johnson in conversation, as he threaded the mazes of a London crowd, was worth hearing; and one would also have liked to see him when some clever rejoinder fell on his ear; as, for example, when after visiting Westminster Abbey with Goldsmith, he had said to his companion, 'Forsitan et nostrum nomen miscebitur istis'—Goldsmith slyly whispered to Johnson, as they stopped at Temple Bar, and he pointed at the grim heads of the executed Jacobites, 'Forsitan et nostrum nomen miscebitur *istis.*'[1]

What a privilege to meet Johnson at the tables of

---

[1] 'Perhaps our names will be associated with *theirs.*' Johnson was a Jacobite at heart.

his friends—at Sir Joshua Reynolds's, General Oglethorpe's, Mrs. Thrale's, and the rest; or at his club at Sams's, No. 40, Essex Street, where the terms were lax and the expenses light, the forfeit for absence being twopence; at the King's Head, Ivy Lane, Newgate Street, where he constantly resorted on Tuesday nights, and played the part of *symposiarch*, till the association was broken up; or at the Literary Club, by far the most illustrious, as it proved the most enduring, first assembling in the Turk's Head, Gerard Street, Soho, and still continued at the Thatched House, according to the standing toast, 'Esto perpetua.' Johnson at dinner, as he engaged with equal earnestness and relish in the practical discussion of plate after plate of good fare, and the philosophical discussion of question after question of manifold kinds, was a spectacle to be long remembered by those who witnessed it; and not less so, Johnson at tea, drinking a dozen cups, and pouring forth streams of shining eloquence, or doubling that number and remaining silent, because his hostess had invited him to serve as a lion to the company.

All this, however, and much more, we must leave, and hasten to the end. Johnson died in the back room first floor of the house in Bolt Court, in 1784. The particulars of his death have been treasured up with the same care as the minutest details of his life. As we peruse the narrative, we feel how melancholy was the new interest which gathered round his favourite abode, as his friends perceived the decline of his health. We see messengers coming up the narrow passage to make inquiries, and many an associate and disciple of the great man hastening with an anxious countenance to hear once more a voice which had so often filled them with admiration. We hear him talking of his will, and making provision for the negro Francis; and eagerly do we listen for all that throws light on the state of the sufferer's mind in reference to religion. Religion had ever been to Johnson a subject of reverential thought. The forms of it he had studiously maintained; but his religious meditations were pervaded by a deep melancholy, and his religious services were tinged with superstition. He had dreaded death, for he had looked to his own performances as a ground of trust. Towards the latter end his views improved; Gospel light shone clearly on his soul, and he became, it may be hoped, another man. On one occasion, when directed to his own good works as a ground of religious hope, he asked the question so well fitted to test that common idea, to expose that fatal delusion: 'But how do we know *when we have done enough?*' 'For some time before his death, all his fears were calmed and absorbed by the prevalence of his faith and his trust in the merits and propitiation of Christ.' 'My dear doctor,' said he to Dr. Brocklesby, who made the above statement, 'believe a dying man—there is no salvation but in the sacrifice of the Lamb of God.' This beautiful testimony to the worth of the Gospel in a dying hour may fitly terminate this chapter on one who, with all his great faults and failings, belongs to the most illustrious group of the shades of the departed that meet us amidst the scenes of Old London. His remains were interred in Westminster Abbey; and as we pause in the Poets' Corner, and think of his rare endowments and acquisitions, all become lost in the infinite importance of his dying words: 'There is no salvation but in the sacrifice of the Lamb of God.'

XII.

EDMUND BURKE.

WE like the Middle Temple. We like to stand on a sunny day beside the fountain, and to watch its scanty jet flinging out spray like so much diamond dust, producing delicious sensations of coolness amidst the burning heat reflected from the old stone walls, and suggesting divers pensive thoughts upon human pleasures, sparkling and brief as the little drops which are every moment forming and disappearing before one's eyes. We like to saunter about the garden and gaze on the exterior of the stately hall—a specimen of the architecture of the sixteenth century, when, in its Gothic form, the art was getting into the sear and withered leaf of autumn, albeit exhibiting some rich flushes of beauty, like the yellow and brown that tint the foliage once covered with virgin green. We like to enter within the walls of the edifice, where its chief magnificence is displayed, and, standing on the daïs at the western end, look up to the timbered roof, with its massive pendants and simple carvings—and round on the painted windows, emblazoned with the arms of illustrious benchers—and on the wall adorned with portraits of English sovereigns—and down upon the stone floor and strong oaken tables, on which, for three long centuries, gentlemen belonging to the famous fraternity of the Middle Temple have eaten their dinners and kept their terms. We like to think of the great ornaments of legal learning connected with the place—of Somers and Hardwicke, Blackstone and Cowper, Thurlow and Dunning, Curran and Tenterden, Eldon and Stowell, of which last two marble busts are preserved in the recess on the north-western side of the noble room. But as we muse upon the shades of the departed, in the venerable hall, one happens especially to strike us, who, though here educated in lawyer-like erudition, is best known to posterity by his consummate abilities as a statesman and philosopher.

Here he comes, in his twentieth year; tall, erect, well-formed, but not very robust in appearance, with a countenance of much sweetness, and esteemed by ladies very handsome. The expression of his face, from its variableness, is what a painter would find it difficult to represent. In a state of quiescence, the marks of intellect are rather vague and indeterminate; but let anything excite him, and at once the symbols of mental strength are manifest on the lines of that broad brow, and in the light of those large eyes. He does not care about dress, and his gait is rather awkward, giving you the idea of a man with *two left legs*. So says Sir Joshua Reynolds, a judge in such matters. His powers of conversation are evidently great, from the spell in which he binds his companion at the table, who seems to forget the good fare before him as he listens to the winged words which fly from the lips of this new student from the bar; nor can the hearty laugh of the hearer fail to tell of the wit and humour of the eloquent talker. Would you know who he is? Then turn to the entry in the books of the Middle Temple, under date April 23rd, 1747. Here it is, rendered into English: 'Mr. Edmund Burke, second son of Richard Burke of the city of Dublin, one of the attorneys of the Exchequer Court of our lord the king in the kingdom of Ireland, is admitted into the society of the Middle Temple, London.'

Letters bring up the mental and moral image of a man as nothing else can do. We have before us one written by Burke on his first arrival in London. 'You'll expect some short account of my journey to this great city. To tell you the truth, I made very few remarks as I rolled along, for my mind was occupied with many thoughts, and my eyes often filled with tears when I reflected on all the dear friends I left behind. A description of London and its natives would fill a volume. The buildings are very fine. It may be called a sink of vice; but its hospitals and charitable institutions, whose turrets pierce the skies, like so many electrical conductors, avert the wrath of Heaven. As to the state of learning in this city, you may know I have not been long enough in it to form a proper judgment of that subject. I do not think, however, there is as much respect paid to a man of letters on this side the water as you imagine. Notwithstanding discouragement, literature is cultivated to a high degree; poetry raises her enchanting wing to heaven; history arrests the wings of time in her flight to the gulf of oblivion; philosophy, the queen of arts and the daughter of heaven, is daily extending her intellectual empire; fancy sports on airy wings, like a meteor on the bosom of a summer cloud and even metaphysics spins her cobwebs and catches some flies; the House of Commons not unfrequently exhibits explosions of eloquence that rise superior to those of Greece and Rome, even in their proudest days. Yet, after all, a man will make more by the figures of arithmetic than the figures of rhetoric, unless he can get into the trade wind, and then he may sail over Pactolean sands. Soon after my arrival in town, I visited Westminster Abbey; the moment I entered I felt a kind of awe pervade my mind which I cannot describe. The very silence seemed sacred.'

This, as far as it goes, is Burke all over. In these extracts we have foreshadowings of what was seen in the man, the orator, and the author, as he was when Fame had seated him beside her on her throne. His keen sensibilities, his sweeping views, his fondness for learning, his majestic fancy, his stately and march-like diction, his love of architecture, his taste for 'the sublime and beautiful,' come out here in unmistakable development, dashed somewhat, it is true, with a juvenile air, which time soon dissipated. Nor can one doubt that the stirrings of oratorical ambition were then felt in his youthful breast, and perhaps some dim vision was even then before him, that the time might come when his voice would add to the honours of British eloquence within the walls of the Commons House of Parliament. Perhaps he was already beginning to attend to figures of arithmetic, as well as figures of rhetoric, with a view to his complete qualification for public life. Certainly, he afterwards showed that he was a master in both respects, proving himself as much at home in calculations touching financial reform as in the resources of imagination wherewith to adorn the most abstract principles of policy and government. His London acquaintances pronounced him 'a remarkably clever and promising young man'—'one possessed of very superior genius and information;' but he was not destined to rank among the Hardwickes and Eldons of the Middle Temple, having an order of mind and a cherished taste decidedly more fitted for the Senate than the Bar —for letters than law.

Having spent a few winters in London, broken by an occasional residence in the country, of which he was passionately fond, he at length gave up all thoughts of the legal profession. His plans remained unsettled, even after his marriage, when we find him taking up his abode somewhere in the village of Battersea, then retaining by the riverside rural charms since faded and gone : and we picture him, on a summer's evening, sitting beside the Thames, or gliding down the stream in a boat, full of such uncertain thoughts as he expresses in the following letter, written August 10th, 1757: 'Apology for my long silence is found in my manner of life, chequered with various designs, sometimes in London, sometimes in remote parts of the country, sometimes in France, and shortly, please God, to be in America.' In America! So among other schemes of this dreamy enterpriser was one for crossing the Atlantic, suggested, it is said, by an invitation from an old college friend settled in Philadelphia. Had he gone, how much would have gone with him! English history would have been deprived of one of the fullest, most interesting, and most valuable chapters of political and literary biography. But he did not go, and we find him in 1759 in Wimpole Street, Cavendish Square—a street, by the way, in which, at No. 67, the 'History of the Middle Ages' was written by Hallam. While there, Burke probably was employed in literary occupation—writing for the *Annual Register*, in the early volumes of which his contributions may be seen, forming materials for the history of that period, of eminent value.

Burke next took up his abode at Plaistow, again evincing his love for suburban scenes; and there in the green lanes we like to picture him indulging his taste for rural objects. A lady, then about fourteen years old, and residing in that neighbourhood, informed one of his biographers that she perfectly remembered him there, that his brother Richard lived chiefly with him, and that they were noticed in the neighbourhood for their talents and sociable qualities, and particularly for having a variety of visitors, who were understood to be authors soliciting a private opinion of their works, and not unfrequently men of rank. In Wimpole Street we afterwards find Burke again, and then in Queen Anne Street, his father-in-law, Dr. Nugent, living with him there. For seven years he occupied the latter residence, when he removed to the neighbourhood of Beaconsfield, so intimately connected with the memory of the great statesman in his latter days.

In our notice of Dr. Johnson, we referred to the formation and progress of the Literary Club. Burke was one of the original members, and therefore his shade haunts the Turk's Head Coffee House, No. 142, Strand—noted in later years as the first London home of George Eliot; now a tourist ticket office. We see in him there a conspicuous star, adding much to the brightness of that celebrated constellation of learning and wit. So very superior was he in conversation, that Johnson, who plumed himself so much on his own gift in this respect, and assumed something like a kingly sway in that chamber of intellectual peers, was wont, in the strongest terms, to laud Burke's good talk, as he often termed it. 'Burke,' he would say, 'is an extraordinary man; his stream of mind is perpetual; he does not talk from a desire of distinction, but because his mind is full. That fellow calls forth all my powers. He is the only man whose common conversation corresponds with the general fame which he has in the world. Take up whatever topic you please, he is ready to meet you. No man of sense could meet Mr. Burke by accident under a gateway, to avoid a shower, without being convinced that he was the first man in England. If you met him for the first time in the street, where you were stopped by a drove of oxen, and you and he stepped aside for shelter but for five minutes, he'd talk to you in such a manner that when you parted you would say, "This is an extraordinary man." Now,' added he, with a modesty he rarely expressed, ' you may be long enough with me without finding anything extraordinary.' Goldsmith, who tried to shine in the same way, was equally enamoured of Burke's skill in conversation, praising it above that of the king of critics, and asking, in reply to an eulogy upon the colloquial achievements of 'the old man eloquent,' 'But is he like Burke, who winds into his subject like a serpent?'

Burke's conversational fame, but still more the literary reputation which he acquired by his 'Philosophical Inquiry into the Origin of our Ideas of the Sublime and Beautiful,' rendered him a man of note in all well-informed circles, before he entered upon the stage of political conflict in the House of Commons, and interwove his name and history with the annals of the British empire. In 1766 he first appeared in

Parliament, and began his career with an augury of success as gratifying to his friends as it was flattering to himself. We remember well the old St. Stephen's, with its close and heavy galleries, its narrow floor, its long benches, the time-honoured chair of the Speaker, and the huge brazen chandeliers containing a vast array of wax candles. It had somewhat of a meeting-house aspect, but it had glorious associations of patriotism, statesmanship, and oratory, in which many a young student of English history, as he sat in the Strangers' Gallery, delighted to revel. We remember it well, and we can almost fancy ourselves in that very house on the night of the 14th of January, 1766, when Mr. Burke made his maiden speech, and took up the American question. He has just sat down amidst great applause, when Mr. Pitt gets up, and observes that 'the young member has proved a very able advocate: he had himself intended to enter at length into the details, but he has been anticipated with so much ingenuity and eloquence, that there is little left for him to say: he congratulates him on his success, and his friends on the value of the acquisition they have made.' That is enough. Such praise is of itself a passport to fame. Cordial congratulations from fellow-members follow that effort; and friends, who have been sitting in the gallery to witness his *début*, perhaps with some anxiety, as soon as the House breaks up, come crowding round him with fervent greetings. The public are loud in extolling the new statesman. A member of the Literary Club, not over-amiable, not fancying Burke very much, indeed, a little annoyed by a recent encounter with him, and envious of his superior powers, expresses some surprise at his political elevation; but he is soon crushed by the dictum of Johnson, who declares: 'Sir, there is no wonder at all. We, who know Mr. Burke, know that he will be *one of the first men of the country*.' As such we propose to follow his 'shade' through the rest of this sketch.

Many characteristic reminiscences of the man and his oratory are connected with the old House of Commons. Were its walls still standing, were they endowed with memory, and could they speak, how would they tell of his famous speeches on American affairs, on financial reform, on Mr. Fox's East India Bill, on the Nabob of Arcot's debts!—pieces of resplendent eloquence, in which reason, knowledge, and imagination vie with each other, all dressed in that livery of stately diction with which his master mind was wont to clothe them as they fulfilled his service. Those walls would tell of that memorable scene of excitement, when he and Mr. Fox, after a firm friendship for many years, broke on the subject of the French revolution; the former exclaiming: 'I know the value of my line of conduct; I have indeed made a great sacrifice; I have done my duty, though I have lost my friend; there is something in the detested French constitution that envenoms everything it touches:' while the latter, bursting into tears, appealed to the remembrance of their past attachment, their reciprocal affection, as dear and almost as binding as the ties of nature between father and son. Those walls would tell of subsequent fierce conflicts between Burke and the Whig party, among whose leading members he had formerly been ranked; and how the violence, not to say bitterness, of speech that sometimes marked the debates between him and them illustrated those well-known words of the wise man, 'A brother offended is harder to be won than a strong city, and their contentions are like the bars of a castle.' Those walls would tell of the significant looks with which Burke was often regarded when he arose to address the House, and how even strangers easily recognized him in his latter days, in the tall elderly gentleman with a tight brown coat, bobwig with curls, and huge spectacles, on the side opposite to Mr. Fox; how occasionally even the eloquence of the great orator had a soporific effect, and an elaborate speech, full of abstract disquisition, extended rather beyond the limit of parliamentary patience, induced honourable members, not accustomed to go so deeply into things, to get up and put on their hats and leave the house; and how, finally, when a young generation appeared, knowing little of the days of Chatham and the applause he yielded Burke, they would sometimes, when he rose, rudely drown his voice with boisterous interruptions. Those walls could also tell of a ludicrous *Irish* incident in the history of Burke's oratory, and with what tact he turned it to account. 'The minister,' said he, 'comes down in state, attended by his creatures of all denominations, beasts clean and unclean; for the Treasury, as it has been managed of late, is worse than Noah's ark. With such, however, as they are he comes down, opens his budget, and edifies us all with a speech. Well, he sits down. What is the consequence? *One half of the House* goes away. A gentleman on the opposite side gets up and harangues on the state of the nation, and in order to keep matters even, *another half* retires at the close of the speech. A third gentleman follows their example, and rids the house of *another half.*' A loud laugh rang through the building at this bull of the great Irishman. 'Sir,' said he, addressing the chair, 'I take the blunder to myself, and express my satisfaction at having said anything that can put the House in good humour.'

Walking up and down Parliament Street—that pathway to the grandest of political arenas—along which so many anxious senators, their brains throbbing with excitement, their hearts bursting with passion, have gone to and fro, we pass and repass the shade of Edmund Burke, and have recalled to our minds two little incidents in this great man's life, connected with that well-known thoroughfare; the one illustrative of his strong feeling of political antagonism, the other of his pitiful and practical benevolence. One wet night, as Mr. Curwen, a supporter of Mr. Fox's views on the French revolution, was waiting for his carriage at the door of the House of Commons, Mr. Burke requested that he would give him a ride home. The former rather reluctantly complied. The two statesman comfortably seated, Mr. Burke began to compliment Mr. Curwen, under the mistaken idea that he agreed with him in his opinion of recent events in the history of France. The latter could not disguise his real sentiments, though he expected that by expressing them he would rouse the indignation of his companion. So it proved; for Mr. Burke, on hearing a declaration of sympathy with Fox, caught hold of the checkstring, and furiously cried: 'You are one of these people—set me down.' They had reached Charing Cross. Mr. Curwen with difficulty prevailed upon the irascible statesman to continue in the carriage till they reached his house in Gerard Street, when, without breaking the silence, which had lasted since his fiery exclamation, he hurried out of the vehicle, and ended for ever all intercourse with the honourable member.

But the breast so susceptible of resentment was equally the subject of generous and kind affections. Going home from the House one night on foot, he was accosted by one of those unhappy beings who haunt the highways of the great metropolis, seeking for a subsistence the wages of vice; and who, wasted by want and sorrow, became a supplicant for charity. In reply to his inquires, she stated that she had been lady's maid in a respectable family, and had been driven through gradations of misery to her present forlorn state, which she confessed to be wretched beyond description, looking forward to death as her only relief. 'Young woman,' said Mr. Burke, as he reached his door, 'you have told a pathetic story; whether true or not is best known to yourself; but tell me, have you a serious and settled wish to quit your present way of life, if you have the opportunity of so doing?' 'Indeed, sir,' she replied, 'I would do anything to do it.' 'Then come in,' said Mr. Burke. 'Here, Mrs. Webster,' he proceeded, addressing his housekeeper, 'here is a new recruit for the kitchen; take care of her for the night, and let her have everything suitable to her condition, till we can inform Mrs. Burke of the matter.' The poor fallen creature was reclaimed through his compassionate care; and we must confess, that on that achievement of mercy our minds rest with a satisfaction and pleasure far beyond what we feel as we dwell on his brilliant intellectual exploits.

Walking past Whitehall, we recollect that Burke, as Paymaster-General in the Rockingham Cabinet, once occupied the office in that building devoted to this department; but there we cannot linger on our way back to Westminster Hall, where we must glance at the great orator on the most celebrated occasion of his life. The part he took in the impeachment of Warren Hastings was characteristic of the man. His imagination was apt to lead captive his reason, to inflame his passions, and to carry him away as on the wings of a storm. He did nothing by halves, and there was no resisting the outbursts of his impetuosity. Impelled by conscientious feelings, though directed by mistaken opinions, a moral power increased the force of the excitement. Hastings, no doubt, had been unrighteous in his administration of Indian affairs, but he was hardly the culprit that Burke made him out to be. The scene of the trial was Westminster Hall; and never since the days of Lord Strafford and King Charles 1. had that edifice witnessed such an array of judicial state. It was fitted up with scarlet hangings, and was surrounded by military pomp. Grenadiers guarded the entrance, and cavalry kept the streets. Peers, in robes of velvet and ermine, were conducted by heralds to their appointed seats. The twelve judges were present in full judicial costume. On green benches, with tables, sat members of the House of Commons, and in a box, especially appropriated for their use, were the conductors of the impeachment. Fox, Sheridan, Windham, and Grey were of the number, all in court dresses. Burke, in like manner attired, was foremost among them. The audience, too, was worthy of the occasion and the actors. It was an assemblage of the beauty, chivalry, and talent of the land. Princesses and peeresses, generals and captains, authors and artists, together with ambassadors from foreign courts, crowded the seats appropriated for spectators. The serjeants made proclamation. Hastings knelt at the bar, while his counsel, including high legal names—Law, Dallas, and Plumer—were at his side. The charges were read. It took two days to read them—a process which, tedious as it was, did not diminish the interest felt in the proceedings. On the third day Burke commenced his harangue. It was a wonderful effort, full of ingenious argument, pictorial description, splendid imagery, and resistless appeals, now swelling into terror, now melting into pathos. The ladies wept; there were hysterical sobs; Mrs. Sheridan fainted; and even the heart of the stern Chancellor was moved. At last came the thunder-clap:—' I impeach Warren Hastings of high crimes and misdemeanours; I impeach him in the name of the Commons House of Parliament, whose trust he has betrayed; I impeach him in the name of the English nation, whose ancient honour he has sullied; I impeach him in the name of the people of India, whose rights he has trodden under foot, and whose country he has turned into a desert; lastly in the name of human nature itself, in the name of both sexes, in the name of every age, in the name of every rank, I impeach the common enemy and oppressor of all.' It was a speech which admirers of rhetorical eloquence rank with Demosthenes' Crown oration.

We must return, before we conclude, to the private life of this eminent man. After he had obtained his rural retreat at Beaconsfield, where he followed his early predilections for agricultural pursuits, and soothed his mind amidst sylvan scenes after the chafings and irritations of political controversy, his residences in London were only temporary and often changed. We find him during the sittings of Parliament occupying houses in the Broad Sanctuary, Westminster; Fludyer Street; Charles Street; Duke Street; and Gerard Street. One of these residences is associated with a well-known story. While staying in Charles Street, he was visited one day by a young man, who with a rich genius had a empty purse. He had come to London as a literary adventurer, and had exhausted all the little stock of money he could scrape together. He wrote a volume of poems, but he had no name to recommend it. In his distress he went to an opulent peer, who did not refuse his patronage, but passed by in total neglect the poet's application for pecuniary aid. The young man thought of Mr. Burke, and wrote a letter to him, 'hearing,' he said, 'that he was a good man, and presuming to think that he was a great one.' He went with a full heart to Charles Street, and there left the letter. He said, 'The night after I delivered my letter at his door, I was in such a state of agitation that I walked Westminster Bridge backwards and forwards until daylight!' The commoner, with far less ample means, did what the nobleman refused. He helped the young man, gave him criticism and advice, sent round members of his family to get subscriptions for his work, introduced him to men of influence, and opened to him a door that led to fame and fortune. The young man was the poet Crabbe, and it was not without tears that he used to tell of Mr. Burke's kindness.

One more locality we must visit. Brompton is a neighbourhood where, formerly more than now, consumptive invalids were wont to repair. Thither many a parent has conveyed his child as a last hope; and as we walk through its squares and streets we feel an air of melancholy come over us, at the thought of domestic joys there crushed—of fair blossoms of promise there torn away. Burke had a son he loved with his whole heart. Disease laid its hand upon him, and the father took him to Cromwell House at Brompton. Here he sunk and died. That blow nearly broke the great man's heart. He never recovered from it. As we go down the gloomy lane by Cromwell House, we are led to ruminate on those pathetic passages in Burke's letter to a noble lord, in he which gives way to his parental grief: 'The storm has gone over me, and I lie like one of those old oaks which the late hurricane has scattered about me. I am stripped of all my honours; I am torn up by the roots, and lie prostrate on the earth. I am alone. I have none to meet my enemies in the gate. I greatly deceive myself if, in this hard season, I would give a peck of refuse wheat for all that is called fame and honour in the world. I live in an inverted order. They who ought to have succeeded me are gone before me. They who should have been to me as posterity are in the place of ancestors.' Poor Burke! Writing to a friend, he said, 'Mrs. Burke seeks tranquillity in prayer!' We hope he did himself. That is the last and best resource for souls stripped of their dearest joys. In communion with the Father of spirits, and approaching Him through the Son with whom He is ever well pleased, the desolate find sympathy, and the wounded heart is healed.

Amidst a cloud of domestic sorrow the shade of the great statesman here leaves us. His last days were spent away from his old London haunts, and his remains rest in the grave of his son and brother in the churchyard of Beaconsfield.

XIII.

JOHN HOWARD.

'On the north side of the Priory of St. Bartholomew,' says John Stowe, in his 'Survey of London,' 'is the Lane truly called Long, which reached from Smithfield to Aldersgate Street.' At the time when our venerable metropolitan topographer recorded this charactistic notice of a well-known locality, it was 'built on both sides with tenements for brokers, tipplers, and such like;' but the brokers had the predominance afterwards, for an annotator upon Strype describes Long Lane as 'a place of note for the sale of apparel, linen and upholsterers' goods, both second-hand and new, but chiefly for old.' It is more than probable that many a thrifty salesman in that queer old neighbourhood made a decent fortune out of his yearly gains, though only one that we know of has attained any celebrity. This is certain, that no fortune was ever laid up by any of the diligent sons of trade in our great metropolis, destined to a better use in the hands of the heir and successor, than the fortune of him to whom we now refer. Many a father has felt what the wise man so touchingly expresses: 'I hated all the labour which I had taken under the sun, because I should leave it to the man who should be after me; and who knoweth whether he shall be a wise man or a fool?' And survivors have witnessed a sad squandering by the new possessor of money scraped together by much toil, amidst not a little of self-denial. But the prosperous tradesman in Long Lane whom we are now thinking of, was honoured as the accumulator of riches, which, instead of 'perishing through sore travail,' became, through the beneficence of his son, the instrument of mercy to England and the world, surrounding his name with a lustre at which generations to come will look back with reverence and praise.

John Howard kept a shop somewhere about the corner of the place so noted for the sale of upholsterers' goods; and when, by diligently following that line of business, he had obtained enough to enjoy his *otium cum dignitate*, he first retired to Enfield, and then removed to Clapton. About 1790 the Clapton residence was described as a venerable mansion situated on the western side of the street, but much decayed, and lately disfigured. Very soon after it was pulled down. There, in 1739, Mr. Howard must have been living in good circumstances, as in that year he paid the fine for not serving as Sheriff of London. He had then a son, about thirteen years old, who was probably born in the Clapton house; though considerable obscurity rests on the scene as well as the exact date of his birth. This son was *the* John Howard on whose name, by universal acclamation, the title of philanthropist has been bestowed—a title far surpassing any which heralds can record or sovereigns confer. We fancy we see him in his father's garden—a lad not tall of his age, yet thin and spare, and rather fragile in his make and appearance, with large nose, and eyes sparkling with benevolence, and compressed lips, which shows that he carries with him a will too strong to be easily broken. Hair cut short in front and curled behind, and costume somewhat like a full court dress in miniature, complete the portrait. Young Howard went to school for seven years with Mr. Worsley, a good Greek scholar at Hertford; and was then removed to the care of Mr. Eames, who was tutor in a seminary conducted in Tenter Alley, Moorfields, for the education of both dissenting ministers and laymen. Mr. Eames possessed rare attainments, was a friend of Sir Isaac Newton, and was pronounced by Dr. Watts to be the most learned man he ever knew. But Howard, with these advantages, never turned out a scholar. Strange to say, he not only knew very little Latin, and less Greek, but he could never write his own language with propriety and correctness. But among his school associations there occurs one of those instances of generosity with which his history abounds. Mr. Densham was assistant to Mr. Eames, and won the respect and gratitude of Howard. The latter, just before setting out on his last and fatal journey, gave his old tutor an unlimited order to draw on his banker for whatever sum he might stand in need of; but the delicate conscientiousness of the poor scholar was as great as the benevolence of his rich friend; for though at the time having only twelve or thirteen pounds a year, he diminished his little capital rather than accept the discretionary privilege.

Howard's father did what few men in his circumstances are wont to do. Though he could leave his son a fortune, he determined to bring him up to trade, and therefore bound him apprentice to Messrs. Newnham & Shipley, wholesale grocers in Watling Street. For that old thoroughfare with a Roman name we must confess some considerable *penchant*. Memories of the time when the great masters of the world had their provinces in Britain, and Roman manners and Roman hearts covered the banks of the Thames, all about that neighbourhood come thick, and fast before the mind's eye, as we sometimes thread that alley-like avenue to London Bridge, in preference to the broader and more crowded highway of Cheapside. Milton's shade, of course, meets us at the corner of Bread Street, and we like to think also of the grocer's apprentice, grown somewhat since we described him at Clapton, who amidst hogsheads of sugar and chests of tea was acquiring habits of application to business of no little use to him in after life. Meditating on this early portion of Howard's history, our thoughts take the shape so well defined by his last biographer: 'No man can foresee even for an hour the turns of fortune.

It is the part of wisdom to be armed and prepared for whatever may befall. Knowledge of a profession is no burden. A gentleman is not the less a gentleman because he is conversant with law, with trade, with medicine; nay, he is then more a gentleman than he otherwise could be, for he is more completely independent. He alone is perfect master of his actions who has a personal means of living—some art or craft, knowledge or skill, of which chance and change cannot divest him; wanting this, his present interest or his fears for the future must often modify his hopes and warp his conscience.'

It would seem, however, as if Howard, who had been well schooled in filial obedience, only *submitted* to the drudgery of the grocer's warehouse, without any liking for scales and ledgers, inasmuch as we find that almost immediately upon his father's death he procured the surrender of his indentures. His apprenticeship obligations were early cancelled upon the payment of a sum of money; but the youth, freed from the yoke of servitude, was by no means disposed to riot in his new-found liberty; with a steadiness and care such as belong to the ripest years of human life, he attended to the preservation, improvement, and proper use of the patrimony he inherited. He personally superintended the repairs of the Clapton house; and as we walk through the main street of that now populous suburb, we think of Howard's visit to the paternal abode, and his recollections amidst the scenes of his boyhood; and call to mind how daily he might be seen close to a buttress of the garden wall, at the hour when the baker was passing with his cart, buying a loaf of the man, and flinging it over the wall, and then, with a laugh, saying to his father's gardener, the playmate probably of his own earlier days: 'Harry, see if there is not something for you there among the cabbages.' The frolicsomeness of Howard in his youth bore the stamp of true kindliness of disposition, and that punctuality in engagements which marked the entire history of Howard in his manhood.

But he did not live in the Clapton house—that was let. His own place of abode was Stoke Newington. He had lodgings there, where he studied and improved his mind. The delicate state of his health required more attentive nursing than he found in the house where he first lodged, so he removed to apartments under the roof of Mrs. Sarah Lowne, a widow of a little property, residing in Church Street, who devoted her time to the care and comfort of the young invalid. He had some rather strange notions, and when they shaped themselves into the form of duty, they always rested upon a very firm substratum of conscientiousness. Though he was only twenty-five, he considered that he could justly repay the lady for her kindness, though she was fifty-two, by nothing less than the offer of his hand in marriage, with the resolution of promoting the happiness of her life who had saved his. The eccentric proposal was at first refused, but being strongly urged, was at length accepted, and Howard amply redeemed his vow. He always expressed himself as having been happy in his choice, though his domestic enjoyment was of a different character from that which he afterwards so richly reaped during the ten years of wedded companionship he spent with his second wife—his beloved Henrietta. The first Mrs. Howard died, in 1755, between two and three years after her marriage, and lies buried in St. Mary's, Whitechapel. Howard felt lonely when this tie was dissolved, and broke up housekeeping, giving away his furniture to the poor of the village.

The old gardener we have mentioned received for his share a bedstead and bedding, a table and half-a-dozen chairs, together with a new scythe—a dividend of the philanthropist's relics which, at a subsequent period, when the donor's fame had spread far and wide, became mightily enhanced in value. We have no means of ascertaining the house where Howard lived at Stoke Newington, but we know where he worshipped. We have a vivid recollection of the old Independent Chapel there, as it appeared about fifty years ago, then much in the same state it had been in from the beginning. The small pulpit, surmounted with a huge sounding-board, and the tall-backed pews and heavy galleries, spoke of other days, constituting an appropriate background for the figure of young Mr. Howard in earnest prayer, or reverently listening to his pastor, the Rev. Micaiah Townsend. The man of whom we write, it should be remembered, was eminent for his spiritual piety no less than his active benevolence. He breathed through his letters and journals a devotional fervour which, while they rebuke the languid religious sentiments of frigid professors of Christianity, are calculated to excite a sympathetic ardour in the hearts of all who have any spiritual sensibility. The motto on his monument in Cardington Church, written by himself, was expressive of his evangelical creed, and his tone of humble confidence from first to last, ' My hope is in Christ.'

Howard removed to lodgings in St. Paul's Churchyard, whence he proceeded to the Continent, and where, we presume, he afterwards returned. That visit to the Continent was a very eventful one. He was taken prisoner and barbarously treated, and detained for some months a captive in France. There he saw and felt what entered into his soul, and afterwards helped to impel him onward in his astonishing career of prison visitation and reform. So strong was the confidence he inspired, he was permitted to return to England to negotiate with the Government for his own liberation. He had pledged his honour to go back to prison if he did not succeed: and when his friends congratulated him on his escape, he desired them to defer their expressions of joy till he had obtained an honourable discharge of his obligations. So the shadow of Howard passes us in St. Paul's Churchyard, out on parole, like another Regulus, prepared to re-enter the land of captivity if he cannot obtain liberty upon terms fair and just. A right noble study is that for the men of commerce, and for all sorts of men who pass by St. Paul's every day : *My word is my bond.* This sentiment, embodied in the conduct even of a heathen, ought surely to guide believers in the Bible, which commends him who 'sweareth to his own hurt, and changeth not.'

In tracing the other London haunts of Howard, we must plunge into the prison world of the last century. Elsewhere in the metropolis, what we know of him for the rest of his life is next to nothing. It is a wonderful progress we have to make, as we follow this illustrious individual in his circumnavigation of charity, ' not to survey the sumptuousness of palaces or the stateliness of temples, not to make accurate measurements of the remains of ancient grandeur, not to form a scale of the curiosity of modern art, not to collect medals or collate manuscripts ; but to dive into the depths of dungeons, to plunge into the infection of hospitals, to survey the mansions of sorrow and pain, to take the gauge and dimensions of misery, depression, and contempt; to remember the forgotten, to attend to the neglected, to visit the forsaken, and to compare and collate the distresses of all men.' The Augean stables which Hercules undertook to cleanse is no unapt symbol of the dens of corruption, tyranny, cruelty, and vice, which Howard resolved to purify and transform, when he entered on his great work of prison reformation. In his book on prisons, he gives the result of his earlier visits to those in London; and from that source, aided by kindred documents, we derive the materials of what for the most part will form the rest of this chapter. The following passages have a graphic character about them, and enable us to catch a glimpse of the philanthropist while engaged in his errand of mercy: 'At each

JOHN HOWARD VISITING A PRISONER.

visit I entered every room, cell, and dungeon, with a memorandum book in my hand, in which I noted particulars on the spot.' 'I have been frequently asked what precautions I used to preserve myself from infection in the prisons and hospitals which I visit. I here answer, next to the free goodness and mercy of the Author of my being, temperance and cleanliness are my preservatives. Trusting in Divine Providence, and believing myself in the way of my duty, I visit the most noxious cells; and while thus employed I fear no evil. I never enter an hospital or prison before breakfast, and in an offensive room I seldom draw my breath deeply.'

A general description of the London prisons by Howard gives a fearful idea of the neglect of discipline which prevailed when he began his researches. The statistics which Howard supplies relative to the prison world of London afford terrible insight into the miseries experienced by the captives.

Newgate was rebuilt between 1778 and 1780. As then erected, and as it still remains, it presents a great improvement upon its predecessor; but, as Howard observed, it was far from being a model, and at the commencement of the present century the gaol fever broke out there, which he predicted would be the result of its defective and faulty arrangements. One shudders on entering the condemned cells which Howard opens for our inspection. There are upon each of the three floors five cells, all vaulted. The strong stone wall is lined all round with planks studded with broad-headed nails; and such is the aspect of these darksome, solitary abodes, that criminals, before unmoved, have been struck with horror, and have shed tears on entering them. Fifteen condemned cells appear to us, now that the criminal law has been reformed, a most unnecessary provision; but alas! when Howard wrote, they seemed not more than to suffice for the demand which was created by the draconic severity of the judicial code. In twelve years 467 executions took place in London, including two by burning, the two culprits being women, one condemned for murder, the other for coining.

The hardened criminal and the juvenile offender were closely associated; and if the latter resisted his initiation into the mystery of the prison-house, he underwent a mock trial by some impudent offender, who assumed the office of judge, and tied a knotted towel on his head to imitate a wig. Prisoners were requested to pay 'garnish,' as contributions to riotous entertainments were called; and the miserable creature who had no money was stripped of his clothes, in discharge of the villainous demand.

A singular relic of the ancient administration of torture is mentioned by Howard as continuing in a form which was observed in his time. When prisoners capitally convicted at the Old Bailey were brought up to receive sentence, and the judge asked, 'What have you to say why judgment of death and execution should not be awarded against you?' the executioner slipped a whipcord noose about the thumbs.

The Fleet Prison stood not far off Newgate, and there the philanthopist discloses some startling scenes of disorder. 'They play in the courtyard at skittles, mississippi, fives, tennis, etc.; and not only the prisoners, for I saw among them several butchers and others from the market, who are admitted here as at another public-house. The same may be seen in many other prisons where the gaoler keeps or lets the tap. Besides the inconvenience of this to prisoners, the frequenting a prison lessens the dread of being confined in one. On Monday night there was a wine club, on Thursday night a beer club, each lasting usually till one or two in the morning. I need not say how much riot they occasion; how the sober prisoners and those that are sick are annoyed by them.'

We are next conducted to New Ludgate in Bishopsgate Street, a prison for debtors free of the city, and for clergymen, proctors, and attorneys. The common side debtors are in two large garrets, the *forest* and *dock*, which have no fireplaces. The prison is out of repair, the walls and ceilings are very black, being never whitewashed. There is no infirmary, no bath. It was in reference to this debtors' prison that the *Spectator* says: 'Passing under Ludgate the other day, I heard a voice bawling for charity, which I thought I had somewhere heard before. Coming near to the gate, the prisoner called me by my name, and desired I would throw something into the box.' Happily it is all now swept away, and so is the Poultry Compter, with regard to which Howard remarks: 'At the roof of the prison are spacious leads, on which the master's side debtors are sometimes allowed to walk; but then the keeper is with them, for the leads communicate with the adjoining houses, one of which affords a ready escape from so close a prison in case of fire.' From this specimen of heedlessness about the security of the prisoners, Howard next takes us to the Wood Street Compter, where all are kept secure enough; there we are shown a room about thirty-five feet by eighteen, with twenty-three beds ranged round the walls, on three tiers of shelves. At one of his visits, he informs us there were in this room thirty-nine debtors, seven of them with their wives and children. The room was swarming with vermin. There was a chapel in the court, and under it a taproom. Within the unwholesome precincts of this place eleven prisoners died in 1773.

We pass on next to Bridewell, where there was no court, and fresh air could be obtained only by means of a hand ventilator, with a tube to each room of the women's ward. It enjoyed a privilege peculiar to itself, that of having an allowance of *rye straw once a month*. 'No other prison in London,' says Howard, 'has any straw or bedding.' In the new prison, Clerkenwell, our reformer noticed some commendable arrangements, but condemned certain cabins or cupboards, five in number, only ten feet by five in measurement, each with a barrack bed for two prisoners: miserably close and unwholesome cells, having no air but from grates over the doors into the gallery. On visiting the Clerkenwell Bridewell in 1777, he found thirty convicts, committed for a term of years. Some of these, and others besides, were sick, and complained of their feet, which were actually turned black. In 1783 five were ill, one was dying with little or no covering on, and in another room one was laid out dead. In the women's sick ward, twelve were lying in their clothes on the barrack bedstead and on the floor without any bedding whatever. In this strange tour about London, which, in proportion as the scenes described shock our sensibilities, must have been to our philanthropist a series of torture, we arrive next at Whitechapel Prison, which presents nothing noteworthy, except the fact of the debtors hanging out a begging box from a little closet in the front of the house, and attending to it each in turn. It brought in only a few pence daily, of which pittance none partook but those who on entrance paid the keeper half-a-crown, and treated the prisoners with half-a-gallon of beer. We hasten by the Tower Hamlets Gaol, in Wellclose Square, and St. Catherine's Gaol, which Howard, though he had visited them repeatedly, only briefly notices; nor can we tarry at the Savoy, with its military guard-rooms, where the philanthropist had seen many sick of the gaol distemper, but where he afterwards found a decided improvement in health, owing to better sanitary regulations. We must, however, relate a striking incident which will ever associate with the history of the Savoy the remembrance of Howard's amazing personal courage and influence over prisoners. During an alarming riot there, the men confined had killed two of their keepers, and no person dared to approach them, until the intrepid philanthropist undertook to do so. Gaolers and friends endeavoured to dissuade him; but in he went to two horrid ruffians, whose savage spirits he so completely subdued by his persuasions, that they allowed themselves to be quietly conducted back to their cells.

At Tothill Fields Bridewell, he informs us, the prisoners washed their hands and faces every morning, before they came for their allowance—a practice that must have been grateful to him, for he ever enforced the strictest cleanliness on those over whom he had any control; and we remember hearing from an old man, who lived at Cardington, how he would notice and reward the children whose hands were clean; and that he once said to a cottager who was not over-fond of self-ablution, 'John Basset, go home and wash your hands, or no dinner.' Howard describes Westminster Gatehouse as empty, but the King's Bench, Southwark, as full to overflowing. It was so crowded in the summer of 1776, that a prisoner paid five shillings a week for half a bed, and many lay in the chapel. The debtors, with their families, two-thirds of whom were within the prison walls, amounted to a population of one thousand and four.

But, perhaps, of all the London prisons, the Marshalsea was the worst, where debtors and pirates were huddled together in dark narrow rooms, four men in each, sleeping in two beds. The taproom was let to a prisoner, and there the inmates of the place, at times, slept on the floor; and to show the habits of drinking which prevailed, it is sufficient to repeat a statement by Howard, that one Sunday six hundred pots of beer were brought in from a neighbouring public-house, because the prisoners did not like the beverage supplied by the tapster within the walls. The spot where we close this melancholy ramble, amidst the scenes of prison life three-quarters of a century since, is the Borough Compter, the last place of confinement of the whole number in London which Howard describes. It was out of repair and ruinous, had no infirmary, and no bedding; while most of the inmates were poor creatures from the court of conscience who lay there till their debts were paid.

It is dreary enough to pursue this pilgrimage from prison to prison; but it is instructive as an illustration of the fallen state of humanity. Where but in a world where things are sadly out of order, and the relations of the creature to the Creator are disturbed, could such flagrant abuses prevail under the colour of political justice? Nor can we help congratulating our country, and blessing the God of nations, for the improved state of things existing in our prisons at the present day, mainly through the instrumentality of him whose shadow we have been following. It was a tremendous stronghold of iniquity that he dared to assault, enough to make the courage quail in even a braver heart by nature than his own; but sustained by help from Heaven he nobly carried through his mission, and crowned it with a success which, if not complete, was signal. His life was a truly earnest one, a battle with wrong, and an errand of richest mercy. 'Tis pleasant to follow poets and painters through their career of elegant literature and art; but we feel ourselves to be in a far different presence, one that gives us inspiring and solemn views of human duty, as we track the footsteps of John Howard. He has something more serious to do than to gather flowers and echo back Nature's sweet music; he has to trample on serpents, to rend asunder chains, and to let rays of light and love into the cells of the captive. Appropriate is the statute to him in St. Paul's, with huge iron manacles and fetters underfoot, and a great key in his hand. But, after all, Howard only walked at a humble distance in the footsteps of Him whom the Hebrew seer described as binding up the broken-hearted, proclaiming liberty to the captives, and the opening of the prison doors to them that were bound. Howard's benevolence was but a reflected beam of His who gave Himself for the redemption of our race out of a bondage worse than that of English or even Algerian gaols. His beneficent course was only an outgrowth of the Gospel he embraced.

The story of Howard's personal exploits almost exhausts our store of London associations in connection with his name. We remember only one more, of a very different character from the foregoing. With this we must close our sketch. Great Ormond Street has been the residence of several celebrities. There lived Hicks, the learned author of the 'Thesaurus;' there lived Dr. Mead, and Dr. Stukeley, and Dr. Hawkesworth; there, too, lived Lord Chancellor Thurlow, when he was robbed of the great seal by a gang of housebreakers; and there, too, for a little while, Howard took up his London abode, in a house left him by his sister. While there, a female of rather forbidding appearance made repeated ineffectual attempts to see the philanthropist. At last she succeeded, and gained admittance to the library. He thought, from the visitor's look, that one of the other sex was come to him disguised, with some evil intent. So he rang the bell and intimated a wish that the servant should remain in the room. But it was quite needless; for the stranger turned out to be a real woman, but a rather enthusiastic worshipper: for she first poured forth a flood of extravagant compliments, and then took her leave, declaring that, after having seen the man she so much admired, she could go home and die in peace.

Christian principle was the foundation of all the excellences of John Howard. He did not adopt religion in later life, when wearied of the world. It was not in his case a last resort after the exhaustion of every other method of seeking happiness. He was the child of religious parents. His father had paid attention to his spiritual culture. He in early youth felt the charms of the service of God. The fresh springtide of his being was devoted to the honour and glory of his Maker. Thus he had a safeguard among such temptations as beset a young man of property entering upon life. When he became, according to common expression, 'his own master,' happily, he felt that there was a very important sense in which he was by no means his own. Freed from the restraint of his guardians, he was conscious of the obligations which he owed his God. The earliest portions of his diary breathe a spirit of fervent devotion, which suffered no abatement, but rather increased, during the subsequent periods of his active life. Religion did not occupy some inferior place in his heart, but it was enthroned in his affections, and ever exerted over his whole nature a supreme sway. He observed the Divine order of duty, 'Seek ye first the kingdom of God, and His righteousness.' No one can study Howard's history without discovering that religion, in his estimation, was the first law, the chief interest, the grand end, and the main happiness of life. Nor was his religion of the ceremonial cast, of the pharisaical order, of the rationalistic stamp—it was thoroughly *evangelical.* It was religion such as is taught in the New Testament, such as was exemplified in the lives of the Apostles, such as is produced by the Spirit of God. Its fresh, earnest, impassioned expression is found in the following extract from his journal, written at the Hague one Sunday night: 'Oh the wonders of redeeming love! Some faint hope I have, through redeeming mercy, in the perfect righteousness, the full atoning sacrifice, that I shall ere long be made the monument of the rich grace and mercy of God, through the Divine Redeemer. Oh, shout, my soul, "Grace, grace; free, sovereign, rich, and unbounded grace!" Not I, not I, a hell-deserving creature; but where sin has abounded, I trust grace superabounds. Some hope have I—what joy in that hope!—that nothing shall separate my soul from the love of God in Christ Jesus. Let not, my soul, the interests of a moment engross thy thoughts, or be preferred to thy interests. Look forward to that glory which will be revealed to those who are faithful unto death. My soul, walk thou with God, be faithful, hold on, hold out; and then—what words can utter?' Thus in broken sentences did his pious feelings find their vent. Thus they came from his heart in sobs and gushes, showing what a fulness of evangelical sentiment there lay deep within him, like a well of water springing up unto everlasting life. It blended with all the other parts of his character, and was the vital spring of his wonderful benevolence. That benevolence, so self-sacrificing, so humble, so irrespective of all temporal rewards, can be accounted for only by recognizing it as the fruit of his faith in Christ, that incarnation of Divine Love.

Such was Howard's character; his end was in harmony with it: he died upon one of his missions of mercy—indeed, he fell a martyr to his philanthropy. He left England for Russia in 1789, on his way to the East to make inquiry into the nature of the plague, with a view to the suggestion of remedies and preventives. The strength and elevation of his Christian faith in the prospect of his perilous enterprise were sublimely manifest in his well-known words : 'The way to heaven from Grand Cairo is as near as from London.' On reaching Cherson, in Russia, he was seized with fever caught while attending a young lady whom, from his well-known skill in medicine, he had been requested to visit. He had to ride several miles on a dray-horse in the midst of rain ; and this, in connection with the contagious nature of his patient's disease, prepared his way to the grave, just after she had been placed there. As death advanced, he contemplated it with perfect composure. Admiral Priestman, who greatly loved and honoured his fellow-countryman, showed him the most devoted attention, and sought to direct his thoughts from the prospect of a fatal termination to his disease. 'Priestman,' said Howard, 'you style this a dull conversation, and endeavour to divert my mind from dwelling on the thought of death; but I entertain very different sentiments. Death has no terrors for me; it is an event I always look to with cheerfulness, if not with pleasure : and be assured the subject is more grateful to me than any other.' He then told his friend that there was no hope; that his constitution could not survive the attack,—he was already too much reduced. 'I have no method of lowering my nourishment,' he added, 'and, therefore, I must die. It is only such jolly fellows as you, Priestman, that get over these fevers.' The old sailor wept, and was silent,—when Howard proceeded to give directions respecting his burial, in beautiful harmony with the humility of his character. He selected a spot in the village of Dauphiney. 'There,' said he, 'lay me quietly in the earth, place a sundial over my grave, and let me be forgotten.' It was the 20th of January, 1790, about eight o'clock at night, that his spirit took its departure from the scene of its labours and sufferings, to find the rest, and receive the recompense graciously promised by the Lord of the Church to all who trust in Him, and do His will, and love His ways.

ECHOES OF WESTMINSTER HALL.[1]

I.

AXE AND HAMMER.

THERE is no music like the voice of an echo. Not the sweetness, richness, or grandeur of its tones, but its mysteriousness, gives it pre-eminence. The idea suggested of some invisible spirit or spirits in the distance, responding to words uttered, or sounds produced, imparts to it a strange and fascinating interest. The memory of many a pleasant spot in fair old England will recur to our readers, where not long since, amidst hills and woods, and beside river streams, they whiled away some pleasant moments, abstracted from busy toils and feverish cares, in listening to strains evoked from the haunts of an echo, by bugle note or human words. How it rolled, and rolled, and died away—thunders softening into whispers! And welcome are the reverberations now caught by

[1] This chapter was written long before the opening of the New Law Courts.

the mental ear, and the pictures of the landscape adorned with mountain, field, and flood, with cottage, tower, and tree, now present to the mental eye, as the quondam tourist, in his easy chair, with loose coat and slippered feet, close to his warm fireside, goes over his travels afresh, repeating in fancy what has been his in realization.

Perhaps of nobler echoes than any our own land can boast of, not a few readers may be thinking, as the title-page of these sketches catches their eye: the Lorelei on the Rhine, with its majestic sevenfold voice throwing down upon your ear, in that romantic rock gorge of the grandest of German rivers, successive undulations of mysterious sound; or the Kœnigsee, not far from Salzburg, that most enchanting of all enchanting lakes, where rock and mountain, forest and water, are arranged in forms of perfect beauty and incomparable grandeur, and where Nature's rarest music mingles with Nature's rarest painting.

But not of such echoes will these chapters treat. To no romantic spot do we purpose to conduct you, but through the crowded, noisy, unpicturesque thoroughfare of Parliament Street down to Westminster Hall, and the lobby of the Senate. And we promise that, though the spot itself be unromantic, some most romantic echoes may be heard within its walls. Or, to make the matter still more easy, and we hope agreeable, our endeavour shall be to bring Westminster Hall to you; and while you retain your comfortable position by the fireside, you shall see the fine old building, more as it has been than as it is, and shall hear echoes of doings within its precincts, gay and grave—our pages serving the office of hill or mountains, in the reverberation of sounds which have long since been silent, but which we shall strive to reproduce for your instruction no less than your amusement.

To catch the earliest echoes, we must go a long way back into the night of time, further into the distant past than Norman or Saxon ages. Well, then, here we are on an island, or rather islet, covered with rushes, weeds, brushwood, and thorns, something like, only wilder and larger than, those bits of land that still peer out of the Thames, the refuge of the rat and water-bird. It lies by the side of the old river, whose waters creep around it; and, untenanted at present by man, its only echoes are the croak of the frog or the cry of the lapwing. But there is some sort of human being coming near it now, with painted skin, like a South Sea Islander, and paddling an odd sort of bark, neither boat nor canoe. It is no other than one of our venerable British forefathers, in his coracle, come out for a day's fishing; not, however, practising such tactics in his art as would entitle the worthy man to hold place in the Isaak Walton line of anglers.

While the splashing of the oar dies away, as he takes his departure to some Celtic village not very far off—let us leap some ages further on to Saxon times, when we find monks very busy clearing away the rushes, and digging up stumps and roots. The foundation-stones of an abbey and church are laid in this island, which they call Thorney; and now, in what has been a terrible place—*in loco terribili*—for the first time you hear axe and hammer; for Sebert, King of the Saxons, having embraced Christianity, and having been baptized by Mellitus, Bishop of London, immediately builds a church to the honour of God and St. Peter on the west side of London. This is the seventh century. And now there are echoes of worship, the chant of psalm and prayer, stealing over the starlit waters of the Thames, while the illuminated altar pours its light through the rude windows. The building is heavy, rude, unadorned, with massive columns and round arches, such as one sees in mediæval MSS., or finds in lingering vestiges here and there in parts of our very oldest churches.

An odd story is told, in connection with that first sound of axe and hammer in the Isle of Thorney—a dreamy fiction—a poetical legend, the like of which may be heard at Venice and other places; and, though now rated at its real value, it was once believed, and we doubt not, was often told in days of yore, by the monks and other folks at Westminster, as they gazed on the later glories of the Abbey Church, whose title, as Minster, gave name to the city. It runs as follows: A fisherman was met by a stranger on the opposite bank of the Thames, and requested to ferry him over, and wait on the side of the Isle of Thorney till he should return. Accompanied by a host of angels, this mysterious personage entered the new church and consecrated it by the light of a supernatural radiance, which filled the walls. The fisherman, startled at the sight of this illumination, trembled at the return of the wonderful priest, who now announced himself to be no other than the Apostle Peter, and told him to go at daybreak to Mellitus, the bishop, and assure him of the consecration. He further gave the fisherman a command to cast a net into the river, and to convey one of the fish to the bishop, assuring him that he should never want fish so long as he dedicated a tenth to the Church. A miraculous draught was the consequence · and Mellitus, on examining the new edifice, found the proofs of the Apostle's visit in the marks of the extinguished tapers and of the chrism. So much for mediæval fables.

But our business is with Westminster Hall, not Westminster Abbey; yet a notice of the founding of the one seems proper as an introduction to the founding of the other, for it originally belonged to the palatial residence of the Saxon kings, which grew up under the shadow of the Abbey, when State and Church were joined in closest bonds. In Canute's time, we find a kingly palace at Westminster, and many think that it was out of a window in this palace that Edric Streon, beheaded by order of the monarch, was cast into the Thames.

Axe and hammer are heard loudly enough at Westminster in the days of Edward the Confessor. The church and monastery are reconstructed; and we are not far off the truth if we add that about the same time the palace was rebuilt, or enlarged and improved, as we have clear proof of the king's residence at Westminster. Heaps of stone, and plenty of scaffolding, and labourers in abundance, with all the buzz and activity which surround a rising edifice, are obvious

WESTMINSTER HALL, IN QUEEN ANNE'S REIGN.

enough on Thorney Island, which may now properly change its name. A pile of Saxon, or more correctly of Norman, architecture—for Edward had a taste for and cultivated Norman art, and Matthew Paris speaks of the building as a new kind of construction—takes the place of thorns and briars, and earlier masonry and scenes of monastic magnificence and regal pomp blend together. Edward pressed on the work very earnestly, having appropriated to it a tenth of his entire substance in gold, silver, cattle, and all other possessions. In the new palatial abode, the Confessor-Prince spends much of his time, holds counsels, seeks refreshment amid the cares of empire in religious meditation and prayer, has strange visions, and at last sickens and dies in the painted chamber—so tradition says.

The Norman came and took possession of this kingly home. The first William left it to the second. There was, no doubt, some large hall for state and festival all along; but now we meet for the first time with the *Great Hall*, which, altered, indeed rebuilt, may, however, be said still to remain. There are faint relics of its Norman character in the outer walls, in the plain thin buttress, and the string course level with the window-sills, which the works of a later period did not efface. Rufus had gigantic architectural ideas, if we are to believe the story told by Matthew Paris. The red-haired king came home from Normandy, and held his court in the New Hall. The warriors, barons, and squires thought it very vast, and expressed their wonder at so grand a place. 'It is not half so large,' quoth he of the red hair, 'as it should have been: it is only a bedchamber compared with what I intend to build.' What he meant to build no one knows; probably he did not know himself. Certainly his subjects would not have wished him to carry out any further these extravagant notions of what befitted a kingly abode; 'for already,' as Fabyan says, 'he filled the spiritualtie and temporaltie with unreasonable tasks and tributes, the which he spent upon the Tower of London and the making of Westminster Hall.'

Time rolls on: Rufus dies, and a long line of kings after him. There are divers architectural and other artistic works in Westminster; stonecutters, and painters, and carvers of wood, ply their toils in adorning the royal chambers; and the Great Hall, of course, comes in for some share in the outlay of skill and money; for it is often used, and one would think, from what we shall see hereafter, somewhat roughly. But we have no particular account of changes in structure and decoration till we arrive at the reign of Richard II., when axe and hammer are heard again more loudly than ever.

The present Westminster Hall is the work of that unjust and unhappy monarch. When the Decorated style was prevalent—when Gothic in England was in its glory and perfection—when the springtide of Early English had ripened into summer beauty, before the rich but decaying autumn season of the Perpendicular order had set in—the mason piled up the walls and ornamental flying buttresses, and the carpenter threw over them the broad oaken roof of cunning work, and the carver shaped the mullions and transoms of the magnificent end-window. A building of rare grandeur is this Westminster Hall, even at the present day, though it lacks the beautiful carving and rows of statues with which it was once adorned; a sight of exceeding splendour it must have been on days of royal festival, when the space of seventy-four feet in breadth, and two hundred and seventy in length—the roof of one span, with no columns to support it—was covered with the gorgeous retinue of a mediæval monarch. It was two years in building, and the expense was defrayed out of moneys levied on strangers and exiles, who, on payment of these demands, obtained licence to remain in the English realm, 'John Boterell being clerk of the works.' So that England was a land of refuge then as now—a home for the homeless, a sanctuary for the oppressed and for the criminal— yielding a precious boon, not without some inconvenience and even evil, but the latter far less than the former; only in Richard's time people had to pay for what they may now get free; and Westminster Hall thus becomes to us a monument of the unchanging sacredness of our old English soil, and of despotic exactions now happily known no longer.

While we listen to the echo of axe and hammer, as Richard's workmen are engaged on the new Great Hall, a novel scene occurs just outside of it. Parliaments meet at Westminster, and have been wont to assemble in this large old chamber of King Rufus, but now that the building is for a while unfit for use, a temporary shed adjoining it is employed for the English senators. The place is open at both ends and sides, that people may hear and see all that is going on; and 'to secure freedom of debate,' as we are told, four thousand Cheshire archers with bent bows, and arrows notched to shoot, surround the house. And so Parliament men, in the reign of King Richard II., appear the mere tools of his despotism; but it is only for a little while. Our Constitution in the hands of brave Englishmen cannot be permanently crushed, and therefore, not long afterwards, in the very hall then approaching its completion, barons and commons plucked the crown from the head of the foolish and misguided tyrant. The hall was completed before Christmas, 1398, when festival was kept in it with right royal splendour and extravagance, with 'every day's justing and running at the tilt, whereunto resorted such a number of people that there was every day spent xxv or xxviii oxen, and ccc sheep, besides fowl without number. Also the king caused a garment for himself to be made of gold, silver, and precious stones, to the value of 3,000 marks.'

A long pause in the architectural history of Westminster Hall here follows. No great changes take place in the building till our own time. Axe and hammer have, indeed, often been heard in the building; but they have been employed in the construction of scaffolding and benches and other appurtenances connected with coronations, festivities, and State trials, of which this hall has been the theatre, and to notices of which the subsequent chapters will be devoted.

Never since the thorns were cleared out on Thorney

Island have there been such architectural works going on there as within a somewhat recent time. In spite of defects, which it is easy to point out, the new Houses of Parliament form a pile of buildings of great beauty and magnificence. With them we have nothing to do in this sketch, save as Westminster Hall forms one of their grand entrances. It is now, in fact, a gigantic porch to the two Houses. Axe and hammer, under Sir Charles Barry's design and superintendence, have somewhat changed the hall of the second Richard. No more fitted for banquetings, the wall and window where the daïs once stood have been removed, and a noble flight of steps now occupy their place, connected with a vestibule or gallery, through which you pass into the Senate chambers of the nation. An enormous arch spans the ascending steps, and behind is a huge window, proportioned to the architectural magnitudes around it. On the left-hand side of these truly royal stairs is another archway cut through the wall, leading into a profusely decorated corridor, ending in the lobby of the House of Commons.

In other respects, the Hall remains as it was, leaving ample scope for genius and taste, while preserving intact its ancient features, to enrich the venerable Hall, and even relieve the broad surface of the floor, with monuments and memorials of men and deeds, which have given a fame to the place far surpassing what anything merely artistic can confer. Nowhere, within the same number of square feet, do such hosts of memories, born on the spot, come starting up to challenge and instruct, to interest and awe, to delight and confound the well-instructed and thoughtful visitor. The antiquary, the lawyer, the statesman, the philosopher, are here all reminded of something associated with their own studies; and such as aspire to none of these titles, but have only average intelligence, and kinship with human kind, and a heart to feel for the joys and sorrows of bygone ages, may here gather lessons of moral wisdom, and learn the vanity of earthly things, and take warning from the ways of ambition, and smile and weep by turns as the pageant and the trial in this strange phantasmagoria of English historical romance in succession come and flit away. To catch echoes of the past will be our endeavour; and among them we shall strive specially to seize and fix on those which proceed from royal feastings—men of the marble chair—bench and bar—old politics and Parliaments—early state trials—the seven bishops, and an Indian viceroy.

II.

ROYAL FEASTINGS.

WALK down to Westminster in winter time, on some cold damp day, when the inhabitants of the city are regaled with a pea-soup fog, and pass through the solemn doorway into the great and venerable Westminster Hall. What a palace of desolation! The outside vapour has penetrated inside the yawning space of the ancient building, in thinner consistency, indeed, but yet of sufficient shade and density to obscure somewhat the massive oak rafters of the roof, the stretch of the walls, the great southern flight of steps, and the figures of all who are passing out and in. Altogether, the genius of the place, if it has any fascination, is of the Medusa kind, and one is glad to get away from Westminster to a snug home and a bright fireside.

Or, drop into this same relic of England's olden times some drizzly night when Parliament is sitting, and some heavy business debate is wearing out the hours on empty benches, and how melancholy looks the hall, despite of gaslamps, and how triste is the silence, only at rare intervals broken by the footfall of a tired-out member eager to get into a cab, whose driver, by the side of his broken-kneed horse, whip in hand, is as eager to catch a fare. And yet this same Westminster Hall, so often dull and dreary, and never now particularly cheerful and joyous, was once the theatre of most brilliant festivities, of banquetings right royal in their way, both at coronations and at weddings, and oftener still at Christmas, Easter, and Whitsuntide. What colours have shone—what gold and silver and jewels have gleamed and sparkled—what armour and arms have glittered—what banners and feathers have waved—what lights have flashed—what minstrelsy has echoed—what shouts of laughter and bursts of song have rolled up the halls and run along the roof, in the Westminster Hall of the Normans, Plantagenets, and Tudors! If few spots have witnessed more of anxiety and sadness, certainly few have seen as much of hilarity and rejoicing.

Let us catch some of the echoes.

Here is the first, proceeding from the black-letter folio of good John Stowe, now before us: 'King William, having returned out of Normandy into England, kept his feast of Whitsuntide very royally at Westminster in the new hall, which he had lately caused there to be builded.' This is all we find recorded. Thus the first of the festive echoes is but faint; but they will soon grow louder.

Henry, the son of Henry II., received the regal crown while his father was alive. He passed through the ceremonies of knighthood and coronation on the same day (A.D. 1170). A banquet followed in the Great Hall, when the father served the son as sewer, bringing up the boar's head, the very crown of the feast, amidst a blast of trumpets. The Archbishop of York—who had crowned the prince, in assumption of a privilege claimed by Becket as Archbishop of Canterbury, with whom the king was at variance—noticed the pride which flushed the cheek of the royal stripling at the honour and service thus done him by his sire, and, turning to him, said, 'Be glad, my son; there is not another prince in the world that hath such a sewer at his table.' The newly crowned scion of royalty gave presage of his after unfilial ambition by asking: 'Why dost thou marvel at that? My father in doing it thinketh it not more than becometh him; he, being born of princely blood only on the mother's side serveth me that am a king born, having a king to my father and a queen to my mother.' Father and son appear about equally foolish in this business; but in the vanity of the latter there was something worse than folly.

On a Sunday in the September of 1189, Richard Cœur de Lion held his coronation feast in the hall, where the citizens of London officiated as the king's butlers, and men of Winchester served up the viands. While archbishops and bishops, earls, barons, and knights, were seated at the royal tables, and the wine-cups went round, and the rude music of the minstrels mingled with the ruder merriment of the numerous guests, a scene occurred outside the walls of the grand banqueting-room in strange contrast to the rejoicings inside, but very characteristic of the state of the times. Richard had given orders that no Jew or Jewess should be present at his coronation, or at the banquet afterwards, 'for fear,' says Stowe, 'of enchantments which were wont to be practised.' But some of the proscribed race, trusting to the gold and the gifts which English monarchs were wont to extort from the children of Israel, whose riches had become proverbial, ventured to approach the royal presence with appropriate offerings—too tempting a bribe to be resisted ; so, in spite of previous orders, they were permitted to enter the hall, and their presents were accepted.

One unlucky wight, however, came into collision with a very zealous hater of the Jewish race, and this led to a general disturbance, whereupon the whole party, who had paid more dearly for their admission than any others, were ignominiously driven out into the street. Public fury against Jews was easily kindled, and when once it burned there was destruction without mercy. Staves, bats, and stones were in immediate request, and the unhappy victims of popular indignation were driven back to 'their houses and lodgings.' Violence grew into massacre ; and that night the streets of Westminster and London were stained with the blood of the children of Abraham. The riot waxed fiercer and fiercer ; the Jews made barricades for their defence, when their enemies proceeded to burn their houses, making a holocaust of the inmates—husbands, wives, and children; or, breaking open the doors, they flung these miserable creatures out of the windows into the midst of blazing bonfires heaped up in the area below. The king caused several of the rioters to be seized, and some of them to be hanged.

What a comment does all this afford on the rudeness of the times, the prejudices against the Jews, the belief in magic, the feeble restraints of law and justice, and the iniquitous partiality and selfishness of the sovereign; for Richard, in sentencing three of the ringleaders to the gallows, expressly declared that it was for having burnt the houses *of Christians!* And when he saw the property, as well as the persons, of the Jews vanishing out of his sight, he declared them under his own gracious and special protection.

The festal echoes become still more distinct as time advances; and in the reign of the third Henry we find numerous detailed records of regal banquetings at Westminster. The marriage of the king with Eleanor of Provence, in 1236, was an occasion on which the festivities of the Great Hall were conducted with unusual splendour. 'The solemnity was resplendent with the clergy and knights properly placed. But how shall I describe the dainties of the table, and the abundance of divers liquors, the quantity of game, the variety of fish, the multitude of jesters, and the attendance of the waiters? Whatever the world pours forth of pleasure and glory was there especially displayed.' So writes Matthew Paris.

In the same reign, we read of dinners given by the king to the poor, both here and in the Little Hall, the weak and the aged being placed on one occasion in the former, and those more strong and in reasonable plight in the lesser, while in the king and the queen's chamber there were great gatherings of the little folks. From Christmas Day to the Day of the Circumcision, in 1247, the Great Hall was filled with poor people, who were there provided with good cheer.

Other adventures, too, there were in those days in the old Westminster Hall, neither festive nor political; for we read of a flood in 1238, when the Thames rose so high that the water entered the building, and the hall was crossed in boats, and people rode through it on horseback to their chambers. After an inundation had occurred at a much later period, the subsiding tide left on the floor of the hall a quantity of fish.

The coronation banquet of Richard II. (A.D. 1377), who rebuilt the hall, was remarkably magnificent. The reader will not care to have the names of all the magnates recorded as being present on the occasion. It will be sufficient to observe that the Lord Steward, the Constable, and the Earl Marshal, with certain knights, rode about the hall on horseback, to keep the people in order; that after the feast the great men, knights, and lords, passed the remainder of the day till supper-time in shows, dances, and solemn minstrelsy; that in the midst of the palace there was set up a marble pillar, crowned with a gilt eagle, from under the feet of which, through four sides of the capital, different kinds of wine gushed out, freely to be taken by all comers, rich and poor.

At the coronation feast of Henry IV. (1399), the champion, in the person of one of the Dymokes, enters at the second course, armed *cap-à-pie*, his horse barbed with crimson housings, a herald proclaiming his challenge with a loud voice, in different parts of the hall. Speaking of that second course, we may add that, thanks to a MS. in the British Museum, we can tell what were the principal dishes in all the three courses of that remarkable dinner. The first included two made dishes called *Braun en Peverarde*, and *Viande Ryal*, and also boar's head, cygnets, capons, pheasant, heron, and sturgeon, with an ornamental preparation styled a *subtlety*, consisting of figures historical or emblematical. The second course comprised venison in frumenty, jelly, young pigs stuffed, peacocks, cranes, venison pasty, tongue, bitterns, fowls gilded, large tarts, and rashers of ham or brawn, winding up, like the first, with a subtlety. The third course comprehended quinces in confection, young eagles, curlews, partridges, pigeons, quails, snipes, small birds, rabbits, white brawn sliced, eggs in jelly, fritters, sweetmeats and eggs, and again the favourite subtlety.

Catherine, the queen of Henry V., was crowned during Lent, and the banquet in the Great Hall on her account was therefore all of fish. Carp, turbot, tench, and perch appeared on the table, and among them there were 'porpies rostyd,' and 'menuys fryed,' which, if we are to take them as meaning roast porpoises and fried minnows, must have formed an odd assortment of viands both as to flavour and size, to say nothing of them as specimens of culinary art. Most elaborate subtleties figured among the fish dishes, and the image of St. Catherine with her wheel, in compliment to the queen, was prominently introduced in each course. Her majesty, we are informed, was with great pomp conveyed into Westminster Hall, and there set in the throne, at the table of marble at the upper end, with the prelates of Canterbury and Winchester on the *right* hand, and the King of Scots on the left.

The young King Henry VI. was crowned here, in 1429. 'At which coronation,' Hall tells us, 'to rehearse the costly fare, the delicate meat, the pleasant wines, the number of courses, the sorts of dishes, the labours of officers, the multitude of people, the estates of lords, the beauties of ladies, the riches of apparel, the curious devices, the solemn banquets, it would ask a long time, and weary you.' No doubt it would; therefore congratulating the reader that the good chronicler's brevity has withheld from us what might have proved too strong a temptation to quote, we pass on to the coronation of Richard III., for which more than ordinary care was taken to render it splendid, both for the personal gratification of the vain usurper, and for the purpose of impressing the people with a sense of that dignity which, though often factitious, doth, in the eyes of the vulgar, like divinity, 'hedge about a king.'

A minute account of the robes worn has been preserved, and the first course of the feast, it is said, was served on dishes of gold and silver. At the second course 'came riding into the hall, Sir Robert Dymoke, the king's champion, his horse trapped with white silk and red, and himself in white harness, and the heralds-of-arms standing upon a stage, among all the company. Then came riding up before the king his champion, and there he declared before all the people, "If there be any man will say against King Richard III. why he should not pretend the crown;" and anon, all the people were in peace awhile. And when he had all said, anon all the hall cried, "King Richard," all with one voice. And when this was done anon one of the lords brought unto this champion a cup full of red wine, covered; and so he took the cup and uncovered it, and drank thereof, and when he had done, anon he casts out the wine, and covered the cup again, and made his obeisance to the king, and turned his horse about, and rode through the hall with the cup in his right hand; and that he had for his labour.'

When Elizabeth of York was married to Henry VII., it is curious to notice that, at the banquet, the queen presided alone—a goodly stage out of a side window having been raised for the king and his mother, 'privily, and at their pleasure,' to see the noble feast and service.

And so again, when Anne Boleyn passed through the dazzling dream of royalty, and sat enthroned in Westminster Hall, the wife of Henry VIII., he, with divers ambassadors, stood to behold the scene in a little closet, made on the right hand out of the cloisters of St. Stephen's.

The reign of Henry VIII. was the very climacteric of that long age of feudal splendour which so often threw its blaze of illusive glory over the sombre and massive hall of William and Richard. A form of mountain-like strength, grave and dark, with cressets sparkling over it now and then, was the feudal system; such, too, was this feudal hall. The spirit began to change in the later Tudor times. Civilization was on the edge of a crisis, and the festivities of English kings, though quaint and proud as ever, came to wear an affected garishness. The growth of one age transplanted into the soil of another altogether different from that out of which it sprang, degenerates into a sickly exotic. What once was natural enough becomes fantastic. The life and meaning of a thing gone out of it, what remains but an unkernelled shell? Mediæval pageantries in modern times are but mouldy husks, empty and rotten.

Westminster Hall, in 1653, witnessed a scene of very different character from regal banquetings—quite a contrast to all feudal pageants—springing out of another state of society, another political spirit, another order of civilization, yet having in it state ceremonial and solemnity—a grand inauguration without a feast. Cromwell was sworn in Lord Protector on the 16th of December, in the Chancery Court in Westminster Hall, which was hung with banners taken from the Royalists at Naseby and Worcester. There was a canopy of state at the south end over the ancient coronation chair, which had been brought out of the Abbey. There was a table before it, covered with pink-coloured velvet of Geneva, fringed with gold. There lay on the table Bible, sword, and sceptre. Members of Parliament were there; the Speaker in a chair beside the table; the Lord Mayor of London and the aldermen, 'with the like,' were there; and his Highness was there in the seat where kings had worn their crowns, his dress rich but plain—a black velvet suit and cloak of the same, and a broad gold band about his hat. 'Fifty-four years old gone April last; brown hair and moustache are getting grey. A figure of sufficient impressiveness, not lovely to the man-milliner species, not pretending to be so. Massive stature; big massive head, of somewhat leonine aspect, wart above the right eyebrow, nose of considerable blunt aquiline proportions, strict yet copious lips, full of all tremulous sensibilities, and also, if need were, of all fiercenesses and rigours; deep loving eyes, call them grave, call them stern, looking from under those craggy brows, as if in lifelong sorrow, and yet not thinking it sorrow, thinking it only labour and endeavour: on the whole, a right noble face and hero face.'

So that great modern man, kingly in his way, sat in Westminster Hall, amidst grave, subdued solemnities, with his Bible and sceptre, and Mr. Lockier, the chaplain, giving an exhortation. But, as a matter of fact, England could not bear the repetition of that sort of thing. Once in the march of centuries it sufficed. The coronation chair went back to Westminster Abbey, and the coronation banquet was restored in Westminster Hall; but the history of the affair becomes dull and tame. It is weary work to go through it. A desperate and costly attempt to revive the mediæval part at the crowning of a modern king was made by George IV. The feast was a fine show—a theatrical exhibition, with nothing real in it but the presence of the Great Duke, to whom the monarch acknowledged that he owed the safety of his crown and the peace of his realm. The coronation of William IV. and of our beloved Queen was without a banquet; and an unlooked-for change must come ere regal feastings will again enliven the old hall. Such festivities as those we have recorded, in connection with our Henrys and Richards, can never more be seen. We by no means wish they should.

III.

MEN OF THE MARBLE CHAIR.

That the king is the fountain of justice is a maxim which obtained, as to the spirit of it, long before it was formally expressed. When a patriarchal sort of sovereign in the oldest times sat in the gate, and every man who had any complaint or cause came to him, that he might do them justice, that venerated ruler, whose prerogatives had not come to be minutely scanned and rigidly bounded, was deemed to be in possession of a legal authority so absolute as to be in some sort divine. And though in less ancient times, and in our western world, other forms of government were blended with the kingly—and among our Saxon fathers, the priest, the earl, and the thane appeared in the royal councils, and had a voice in judicial and legislative decisions—for during a long season they were blended, and an accurate distinction between them in practice and theory is a comparatively modern refinement—yet the crowned head was thought fullest of wisdom, as the rudely sceptred hand surpasses others in strength. By common consent, the king was most knowing and most able. There were inferior courts of justice in our old Anglo-Saxon land, for the king could not be everywhere himself; but all the streams of justice were acknowledged to flow from him as the original source; and when these were multiplied, still he sat at certain times in the great hall of his palace, administering justice with his own lips; and litigants came and told their tale in the royal ear, and sought the termination of their quarrels from his behest. So sat Edward the Confessor, in his palatial hall at Westminster, the great father-judge of the realm, his people bowing to his decisions with reverence, if not always with satisfaction.

Kingship in England lost nothing of individual power by passing from the Saxon to the Norman; on the contrary, William, amongst his barons, sat more potent than Edward amongst his thanes. He was feudal lord of the land, and transferred to his court at Westminster notions and usages such as prevailed in Normandy and throughout France. As monarch over his new kingdom, he was an exaggerated impersonation of the feudal power, which reigned in every baron's castle, meting out justice, according to its own fashion, among the members of the household. England was for a while a sort of Norman fortress, and the subjects of the king were dealt with as his children, his servants, and his retainers. In 1069, the Abbot of Peterborough was tried in person before the king at Westminster—the first particular notice we have of a law court on the spot, the first judicial scene which appears amidst the festivities of Norman times, and a prelude to manifold legal transactions and proceedings, which impart to Westminster Hall nobler memories than arise out of its most gorgeous coronation banquets. In 1234 we find a curious case tried before Henry III. in person, many of his bishops and principal subjects being present on the occasion. Seven Jews were brought before him, absurdly charged with having stolen and circumcised a boy at Norwich, keeping him in confinement, with a view to his crucifixion at the following passover. Matthew Paris says: 'They were convicted of this crime, and in the king's presence confessed themselves guilty, and were detained in prison afterwards, to await his pleasure.' According to another authority—Fabyan—they were released without punishment.

In 1256, John Stowe tells us that 'King Henry sat in the Exchequer of this Hall, Westminster, and there set down order for the appearance of the sheriffs and bringing in of their accounts; and there were five marks set on every sheriff's head, for a fine, because they had not distrained every person that might spend 15*l.* land by the year, to receive the order of knighthood, according as the same sheriffs were commanded.'

The express mention of the Court of Exchequer indicates that the rudimental administration of justice had given place to something more definite and artificial. At an early period matters relating to revenue seem to have been separately considered, and to have come under distinct adjudication. A particular chamber was set apart, and at particular seasons the great lords of the king's court there met the monarch; and so arose the Court of Exchequer.

Another court, branching out of the *curia regis*, appears in the reign of King John, before Magna Charta; this was the Common Pleas. King's Bench and Chancery are recognizable in the reign of Edward I. Physiologists inform us that the higher organs of animal life are found undeveloped in the lower types of animal existence; and so, seminally, are found in the primitive constitution of the Norman king's court, powers which have unfolded themselves under the culture of later civilization, into the elaborate formation of our modern law practice. But the worthies who sat judging in the earliest Westminster Hall little dreamt of the manifold distinctions, divisions, intricacies, and subtleties in which their descendants of the ermine and coif would become involved in the nineteenth century.

Even among the officers of the Saxon kings we find a Chancellor—shall we say s ocalled from his power of cancelling the king's letters-patent, when granted contrary to law? or from the *cancelli*, the lattice-work, or crossbars which separated the multitude from the chancel or recess in which he sat?

This now important functionary at first was far from being *Lord High* Chancellor: he was little more than clerk of the king's closet. In Norman times, for a good while, the Lord High Justiciary was the chief law officer of the Crown. The Saxon chancellor had, however, his legal functions, and the earliest reported decision of a Chancery lawyer is, we believe, that of the renowned St. Swithin, of moist memory, who, when he held the Great Seal, had an old woman come before him seeking redress in equity, for a rude assault committed upon her, whereby she had been shoved about on her way to market, so that all the eggs in her basket were crushed to pieces. Lord Chancellor Swithin's decision was more practical, as it was more marvellous, than those of his successors are wont to be : for, according to the report of this great case, in William of Malmesbury, the saint, while he gave judgment against the aggressor, made over the eggs the sign of the cross, and thereby miraculously consolidated shell and yolks ; so that we doubt not the good market-woman went away from that Court of Chancery far merrier than people since have done, for she brought out a far better estate than had been thrown in.

The chancellors at first were clerical personages ; but in the reign of Henry III. we are presented with the variety of a lady Keeper of the Great Seal, in the person of Queen Eleanor, who actually sat in judgment in the Aula Regis, except when the private domestic affair of the birth of a young prince kept her at home.

Anciently, the king's court migrated with his majesty from place to place, and was held at Westminster, Winchester, or Gloucester, as the case might be ; and the same custom was observed with regard to the distinct branches into which the original court became divided, until the manifest inconveniences of the arrangement produced a change; and in the reign of Edward III. Chancery settled down at Westminster. A corner of the Great Hall had already been allotted to the Common Pleas; and now at the upper end, and on the right-hand side, in a recess left open, with only a bar to keep off the suitors and people, the hitherto movable authority was fixed. A marble table on an elevated floor, reached by five or six steps, with a marble chair close to it, were the visible signs of this dignified court. Writs and letters patent were signed on the table, and my lords were inaugurated by being solemnly seated in the chair. These memorials of Chancery justice existed in Dugdale's time, and are are said to have been displaced when the Chancery Court was enclosed.

The first layman who sat in the marble chair was Sir Robert Bourchier, knight, who took the place of Robert de Stratford, and who, with his royal master Edward III., sought to exclude the ex-chancellor from his seat in Parliament; whereupon one day a sad *fracas* occurred in Westminster Hall. When Stratford, Archbishop of Canterbury, appeared in pontifical robes, with his crosier, demanding admittance to the Chamber of Peers, he was seized and carried to the bar of the Court of Exchequer. After this, taking up his position in Palace Yard, he declared he would not stir till the king admitted him to Parliament. 'Thou art a traitor; thou hast deceived the king, and betrayed the realm!' exclaimed some of the royal party. 'The curse of the Almighty, and of His blessed mother, and of St. Thomas, and mine also, be upon the heads of them who inform the king so!' rejoined the vengeful priest.

The installations of Simon de Langham and Sir Robert Thorpe are specially mentioned in the reign of Edward III., the former as extraordinarily magnificent, the latter as graced by the presence and assistance of his predecessor, the renowned William of Wickham. Archbishop Arundel's occupation of the marble chair was remarkable for the trial of William Thorpe, a priest, for heresy. 'Being brought before Thomas, Archbishop of Canterbury and Chancellor of England, when that I came to him,' says the poor priest, 'he stood in a great chamber, and much people about him, and when that he saw me he went fast into a closet, bidding all secular men that followed him to go forth from him.' After a long colloquy, the chancellor said: 'Be this thing well known to thee, that God, as I wot well, hath called me again and brought me into this land for to destroy thee and the false sect that thou art of, as, by God (such was his awful blasphemy) I shall pursue you so narrowly, that I shall not leave a step of you in this land.' After this loving address, the Lollard confessor replied: 'Sir, the holy prophet Jeremy said to the false prophet *Anany*, "When the word that is the prophecy of a prophet is known or fulfilled, then it shall be known that the Lord sent the prophet in truth."' The chancellor was little pleased at this sharp kind of rejoinder, in which so many of the early English so-called heretics excelled, and with another oath, and a coarse threat, dismissed the accused to a 'foul unhonest prison,' where, it is to be feared, William Thorpe ended his days.

Among the men of the marble chair, Cardinal Beaufort appears conspicuous in the reign of Henry V., not for any good qualities, but for his pride and rapacity. So great was his wealth and so keen his avarice, that when the king sought from him pecuniary help in his troubles, this keeper of both royal conscience and royal seal would not give a farthing, but only lend—nor that without the first security. The king preferred to offer his crown rather than not get the gold he wanted; and we have thus the strange fact of a sovereign of England pawning his crown to a lord chancellor.

The reign of Henry VIII. presents to us two of the most remarkable men that ever filled the marble chair—one immediately succeeding the other, an unparalleled succession—both great, very great, but exhibiting each his own kind of greatness, between which, as to superiority, the reader will very soon decide—Cardinal Wolsey and Sir Thomas More.

In connection with the former, we have a description of two very characteristic scenes associated with the marble seat at Westminster. Cavendish, his biographer and one of his household, thus quaintly describes the first:—

'Having risen by daybreak and heard mass, he returned to his private chamber, and his public rooms being now filled with noblemen and gentlemen attending his *levée*, he issued out into them, apparelled all in red, in the habit of a cardinal, which was either of fine scarlet or else of crimson satin, taffety damask, or caffa, the best that he could get for money; and upon his head a round pillion, with a noble of black velvet set to the same in the inner side; he had also a tippet of fine sables about his neck; holding in his hand a very fine orange, whereof the meat or substance within was taken out, and filled up again with part of a sponge, wherein was vinegar and other confections against the pestilent airs, the which he most commonly smelt unto passing among the press, or else when he was pestered with many suitors. There was also borne before him, first, the Great Seal of England, and then his cardinal's hat, by a nobleman or some worthy gentleman, right solemnly bareheaded. And as soon as he was entered into his chamber of presence, there were attending his coming to await upon him to Westminster Hall, as well noblemen and other worthy gentlemen, as noblemen and gentlemen of his own family; thus passing forth with two great crosses of silver borne before him; with also two great pillars of silver, and his pursuivant-at-arms with a great mace of silver gilt. Then his gentlemen ushers cried and said, "On, my lords and masters, on before! make way for my lord's grace!" Thus passed he down from his chamber to the hall;

and when he came to the hall door, there was attendant for him his mule, trapped altogether in crimson velvet and gilt stirrups. When he was mounted with his cross-bearers and pillar-bearers also upon great horses trapped with fine scarlet, then marched he forward with his train and furniture, in manner as I have declared, having about him four footmen with gilt pole-axes in their hands; and thus he went until he came to Westminster Hall door, and there alighted and went after this manner up through the hall into the Chancery; howbeit he would most commonly stay awhile at a bar made for him a little beneath the Chancery on the right hand, and there commune some time with the judges, and some time with other persons. And that done he would repair into the Chancery, sitting there till eleven of the clock, hearing suitors and determining of divers matters. And from thence he would divers times go into the Star Chamber, as occasion did serve, where he spared neither high nor low, but judged every one according to their merits and deserts.'

As to his last public judicial appearance, Lord Campbell observes: 'On the first day of Michaelmas term, which then began in the middle of October, he headed the usual grand procession to Westminster Hall, riding on his mule, attended by his crosses, his pillars, and his pole-axes, and an immense retinue to defend the Great Seal and the cardinal's hat. It was remarked that in the procession, and while sitting in the Court of Chancery, his manner was dignified and collected, although he, and all who beheld him, knew that he had touched the highest point of all his greatness, and from the full meridian of his glory he hastened to his setting.'

Sir Thomas More being neither cardinal, archbishop, nor a dignitary of the realm, but simply a wise man and a learned lawyer, though very popular among those who could appreciate his character and qualifications, it was thought necessary to induct him into the chancellor's office with state and dignity, for the purpose of impressing the vulgar mind, which had been dazzled with the pageantry of his predecessor. The procession was headed by the Duke of Norfolk, the first peer, and the Duke of Suffolk, the king's brother-in-law: the nobles and courtiers in and about London, together with the most distinguished members of the legal profession, followed in order. On reaching Palace Yard, the new chancellor in his robes was conducted by the two great dukes to the marble chair, when Norfolk, by the king's command, made an oration in honour of More, vindicating the royal choice of a man who belonged to neither the church nor the nobility, but was one who had both wife and children. A speech is there reported as having been delivered by Sir Thomas, in the course of which, turning to the marble chair, he made the following remarks :—

'But when I look upon this seat—when I think how great and what kind of personages have possessed this place before me—when I call to mind who he was that sat in it last of all—a man of what singular wisdom, of what notable experience, what a prosperous and favourable fortune he had for a great space, and how, at last, dejected with a heavy downfall, he hath died inglorious—I have cause enough, by my predecessor's example, to think honour but slippery, and this dignity not so grateful to me as it may seem to others; for both it is a hard matter to follow with like paces or praises a man of such admirable wit, prudence, authority, and splendour, to whom I may seem but as the lighting of a candle when the sun is down; and also the sudden and unexpected fall of so great a man as he was doth terribly put me in mind that this honour ought not to please me too much, nor the lustre of this glittering seat dazzle mine eyes. Wherefore, I ascend this seat as a place full of labour and danger, void of all solid and true honour, the which by how much the higher it is, by so much greater fall I am to fear, as well in respect of the very nature of the thing itself as because I am warned by this late fearful example.'

This speech looks too much like one made for the hero; and we share in the suspicion that Master Roper, the reporter, had more to do with it than his grandfather the chancellor. However that may be, no one before had so worthily filled that seat of honour and responsibility as he who was now installed. In days when the saying, as true as ever, had grown old, that 'no one could hope for a favourable judgment, unless his fingers were tipped with gold,' he administered justice with as much impartiality as diligence. 'Having heard causes in the forenoon between eight and eleven, after dinner he sat in an open hall, and received the petitions of all who chose to come before him, examining their cases and giving them redress where it was in his power, according to law and good conscience; and the poorer and the meaner the suppliant was, the more affably he would speak unto him—the more heartily he would hearken to his cause, and with speedy trial despatch him.'

'It happened on a time that a beggar-woman's little dog, which she had lost, was presented for a jewel to Lady More, and she had kept it some se'nnight very carefully; but at last the beggar had notice where her dog was, and presently she came to proclaim to Sir Thomas, as he was sitting in his hall, that his lady withheld her dog from her. Presently my lady was sent for, and the dog brought with her, which Sir Thomas, taking in his hands, caused his wife, because she was the worthier person, to stand at the upper end of the hall and the beggar at the lower end ; and saying that he sat there to do every one justice, he bade each of them call the dog; which, when they did, the dog went presently to the beggar, forsaking my lady. When he saw this he bade my lady be contented, for it was none of hers; yet she, repining at the sentence of the lord chancellor, agreed with the beggar, and gave her a piece of gold, which would well have bought three dogs; and so all parties were agreed, every one smiling to see his manner of inquiring out the truth.'

Never since his time, we may add, has anything of the kind been seen more morally beautiful in Westminster Hall than the well-known demeanour of More towards his aged father, then puisne judge in the Court of King's Bench. 'Every day during term time, before the chancellor began business in his own court, he went into the Court of King's Bench, and, kneeling before his father, asked and received his blessing. So, if they met together at readings in Lincoln's Inn, notwithstanding his high office, he offered the pre-eminence in argument to his father, though, from regard to judicial subordination, this offer was always refused.'

The heart of the man Wolsey is seen in the gay pageant of his installation, as the heart of the man More is seen in the filial love and reverence which he cherished for his aged parent. With all More's infirmities and errors, making due deduction for his sympathy with a persecuting age—for alas! he did, by his severity to some Protestants brought before him, practically deny the principles of tolerance which, with such fair and beautiful eloquence, he had illustrated in his 'Utopia'—this upright chancellor, in the reign of the most tyrannical of monarchs, must impress us as an embodiment of high moral grandeur—as a really honest man. How all Wolsey's grandeur fades away, and his moral meanness comes out to the eye of posterity! How to the same eye, amidst the gloom of his affliction, emerges the radiant form of More! Time destroys many illusions, rectifies many errors, and often anticipates the judgments of another world.

IV.

OLD PARLIAMENTS AND POLICY.

'A TOURIST,' says Sir Francis Palgrave, in his interesting volume, 'The Merchant and the Friar,' 'a tourist living in those happy days when a monkey who had seen the world was a rarer animal than any of the present tenants of the rival Zoological Gardens, and then enjoying much unmerited reputation, the author of "Zeluco," exemplifies the ignorance of the Continental *noblesse* by telling an anecdote of a Neapolitan lady of high rank, who, hearing an Englishman discourse, with much animation, respecting Parliament, exclaimed, in reply, "Parliament! what is it? a *corso*? a horse-race?" She was not able to suppose that any other matter could excite so much interest and be remembered with so much pleasure.'

The story, as it is here told, certainly looks somewhat improbable; but that a good deal of ignorance about Parliaments should exist in the kingdom of Naples is by no means surprising. What Parliaments *are*, and the very great advantages which from them accrue to the public welfare, is happily known by most persons in this free country—Parliaments being the palladium of our freedom; but what Parliaments *were* in early days, when they used to meet in Westminster Hall, is perhaps by a good many persons quite unknown. We do not mean to draw a parallel between the Neapolitan lady and any of our readers: she had no idea of a Parliament at all; but it is possible that some one reading these sketches may imagine that Parliaments at first were very much like what Parliaments are now.

It is true we catch but very indistinct echoes of the voices and doings of the early Parliaments in the hall of Rufus. The sounds are in themselves feeble, and then we have the difficulty of catching them augmented by historical critics and legal commentators, who raise in our ears a loud buzz and bewildering din in their conflicts with each other, under pretence of clearly repeating to us what the echoes say.

Thus much is clear, that Parliaments, in the very old time, were for a good while far more judicial than legislative. The writer just quoted describes in a lively manner a proclamation of the opening of Parliament in the time of Edward II. A grave-looking personage, standing in the midst of a crowd in Eastcheap, reads with a loud voice from a parchment roll, the 'crye' that on the octave of St. Hilary now next ensuing, our lord the king will hold his High Court of Parliament at Westminster. All who had any grace to demand of the king in Parliament, or any complaint to make to the king in Parliament of matters which could

not be redressed or determined by ordinary course
of the common law; or who had been in any way
aggrieved by any of the king's ministers, the king's
justices, the king's sheriffs, or their bailiffs, or any
other officer; or who had been unduly assessed, rated,
charged, or surcharged, to aids, subsidies, or taxes,
'are to deliver their petitions to the receivers whom for
that purpose our lord the king hath appointed, and
who will sit openly from day to day ready to listen to
you, ready to attend to you, in the Great Hall of the
king's palace of Westminster, at the foot of the staircase on the left-hand side, just as ye enter the same.'
Whereat there is much rejoicing and throwing up of
caps, and vociferous shouts of 'Long life to his
Majesty;' and, perhaps, among the dirty boys and
greasy butchers—the sooty smiths and begrimed cord-
wainers—among the fishermen and sailors that have
just come from the river-side—among the men-at-arms
and baronial retainers—among monks and friars, pretty
plentifully sprinkled in all street gatherings—there are
substantial citizens, and even humbler folks, who have
some heavy wrong chafing their spirit, and who are
panting for redress, and who, as they hear the welcome
'crye,' resolve that, on the octave of St. Hilary, they
will be at the foot of the staircase, on the left-hand side
of the Great Hall.

Let us go down ourselves on the appointed day.
As well as the crowd about the door will let us, we
elbow our way into the hall. Here are people of all

sorts, come to ask for justice at the hands of the triers who are sitting, in the king's name, to hear complaints and give decisions in these cases of appeal. Here are people come to complain of some wrong done them in the exaction of dues by the officers of the king—of their being defrauded of their property through some misjudgment in the lower courts—of some loss for which they have in vain sought elsewhere for compensation—of some unfair outlawry, proclaimed by the coroner of a certain county—of some violence done by the lord of a manor to one of free birth and blood, under an assumed and illegitimate claim of villanage.

These Parliaments have very extensive powers, and are very busy in putting everybody and everything to rights. But not to dwell any longer upon these judicial associations of the old Parliaments in Westminster Hall, we would just remind the reader of the relic of these old usages in the existing authority of the House of Lords, as the final Court of Appeal in the English realm.

The Commons began to sit in Parliament in Westminster Hall in the reign of Henry III., and their functions at first, it should be observed, were scarcely deliberative. They petitioned for the redress of grievances, and provided for the necessities of the crown. Their hold of the purse gave them power as petitioners. There is the secret of many of the acquisitions on the side of popular liberty made in the history of the English Constitution. The Commons and the Barons at the beginning sat together in the same great hall; but probably there always was some distinction made between them—the upper body of the great national council sitting at the top, the lower at the bottom. The distinction becomes clear enough between Lords and Commons in the reign of Edward III., when the Speaker is mentioned, the first person in that office of whom we have any account being Sir Thomas de Hungerford. It is curious to notice that there occur among the early summonses to meet the barons at Westminster, writs addressed to certain ladies—Maria Countess of Norfolk, Eleanor Countess of Ormond, Philippa Countess of March, Agnes Countess of Pembroke, and Catherine Countess of Atholl, as well as to four abbesses—though it does not appear that any of these noble dames actually took their seats among the Peers; and it is also curious to remark how the Commons were paid for their attendance in Parliament—knights of the shire receiving, in the reign of Edward II., generally four shillings a day, but sometimes only three-and-fourpence, and in one instance only two-and-sixpence. The charges of their coming to Westminster and returning home were also allowed.

The earliest echoes of parliamentary proceedings which ring in Westminster Hall on the side of legislation have in them a decided tone of grumbling; but then it is that noble sort of grumbling to which our ancestors were addicted—grumbling about unquestionable grievances, grumbling against the encroachments of despotism on liberties solemnly conceded by charter and confirmed by oath. Westminster Hall witnessed many a scene of earnest complaint and firm resistance in the time of Henry III., for which Englishmen ought to be thankful. He gave his Parliament an uncommon deal of trouble by his faithlessness. When his money was gone, he would call together the estates of the realm. In 1248 they met him when he was in deep pecuniary distress. He asked for a subsidy 'in relief of the great charges which he had in divers ways sustained.' But the barons, who looked for reformation in his doings, told his majesty 'that they would not impoverish themselves to enrich strangers, their enemies,' upon whom, in his prodigality, he had wasted much of his revenue. He promised amendment, and adjourned the Parliament. When the Parliament met again, he renewed his demands of money; but the Commons, seeing no amendment in their royal master, renewed their refusal.

One of the most awfully dramatic scenes ever witnessed in Westminster Hall was performed by Henry and his Parliament in the midst of their conflicts, arising out of his violation of the Great Charter, so prized by the barons, so disliked by the king. There they were assembled in solemn order on the 3rd of May, 1253—Henry himself and his brother Richard of Cornwall, and the Earls of Norfolk, and Suffolk, and Hereford, and Oxford, and Warwick, and other great barons, together with the Archbishop of Canterbury, and the Bishops of London, Ely, and Lincoln, and many more—these latter all dressed in pontifical robes, with lighted candles in their hands. The barons had come to hear, and the priests to pronounce, in the presence of the monarch, the sentence of excommunication against any who should encroach on the liberties of the Church and State, especially those confirmed in the Great Charter of the kingdom of England and the Forest Charters. Terrible was the sentence :—' In the name and authority of Almighty God, the Son, and the Holy Spirit; in the name of the Virgin Mary and the blessed Apostles; in the name of St. Thomas of Canterbury and all the Martyrs and Confessors and Virgins, it anathematized, sequestered, and drove from the threshold of Holy Church every one who knowingly and maliciously should so transgress.' The king listened calmly, placing his outspread hand on his breast, in token of assent, till the fearful sentence had terminated. A candle had been offered to him as well as the rest, but refusing to hold it, and putting it into the hand of one of the prelates, he observed : ' It does not become me to hold one, as I am not a priest.' The royal hand laid on the heart sufficed to express his testimony. The bishops threw their candles on the floor ; as they lay flickering and smoking, reflected on the embroidery of rich canonicals, the ornaments of courtly robes, the surface of polished armour, the points of spears and battle-axes, the heads of crosses, and the tops of crosiers—as the lights became extinguished, and the stench of the wicks spread over the hall—each one said: 'So let him who incurs this sentence be extinguished, and smoke and stink in hell.' And then the king exclaimed: 'As God shall help me, I will keep these charters inviolate, as I am a man, as I am a Christian, as I am a knight, as I am a crowned and anointed king!' However earnestly the barons and bishops played their parts in this solemnity, the sovereign performed his insincerely or inconsiderately; or perhaps, what may be nearer the mark, he uttered his vow honestly at the time, but soon changed his mind; for ere long we find him going back to his old ways, after getting a dispensation from his oath; and, seen in the light of what followed, the tragic drama of Westminster Hall becomes very much like a farce.

In 1255 Henry met his Parliament again at the Feast of St. Edward, almost all the great men of the kingdom being present. The session was prolonged day after day by the king, in the hope of getting what he wanted, but in vain; after which he had recourse to his old tricks, and mulcted Jews and citizens, extorting eight thousand marks from the former, under pain of hanging them if they did not speedily pay. 'And when,' as Holinshead says, 'he had fleeced them to the quick, he set them to farm under his brother Earl Richard, that he might peel off skin and all.'

Again the spirit of resistance breaks out, and we

have in Westminster Hall another scene. In 1258 the barons come to Parliament in complete armour. There they are, clothed in steel from top to toe. Helmets, breastplates, shields, swords, and spears, look rather alarming. 'Am I then a prisoner?' asks the monarch, a little daunted. 'Not so,' replies Roger Bigod, Earl of Norfolk and earl marshal, a right brave man, a champion for his country's liberties, and ready to beard the royal lion, when putting his paw on the rights of his subjects—'Not so; but as you, sir, by your partiality to foreigners, and your own prodigality, have involved the realm in misery, we demand that the authority of the State be delegated to Commissioners, who shall have power to correct abuses and enact salutary laws.' The king stormed, but it was useless. A Parliament soon after assembled in Oxford, when a council of safety was appointed, consisting of barons and prelates, assisted by *representatives* of the people; which was the beginning of the authority of Commons representation, as an integral part of the Constitution of the empire. Simon de Montfort was the leader of that business: and we may here relate the following story in illustration of his power, and the awe which he inspired in the mind of King Henry.

The king, going out to dinner, left his palace, and took a boat at Westminster. The sky grew dark, and the wind grew fierce, the rain grew heavy, and the Thames grew rough, and thunder and lightning grew loud and strong. The king, who was always frightened at a storm, grew more and more fearful, and commanded the rowers to put him ashore. They were just by the Bishop of Durham's palace, in which Simon de Montfort then lived. The earl, seeing the monarch's approach, ran out to the river-stairs to meet him, and after respectful salutations inquired why his majesty looked so terrified now that the storm had ceased. 'Above measure,' he gravely answered, 'I dread thunder and lightning;' but, with his accustomed oath, added, 'I am more in terror of you than of all the thunder and lightning in the world.' Perhaps he had cause to be.

Westminster Hall, in the reign of Edward II., again rings with the echo of complaint. The charters are still violated. This is the tone in which Parliament expresses itself—rather humble, it must be confessed: 'The good people of the kingdom who are come hither, pray our lord the king, that he will, if it please him, have regard to his poor subjects, who are much aggrieved by reason that they are not governed as they should be, especially as to the articles of the Great Charter: and for this, if it please him, they pray remedy; besides which, they pray their lord the king to hear what has long aggrieved his people, and still does so from day to day, on the part of those who call themselves his officers, and to amend it if he please.'

Things improve in Westminster Hall under the third Edward; but there is sad confusion under his grandson Richard II., which ends in the transfer of the crown to

Henry IV. A famous scene is connected with this transaction. The first most memorable act in the edifice which Richard had caused to be renewed and adorned, was one which extinguished his royal authority.

On September the 30th, 1399, Parliament assembled in the Great Hall, 'which they had hung and trimmed sumptuously, and had caused to be set up a royal chair on purpose to choose a new king, near to which the prelates were sat; on the other side sat the Lords; and, after the Commons, in order, first sat the Duke of Lancaster, then the Duke of York, and after him other great dukes and earls; but the Earls of Northumberland and Westmoreland sat not, but went up and down, ofttimes kneeling, in doing their offices,' says our informant, John Stowe, whose pictorial narrative we here chiefly follow. Arundel, Archbishop of Canterbury, preached a sermon in Latin on the blessing of Jacob by his father; after which a doctor of law stood up and read an instrument, to the effect that Richard, by his own confession, was unworthy to reign, and would resign the crown to anyone fitted to wear it. Then the archbishop persuaded them to proceed to the election of some one to occupy the vacant throne, which those present deemed very proper, except about four of Richard's party, who durst not speak. Then came the delicate question, Who should the new sovereign be? 'Shall it be the Duke of York?' asked the archprelate; and they answered, 'No.' Then he inquired if they would have his eldest son, the Duke of Aumerle, and they said, 'No.' Would they have his youngest son? And they said, 'No.' Others were named, and were likewise rejected. So, staying awhile, at last his grace asked, if they would have the Duke of Lancaster; and then all answered that they would have no other. The demand was made thrice, and then certain instruments and charters were read in the presence of all. Then the archbishops, coming to the duke, fell on their knees, declaring to him that he was chosen king, and wished him to say if he would consent thereto. Then the duke, being on his knees, rose and declared he accepted the realm, since it was ordained of God. According to the Parliament rolls, he also asserted that he had a right to the crown. 'In the name of Father, Son, and Holy Ghost'—so runs the record of his declaration—'I, Henry of Lancaster, challenge this realm of England, and the crown, with all the members and appurtenances, as that I am descended by right line of the blood, coming from the good lord King Henry III., and through the right that God, of His grace, hath sent me, with help of my kin, and of my friends, to recover it, the which realm was in point to be undone for default of governance and undoing of the good laws.'

The archbishop, Stowe goes on to tell, read what the new king was bound unto, and with certain ceremonies signed him with the cross; then he kissed the archbishop, and they took the ring with which the kings of England are wedded to the realm, and bare it to the

Lord Percy, who was constable; and he receiving it, showed it to the whole assembly, and then put it on the king's finger. The king kissed the constable, and then the archbishops led the king up into the empty throne. The king made his prayers on his knees before it, and then delivered a speech, first to the prelates, and then to the Lords, and then to the commons, and so sat him down on his seat. He sat a good while in silence, and so did all the rest, for they were in prayer for his prosperity; and when they had ended, he filled up such offices of state as had become vacant. After this, the archbishop spake certain things in Latin, praying for the king's prosperity and for the realm's; and afterwards, in English, he exhorted all present to pray the like, after which every man sat down. With all this, there were shouts and acclamations, and it was announced that a Parliament should be held in the same place on the Monday next following, and that on St. Edward's Day the coronation should be celebrated.

Another irregular succession to the crown occurred in the case of Richard III. Entering the hall in great state, he placed himself in the marble chair, and declared he would take the crown in that place, where the laws were administered, in the king's name, and where of old the king did preside in person. Dwelling upon the evils of discord, and the blessings of union, this royal fisher for popularity proclaimed his forgetfulness of enmities and his pardon of all who had offended him. In proof of sincerity, he sent for one Fog, towards whom he had long had a deadly enmity, and publicly took him by the hand, 'which thing the common people rejoiced at and praised, but wise men took it for a vanity.'

Almost every Parliament from the 28th of Edward III. was opened in the Painted Chamber, and the general place of assembly for the Peers and great men was the White Chamber. The Commons often sat in the Painted Chamber, but in the last two Parliaments they were directed to withdraw to their ancient place, in the Chapter House at Westminster. St. Stephen's Chapel did not become appropriated, as the place for the Commons House, until the dissolution of the abbeys in the reign of Henry VIII.

V.

BENCH AND BAR.

It is remarked that through Chancery Lane, 'the connecting link of all the Inns of Court, there must have passed all the great and eminent lawyers, from Coke and Hale to Erskine and Romilly; Sir Thomas More with his weighty aspect, Bacon with his eye of intuition, the coarse Thurlow, and the elegant Mansfield.' The *silent* shadows of the men do very solemnly come before us as we enter that busy thoroughfare. With thoughtful countenance—with looks deeply fixed in meditation—principles, cases, opinions, revolving in their minds—the great ones of the Bench and Bar cross our path in mute majesty, as, in our walks from Fleet Street to Holborn, we turn from the present to the past—from the crowds of the unknown living to the assemblage of the illustrious dead. We see them there as students—students in the conventional sense, as young men reading law before entering on practice—or as students in the general sense, as men matured and aged, with their hands full of business, but with their intellects still, and, especially just now, tasked to the very utmost in the severest exercises of acquisition or application, preparing some momentous plea or great decision. They are seen there on the way to speech and action. The inward treasure is being just unlocked. The fountain is rising from its hidden depths. The fire is kindling up—the flame will come.

The remark about Chancery Lane is true of Westminster Hall, with this difference—that in the latter case we find these same great men in the midst of the arena, where they display before the world the results of their learning and experience. The thinkers are actors here. Those who have studied in the Inns of Court speak in the Courts of Westminster. They wrestle in hard conflict. Earnest are their debates; pleas are urged; appeals are uttered; decisions are claimed and expressed; thought is embodied in eloquence; the jurist becomes orator. There are words of wisdom; treasures are poured forth; streams gush from the spring; the fire blazes as it burns. The past at Westminster is not a religion of calmness and silence, like that in the City. There are not merely *forms* peopling it; it rings with *voices*. Westminster has its echoes, as well as its shadows. Perhaps no spot on the face of the earth has so resounded with eloquence; certainly not any, if we connect St. Stephen's Chapel with the law courts. When the much-talked-of New Zealander, after sitting on the ruins of London Bridge, soliloquizing on

St. Paul's, shall come down to Westminster to do his duty there, he will have illustrations of the beauty, music, and power of human words associated with the spot, which will surpass even those which now occur to the classical traveller, as, at Athens, he makes his way through fields of bearded barley, to the *bema* of Demosthenes.

'The Bench and the Bar,' in even something like their present meaning, are terms inapplicable to the early days of judicial proceeding in this country, when the king sat in person in his hall to dispense justice; but we may employ them in reference to the early times, when the distinct judicatures were developed out of their primitive normal condition. The words 'Bench and Bar,' as now commonly used to denote judges and barristers, seem to be derived from the Inns of Court, which originated when the Common Pleas were established at Westminster. Those Inns constituted, in fact, a university for the study of law —such a university being rendered needful by the prejudices at Oxford and Cambridge against the studies necessary for preparing men to practise in the new court. There were Benchers in those Inns, the superiors of the house, who occupied the upper end of the hall on public occasions, and sat on a daïs.

This part of the building was separated from the rest by a bar; below that sat the students who had attained a certain proficiency and position, and were called out of the body of the hall to sit near the bar, for the purpose of taking part in the mootings or disciplinary pleadings—exercises which formed a part of legal education, with a view to preparing men for their appearance in the Courts at Westminster. Those so distinguished were termed *utter* or outer barristers; while the rest of the students, who sat in the centre of the hall, were styled *inner* barristers. At first this arrangement did not regulate the method of proceeding at Westminster. The utter barrister, as such, had no right to practise there. They do not appear to have attained that right till the time of Elizabeth. In old law reports, the term 'barrister' is not used. Pleaders are called serjeants and apprentices-at-law.

The terms 'Bench and Bar,' then, strictly speaking, belong to the Inns of Court, rather than to the Courts of Westminster, till the time of Elizabeth; but as the words, in the sense we use them, are derived from usages in those Inns almost as ancient as the origin of those Courts, and as men connected with those Inns, though not simply by virtue of that connection, practised in those Courts, we shall take the liberty of employing the words in relation to early times at Westminster. Even in the Aula Regis there were serjeants-at-law who were assessors with the chief justiciar, and advocates for the suitors. When distinct courts were instituted, the judges were chosen from among these serjeants. From the Conquest to the time of Edward I. serjeants were the only advocates; from that time to the fifteenth century, law apprentices, as they were called, were allowed to practise in certain courts; then, these law apprentices were merged in the utter barristers.

The medley dress worn by the serjeant in Dugdale's time was of three colours, murrey or dark red, black furred with white, and scarlet. Dress, indeed, seems to have been a grand study with the old lawyers, if we may judge from the sumptuary regulations enacted respecting them:—'To check the grievance of long beards, an order was issued by the Inner Temple that no fellow of that house should wear his beard above three weeks' growth, on pain of forfeiting 20s.' The Middle Temple enacted that none of that society should wear great breeches in their hose, made after the Dutch, Spanish, or Almain fashion, or lawn upon their caps, or cut doublets, under a penalty of 3s. 4d., and expulsion for the second offence. 'In 3 and 4 Philip and Mary, it was ordained by all the four Inns of Court that none, except knights and benchers, should wear in their doublets or hose any light colours, save scarlet and crimson, nor wear any upper velvet cap, or any scarf or wings in their gowns, white jerkins, buskins, or velvet shoes, doubles, cuffs in their shirts, feathers or ribbons in their caps; and that none should wear their study gowns in the City, any further than Fleet Bridge or Holborn Bridge; nor, while in commons, wear Spanish cloaks, sword and buckler, or rapier, or gowns and hats, or gowns girded with a dagger on the back.'

The distinguishing head-gear was the coif or black

cloth cap. Barristers' wigs were inventions imported from France after the Restoration ; and it appears that at first the Bench frowned on these now cherished ornaments of the Bar. When a celebrated lawyer once argued a great privilege case, having to speak sixteen hours, he obtained leave to speak without a wig, but under the condition that 'this was not to be drawn into a precedent.'

Coifed and robed, in the old time the serjeant might be seen, deep in official business, not only at the Inns of Court and in Westminster Hall, but in St. Paul's Cathedral, where, by a chosen pillar, he listened to his clients, and took notes of their causes on his knee. There were his 'chambers,' and without the interpoposition of an attorney there he held consultations; and some relic of the old connection between serjeants and St. Paul's remained to the time of Charles II., when, on the elevation of a lawyer to the degree of the coif, he marched in procession to the cathedral and selected his pillar.

There are echoes of strange sounds down at Westminster, as we dwell on the scenes in the hall, and on the treatment and doings of men on the Bench. The first chief justice who acted simply as judge was Robert de Brus, in 1268. In the next year we meet with the following incident :—The Earl of Surrey had a quarrel with Sir Alan la Zouche about a certain manor. They came before the judges on the Tuesday after St. John the Baptist's day. People then seem to have had less control over themselves than they have now; and so the earl and Sir Alan not only came to high words with each other, but actually they began to fight in the presence of the court. The domestics of the earl joined in the fray, and presently the hall became a scene of confusion, wonderfully contrasting with the decorum maintained in our modern courts. The servants attacked Sir Alan, chased him when he fled from before the Bench, followed him into the royal chamber, and there wounded him till he was half dead. The poor man afterwards expired from fever, brought on by the hot weather and the injuries he received. His son also was much hurt. The earl and his retainers made their escape, but were pursued and overtaken; and on the Sunday after the Feast of St. Peter and St. Paul we find the culprit brought to court to receive justice. He was fined 7,000 marks, and was required to walk from the New Temple to Westminster, there to swear that the deed had not been done from premeditated malice.

In 1289 judges themselves were found culprits. The ermine was stained with deep corruption. Nearly all on the Bench were accused of illegal practices, for which a motive, though no excuse, may be found in the smallness of their salaries, the Lord Chief Justice receiving only sixty marks a year. De Weyland then possessed that dignity, and on being apprehended for his malpractices, he managed to escape in the disguise of a monk, preferring to abjure the realm rather than to stand a trial. After forfeiting all his property to the

Crown, he marched barefooted and bareheaded, with a crucifix in his hand, down to Dover—a very curious spectacle to the people of Kent, all along the road. The king, to put a stop to the iniquity of taking bribes, made the judges swear that they would for the future take neither money nor any kind of present, unless it was a breakfast, which they might accept, provided there were no excess.

In the reign of Richard II. another disgraceful circumstance occurred in connection with the judicial Bench. The judges—with the exception of Sir William Skepwith, and Chief Justice Tresilian, who was not to be found—were arrested while sitting on the very throne of judgment, for having prostituted their high office in the service of an unprincipled monarch and his worthless court. Sir Nicholas Brambre, one of the chief persons accused, was formally impeached and tried in Westminster Hall; and what is most curious and remarkable, Tresilian, who had successfully concealed himself, now came in disguise to witness the trial of his colleague. He had got upon the top of an apothecary's house, close by Westminster Palace. Descending the gutter, to see who passed in, he was detected by some of the peers. This is one account. Another states that he lodged at an alehouse, 'right over against the palace gate,' and there looked out of a window to watch the notables on their way to the trial. At any rate he was seen and recognized. A squire of the Duke of Gloucester, Froissart tells us, observing the judge under his disguise, cunningly contrived to catch him. After obtaining an interview, through the landlady, to make sure of his identity without giving rise to suspicion, he informed his master the duke. 'Then the squire went forth and took four serjeants with him, and said, "Sirs, follow me afar off, and as soon as I make to you a sign, and that I lay my hand on a man that I go for, take him, and let him not escape." Therewith the squire entered into the house where Tresilian was, and went up into the chamber; and as soon as he saw him, he said, "Tresilian, you are come into this country on no goodness; my lord the Duke of Gloucester commandeth that you come and speak with him." The knight would have excused himself, and said, "I am not Tresilian; I am a farmer of St. John of Hollands." "Nay, nay," quoth the squire, "your body is Tresilian, but your habit is not;" and therewith he made tokens to the serjeants that they should take him. Then they went up into the chamber and took him, and so brought him to the palace.'

The miserable creature is described by a chronicler as having his hair and beard overgrown, and wearing old clouted shoes and patched hose, more like a beggar than a judge. In the end, Brambre was beheaded and Tresilian hanged. What occurred when the latter was executed is very horrible. He would not go up the ladder till he was well beaten with bats and staves, and then he said he would not die with his clothes on. So he was stripped, and hanged naked. The next morning his wife, having a licence of the king, took down his body, and carried it to the Greyfriars, where it was buried.

The judges' robes were not always pure in times succeeding those of Tresilian. We might tell other tales of judicial dishonesty; but the time has long since passed away when any reflection could be fairly cast on any of the wearers of the SS collar, or their brethren of puisne rank.

A very different incident from those just mentioned occurs in connection with the judicial history of Westminster Hall, during the early history of Henry V. When, as Prince of Wales, he was leading a dissipated life, one of his servants was arraigned at the King's Bench for some act of felony. The master took the servant's part, and appeared beside him before the throne of judgment, demanding that he should be set at liberty. Chief Justice Gascoigne, nothing terrified by the presence of the king's son, proceeded to mete out justice in the king's name. Henry, chafed by the judge's resoluteness, threatened to do him violence, and for that purpose was ascending the bench, when Gascoigne, in a dignified manner, rebuked his presumption, and ordered him to be imprisoned in the King's Bench for contempt of the king's justices. The prince, overcome by this kind of courage and majesty, 'laying his weapon apart, doing reverence, departed, and went to the King's Bench as he was commanded.' 'O merciful God!' exclaimed his father, on hearing of it, 'how much am I above all other men bound to your infinite goodness, specially for that He hath given me a judge who feareth not to minister justice, and also a son who can suffer patiently and obey justice.'

On reaching the times when the words 'Bench and Bar,' in their present meaning, may be applied to the Westminster Hall Courts, we catch distinct and loud echoes—the echoes of names familiar to the schoolboy, pronounced in every intelligent household in England. Sir Edward Coke was the greatest of English lawyers. We find him at the Bar in the reign of Elizabeth. He was made Attorney-General in 1594, and knighted by James I. His heart seems to have been hard as his head, and 'brutal' is not too strong a term to be applied to his conduct on the trial of the Earl of Essex. His behaviour towards Raleigh, when conducting his prosecution, was of the same description. The most unmeasured abuse was poured on the prisoner. He was 'the notoriest traitor that ever held up his hand at the bar,' and 'a monster with an English face, but a Spanish heart.' This dignified Attorney-General declared he would lay Raleigh 'on his back for the confidentest traitor that ever came to a bar;' adding, 'I want words sufficient to express thy viperous treason.'

Such cruel treatment of one arraigned at the bar was of a piece with Coke's arrogant behaviour towards his brethren of the long robe. Bacon was his contemporary and rival, and fierce were the contests between these memorable barristers.

'Mr. Bacon,' said the Attorney-General, 'if you have any tooth against me, pluck it out, for it will do you more hurt than all the teeth in your head will do you good.'

'Mr. Attorney, I respect you,' said Bacon, 'but I fear you not; and the less you speak of your own greatness, the more I will think of it.'

He replied: 'I think scorn to stand upon terms of greatness towards you, who are less than the little, less than least.'

'He gave me,' says Bacon, who relates the dialogue, 'a number of disgraceful words besides, which I answered with silence, showing that I was not moved by them.'

This style of abuse prevailed at the Bar at a later period, and even on the Bench was continued by the infamous Jeffreys—a far different person, however, from Coke, as in learning and ability, so in moral character; for Coke, with all his harshness and pride, was a man of worth and honesty, an upright judge, and a stern patriot.

The transfer from the Bar to the Bench was a very grand ceremony in those days. It was akin to the scenes witnessed at the installation of men in the marble chair. Coke had no liking for show, so he procured a dispensation of the honour of riding from Serjeants' Inn to Westminster in his 'parti-coloured robes.' When Chief Justice Montague received the collar of SS, the procession was very grand. First went on foot the young gentlemen of the Inner Temple ; after them the barristers according to their seniority ; next the officers of the King's Bench; then the said Chief Justice himself on horseback in his robes, the Earl of Huntingdon on his right hand and the Lord Willoughby of Eresby on his left, with above fifty knights and gentlemen of quality following. On entering the Court of King's Bench, he first presented himself at the bar, with a serjeant on each hand. The Lord Chancellor, on the bench, produced the writ by which he was constituted Chief Justice, and delivered a speech on the duties of the office, to which Montague replied. The writ being read, he took the oaths, mounted the bench, and was placed in the seat of Chief Justice.

Among all the names which occur in connection with Bench and Bar, no one is equal in combined greatness and excellence to that of Matthew Hale. 'What but Christianity,' said the late Mr. Knox, ' could have given to Judge Hale that uniform ascendency over everything selfish and secular, by means of which he so undeviatingly kept the path of pure heroic virtue, as to be alike looked up to and revered by parties and interests the most opposite to each other? Is there in human history any fact more extraordinary than that the advocate of Strafford and Laud, and of King Charles (had liberty been given for pleading), should be raised to the Bench by Cromwell? And, again, that a judge of Cromwell's should be not only reinstated by Charles II., but compelled by him, against his own will, to accept of the very highest judicial trust? Such is the triumph of genuine Christianity, a triumph which is in some degree renewed wherever the name of Hale is even professionally repeated; since the appeal is evidently made not more to the authority of the judge than to the integrity of the man.'

Once a duke called on Chief Baron Hale, pretending to inform him respecting a case shortly to be tried in his court. 'Your grace,' said the judge, 'does not deal fairly to come to my chamber about such an affair, for I never receive any information of causes but in open court, where both parties are to be heard alike.' The duke reported this to the king, who replied: 'Your grace may well content yourself that it is no worse; and I verily believe that he would have used myself no better, if I had gone to solicit him in any of my own causes.'

Once a banker who was Lord Mayor of London, and a courtier to boot, delayed making a return to a *mandamus*, whereupon the prosecutor moved for an attachment. Howel, the Recorder, appeared on the behalf of the City chief magistrate, and urged the inconvenience of such a personage being imprisoned. But all mayors and all men were alike to Hale on the bench. Putting his thumb to his girdle, as he was wont, he said: 'Tell me of the Mayor of London; tell me of the Mayor of Queenborough.'

He neither clung to a judgeship from selfishness and pride, nor resigned it from idleness and prospect of pension. When enfeebled by disease, he might be seen slowly walking into Westminster Hall, supported by his servants, or retiring oppressed with fatigue from the bench he so much adorned. He at length applied for a 'writ of ease,' which the king unwillingly granted, offering to let him hold his place and do what business he could in his chamber; but he answered, that he could not any longer, with a good conscience, continue in it, since he was no longer able to discharge the duty belonging to it. There was no allowance for retiring judges then, but the king insisted upon the continuance of Hale's salary as long as he lived. He died very shortly after his resignation of office. Wonderful was the sanctity attached to his name; people regarded him as a saint, and 'they thought there was virtue in touching his coffin.' 'In popish times,' says Lord Campbell, 'miracles would have been worked at his tomb, and he would have been canonized as St. Matthew of Alderly,' the village where he died and was buried.

Westminster Hall, in term time, was a busy place during the last century—busy in more senses than one. The law courts occupied a large space at the upper end of the Great Hall; but there was also a range of counters, stalls, and cases for the sale of books, prints, and mathematical instruments. This would remind us of a modern railway station; but the traffic in Westminster Hall went further still, and we are informed that sempstresses and others there exposed their wares, giving to the great judicial vestibule the appearance of a market or fair. Then, amidst all this bustle there was a side bar, where certain formal motions might be made, of which a vestige remains in the phrase 'side bar motions.' The black robe and the wig intermixed with the booksellers, sempstresses, and haberdashers, strike us as an odd variety; and then, as we go on to think of those times, the shadows of Lord Hardwicke, and Chief Justice Sir Dudley Ryder pass by, with others less known to fame, and whose voices have left a fainter echo behind them.

Proceeding to the latter half of the last century, as we enter the old Court of King's Bench, we see occupying the Bench the most remarkable by far of the modern wearers of the scarlet robe and ermine, the coif and SS collar. Lord Mansfield was perhaps the most maligned of any judge that ever lived. Junius fixed his fangs on him with merciless severity; and we remember, in our younger days, after reading the eloquent diatribes of that most factious writer, picturing Lord Mansfield to ourselves as a very monster of injustice. But true history tells quite another tale; and Lord Brougham justly pronounces, that it may be doubted if, taking both the externals and the more essential qualities into the account that go to form a great judge, any one has ever administered the laws in this country whom we can fairly name as his equal. To a calm, clear, and winning manner, more suited to the repose of the Bench than the excitement of the Bar, he added the strictest justice, as well as very extensive juridical learning. Lord Campbell follows on the same side, acquiescing fully in the eulogium pronounced on him in his lifetime as 'the great Lord Mansfield.' The estimate of contemporaries in general must not be judged of by the abuse of Junius, for the greatest homage was done to Mansfield as a judge, from the first experience which the public had of his eminent merits. Crowds flocked to hear him pronounce judgment; and in his time began the practice of reporting in newspapers charges addressed to juries, from the very beautiful, correct, and impressive manner in which he discharged that function of his office. So great was the public confidence in his integrity, that suitors crowded his court with business, so as to leave the rest almost forsaken.

Approaching the end of the century, we meet with one at the Bar as pre-eminent there as Mansfield had been on the Bench. This was Mr. Erskine, whose noble figure, expressive countenance, sparkling eye, and graceful form, so kindles the eloquence of Lord Brougham in describing the statesmen of the time of George III. 'Juries have declared that they felt it impossible to remove their looks from him, when he had riveted and as it were fascinated them by his first glance; and it used to be a common remark of men who observed his motions, that they resembled those of a blood-horse, as light as limber, as much betokening strength as speed, as free from all gross superfluity or encumbrance. Then hear his voice of surpassing sweetness, clear, flexible, strong, exquisitely fitted to strains of serious earnestness; deficient in compass, indeed, and much less fitted to express indignation, or even scorn, than pathos, but wholly free from either harshness or monotony.' And this was but the outer frame of high intellectual qualities, penetration, memory, reason, and fancy; this was but the vehicle which conveyed consummate knowledge, argument, pathos, and persuasion, and all employed in the service of the cause of liberty against injustice, tyranny, and oppression. No echo rings in old Westminster Hall more rich and noble than that of Erskine's eloquence.

VI.
STATE TRIALS.

It is the 7th of June, 1380, and all London is astir. Not only are citizens, high and low, hastening down to Westminster, but lords and country folk of all degrees are coming in from every quarter. Kentish men and men of Kent are jostling each other on London Bridge, where other southern counties are contributing to the troops of sightseers. They are coming from Essex and Hertfordshire down to the Strand, where the crowd thickens: and then, what tributary streams roll in at Charing Cross, out of the Oxford and Windsor roads! and there they are in bright array and holiday costume —knights and squires, yeomen and peasants, all glittering in the summer sun, with the fresh green trees, oak, elm, and ash, and picturesque hostels, here and there, forming a background to the animated pageant. There are more people here, they say to one another, than were seen at the king's coronation.

Before the palace at Westminster there is to be a grand judicial combat between a knight and a squire, the latter charged by the former with treason. The knight is Sir John Annesley, and the squire is Thomas

Katrington; and the treason charged is, that the said squire has delivered up the castle of St. Sauveur le Vicomte, in Normandy, of which he was governor, into the hands of the French. The castle would have come to Annesley, if it had not been given up by Katrington: so Annesley has accused Katrington before the lord the king, and thrown down his gauntlet in the court, offering, by duel, to justify his accusation; and now the two are going to fight it out in the presence of his majesty King Richard II. and the lords of the realm. All the preliminaries have been settled according to feudal and chivalrous usage; and to witness the issue are the people come.

The lists are set up; pavilions are built for the accommodation of the royal party and the ladies of the court, on the pavement in front of the palace; and all looks as grand as painting, and gilding, and tapestry, and flags, and dresses of rich colour, elaborate device, and whimsical ornament can make it. The lists are railed in by substantial barriers, to keep off the crowd, who are wedging and pressing toward the arena on all sides, while from walls and battlements, from windows and roofs, curious eyes are looking for the arrival of the combatants. And here they come! Sir John Annesley, armed and mounted on a fair courser, trapped in seemly fashion, advances as appellant, waiting for his antagonist.

Hush! Three times the herald, with his rich tabard of crimson and gold, and coat of arms, cries out,

'Thomas Katrington, defendant, come and appear to save the action for which Sir John Annesley, knight and appellant, hath publicly and by writing appealed thee.' At the end of the third call appears the defendant, riding on a courser covered with trappings embroidered with his arms. He alights from his horse before entering the lists, lest the Lord High Constable should claim the horse; for, according to the law of arms, if the squire brings his horse within the barrier, it is forfeit. But his precaution in this instance fails; for the good steed, pressing after his master, thrusts his head over the posts, and the constable thereupon demands at least so much of the animal as has transgressed within the bounds; wherefore, as the body will be of little use without the head, the whole is adjudged to his lordship.

An indenture, according to custom, has been drawn up and sealed by the parties, and is now read in the public hearing. Katrington, not quite satisfied with himself and his cause, makes exceptions to the terms, though he has already subscribed them; in consequence of which the Duke of Lancaster, who has befriended him, is very angry, and declares, if he will not accept what he has already agreed to, he shall at once be held guilty of treason, and accordingly executed. The people shout at that, and the squire is forced to say that he dares fight his enemy on the point in question, and all others whatever. Now, so far as strength is concerned, he seems to have the advantage, for he is a great, tall, muscular man, and the knight Annesley is little of stature. Moreover, he has some brave men on his side—my Lord Latimer, my Lord Basset, and others.

Both combatants make oath of the goodness of their cause, and disclaim the use of magical arts for protection. It is to be a fair fight; and, offering up prayers, they begin. First, their spears are launched, and after some rough work with these weapons, their swords are drawn and crossed, and there is abundance of clashing, not without wounds; and then come the daggers with deadly thrusts. They struggle dreadfully together, and at last the knight disarms the squire, and throws him down, when, blinded with perspiration, that has wetted his vizor, he tumbles over his adversary, and there they lie, sprawling and worrying one another on the ground like a couple of exasperated dogs. The king orders the combatants to be parted, but the squire is unable to stand, and has to be placed in a chair. Little Annesley, who seems still fresh, begs the king to let them fight again. He will lie down just as he was, with Katrington over him. But Katrington is too weak to do anything more: he faints away. His armour is taken off. Restored to consciousness, he gazes wildly round, and there, standing before him, is the knight, still full-armed, calling him traitor and perjured, and daring him to renew the contest. Katrington is exhausted, and can say nothing. The battle is declared to be at an end. Annesley has won it, and the people disperse, talking the matter over, and mostly taking part with the victor; and the next day the defeated squire dies mad,—his dead body is hanged at Tyburn.

There are more trials of this kind connected with the old hall; but our main business is with other associations within, and there some notable trials demand our attention—trials that have made the world ring, that have filled posterity with wonder, and that have themselves been tried over and over again as to their legality and issues—certain of which still remain moot-points in history, that have affected most powerfully all after times, and that are producing effects even now. Into the legal and political questions involved we do not here enter. The bare facts alone belong to these sketches.

We have seen Sir Thomas More in 'the marble chair.' In 1534, he was tried for denying the king's ecclesiastical supremacy. The subjoined description of his appearance on the occasion is admirable. 'On the morning of the trial,' says Lord Campbell, in his 'Lives of the Chancellors,' 'More was led on foot in a coarse woollen gown, through the most frequented streets, from the Tower to Westminster Hall. The colour of his hair, which had become grey since he last appeared in public; his face, which though still cheerful, was pale and emaciated; his bent posture and his feeble steps, which he was obliged to support with his staff, showed the rigour of his confinement, and excited the sympathy of the people, instead of impressing them, as was intended, with dread of the royal authority. When, sordidly dressed, he held up his hand as a criminal in that place where, arrayed in his magisterial robes and surrounded by crowds who watched his smile, he had been accustomed on his knees to ask his father's blessing before mounting his own tribunal to determine, as sole judge, on the most important rights of the highest subjects in the realm, a general feeling of horror and commiseration ran through the spectators; and after the lapse of three centuries, during which statesmen, prelates, and kings have been unjustly brought to trial under the same roof, considering the splendour of his talents, the greatness of his acquirements, and the innocence of his life, we must still regard his murder as the blackest crime that ever has been perpetrated in England under the forms of law.'

More's defence, as he sat in a chair, being too infirm to stand, was very able and touching, and made such an impression that he was near being acquitted, when Rich, the Solicitor-General, leaving the bar, presented himself as a witness, to bear testimony against the chancellor. This extraordinary proceeding was enough to startle even prejudiced jurors, and the reply of More to the evidence so tendered produced a deep impression, in consequence of which the cause of the prosecution was again imperilled; but the Chief Commissioner Audley came to the rescue of the court, and by his summing-up procured a verdict of guilty against the prisoner.

No state trial which had ever occurred before produced such excitement as attended that of Lord Strafford in the reign of Charles I. We have described the crowds which flocked to the judicial combat outside the hall, in the days of Richard II.; but that was the index of a local and confined interest, compared with the widespread feeling of the seventeenth century, when the liberties and religious rights of the country had been assailed by the arbitrary proceedings of the Star Chamber, which have made that place a name of notoriety and infamy. At the same time, too, the three kingdoms were agitated by the great question of the relative powers of parliaments and of kings. In attacking Strafford, a principle was involved as well as a person; and great and important as was the person, the principle was infinitely greater and more important still. All Europe and the whole world might well look on with throbbing interest when this remarkable man was tried. A throne was erected in Westminster Hall for the king; cabinets hung with arras were placed on each side; before the throne were seats for the peers, and woolsacks for the judges, and stages for the House of Commons. The Scotch and Irish commissioners were to be present, and to occupy the two upper rows of benches. An enclosed dock and bench, fenced in, were appointed for the prisoner.

On Monday morning, March 22nd, at seven o'clock,

Strafford was brought from the Tower, with a procession of barges, containing one hundred soldiers. Landing at Westminster, he was conducted to the hall by two hundred of the trained band, all the avenues to the place being guarded by constables and watchmen from before daylight. Charles I., the queen, and the prince, came about nine o'clock, and sat in the enclosed cabinets, where they were scarcely seen and little noticed. The king had expressly forbidden that the axe should be carried before Strafford, as was common on such occasions; so he appeared in the dock without that appendage to the ceremonial of a trial for treason. The whole of the first day was employed in reading the impeachment, the king and prince staying all the time. Day after day the trial went on, the interest in it increasing, and public opinion becoming divided. Pym was the chief conductor of the prosecution, and employed all his abilities against the accused. The royal family attended; and the king, we are told, impatient at having his view and hearing interrupted by the trellis-work put up before his closet for secrecy, tore it away with his own hands, and thus became visible to the assembly. The courtiers were on the side of Strafford, and so were the ladies generally, being touched by his gallant bearing, his handsomeness, grace, and eloquence. There they were, writing down notes day after day, and earnestly debating points of law and fact as they arose on the trial. We cannot say much for the gravity and decorum of some of the gentlemen who were present. Baillie tells us that after ten o'clock there was much public eating, not only of confections, but of flesh and bread, bottles of beer and wine going thick from mouth to mouth without cups, and all this before the king's eyes.

After weeks spent in adducing evidence and arguments in support of the charge of high treason, Strafford was allowed to make his defence, which was certainly most able and eloquent. One part of it is well known, but must be related here among the memorable echoes of the old hall. The children of the prisoner were at hand during the trial, and pointing to them with tears, the prisoner exclaimed: 'My lords, I have troubled you longer than I should have done, were it not for the interest of these dear pledges a saint in heaven hath left me. What I forfeit myself is nothing; but that my indiscretion should descend to my posterity woundeth me to the very soul. You will pardon my infirmity: something I should have added, but am not able; therefore let it pass. And now, my lords, for myself I have been, by the blessing of Almighty God, taught that the afflictions of this present life are not to be compared to the eternal weight of glory which shall be revealed hereafter. And so, my lords, even so, I freely submit myself to your judgment, and whether that judgment be of life or death—*Te Deum laudamus.*'

The Bill of Attainder passed the Commons on the 21st of April, and on the 7th of May it passed the

Lords. Strafford appealed to the king; but the royal assent was given to the bill on the 10th of May. Charles made a feeble appeal by letter on his behalf to the House of Lords, asking that Strafford's life might be spared, 'if it might be done without the discontent of his people;' adding in a postscript, 'If he must die, it were charity to reprieve him till Saturday.' Neither request was complied with; and the king said, 'What I intended by my letter was with an *if* it might be done with contentment to my people. If that cannot be,' he added, 'I say again, *Fiat justitia*. My other intention proceeding out of charity for a few days' respite, was upon certain information that his estate was so distracted that it necessarily required some days for settlement.' On the 12th Strafford perished on the scaffold.

That Westminster Hall tragedy was not long after followed by another: Charles himself was arraigned at the bar. Into anything beyond the incidents of the trial we do not propose entering. A high court of justice was appointed for the occasion, consisting of one hundred and twenty-five commissioners, of whom not more than eighty assembled at one time. Serjeant Bradshaw was voted president, under the title of 'Lord President.' The hall was specially fitted up for the occasion. At the further end sat the commissioners in rows, with high-crowned hats and cloaks. On each side were galleries for spectators. In the front of the commissioners, on an elevated platform, sat Bradshaw, with John Lisle and William Say as assistants. 'He was afraid,' it is said, 'of some tumult, upon such new and unprecedented insolence as that of sitting judge upon his king; and therefore, besides other defence, he had a thick, big-crowned beaver hat, lined with plated steel, to ward off blows.' The hat, with a Latin inscription on it, is now to be seen in the Museum at Oxford.

Immediately before the Lord President was a long table, at which sat the clerks of the court, the mace and sword lying on the table. A chair was provided for the king within the bar, and at his right hand stood three councillors, to conduct the prosecution in the name of the Commonwealth. Royal banners, taken at Naseby, were hanging as Parliamentary trophies over the head of the royal captive. The great door was thrown open for the admission of the people, and the hall was everywhere well guarded by soldiers.

On the 8th of January, the commissioners had marched to their places, amidst beating drums and sound of trumpets, to make proclamation of the opening of proceedings. On the 19th the king had been brought from Windsor, and on the 20th he was conveyed, in a sedan chair, to the bar, where he took his seat on a chair covered with velvet. He looked sternly on the people and the court, without moving his hat. They returned like looks, and continued to sit covered. Bradshaw stated the cause of the trial. Coke, as leading counsel, stood up to speak, when Charles cried, 'Hold, hold!' at the same time touching him on the shoulder with his cane, the gold head of which dropped off as he was doing it—an ominous incident, to be coupled with the blowing down of the royal standard when first raised at Nottingham! The clerk began to read the indictment, when the king again cried, 'Hold!' but at the order of the president the clerk went on, 'the king looking sometimes on the high court, sometimes up to the galleries; and having arisen again and turned about to behold the guards and spectators, sat down again, looking very sternly, and with a countenance not at all moved till the words naming "Charles Stuart to be a tyrant and traitor," were read, at which he laughed as he sat, in the face of the court.'

The whole being finished, the king demanded the authority of the court, the illegal constitution of which was the point he insisted upon throughout. He refused to plead before such a tribunal. Beyond that preliminary they could not get him to advance. After adjournments and re-sittings, and the hearing of witnesses in the Painted Chamber—the king all the while declining to acknowledge the jurisdiction of the parties who had summoned him to the bar—on the seventh day the High Court of Justice sat for the last time. President Bradshaw had then changed his black robe for a red one, and the other commissioners appeared in their best habits. The king—amidst cries from the soldiers and people, of 'Justice, justice! Execution, execution!'—sat down in his chair, still with his hat on.

The appearance of things betokened the approaching catastrophe, and Charles felt it. He demanded to be heard. Bradshaw insisted that the court should be heard first, remarking how he had refused to make answer to the charges against him, brought in the name of the people of England. 'No, not half the people!' shrieked a female voice, supposed to be that of Lady Fairfax, wife of the Lord General. Charles requested to be heard in the Painted Chamber, *before the Lords and Commons;* to which Bradshaw replied by urging that all this was a continued contempt of court.

John Downes, citizen of London, one of the commissioners, now got up and exclaimed, 'Have we hearts of stone? Are we men? My lord, I am not satisfied to give my consent to this sentence. I have reasons to offer against it. I desire the court to adjourn to hear me.' The court retired, and then returned, determined to proceed with their purpose. Many words followed between the president and the prisoner, all involving the primary question as to the legality of the trial. The king was startled at being called 'tyrant, traitor, murderer,' and uttered that memorable cry of 'Hah!' which still seems to echo round the old hall. The king wanted to be heard in arrest of judgment; but the president replied it was too late, as he never admitted the jurisdiction of the court. The clerk was told to read the sentence, when Charles again claimed to be heard, and was refused. 'Sir, you are not to be heard after sentence.' 'No, sir?' 'No, sir, by your favour.

Guards, withdraw your prisoner.' 'I may speak after the sentence, by your favour, sir; I may speak after the sentence even. By your favour.'—'Hold!'—'The sentence, sir'—'I say, sir, I do'—'Hold.' These broken words, with stammers—for the king had a hesitancy in his speech—wound up the terrible trial; and then he retired, saying to himself, 'I am not suffered to speak; expect what justice other people will have.'

As to the *mode* of conducting the trial, and the behaviour of the president, the opinion of a modern judge, of great experience and discretion, carries weight, and with that we conclude our sketch:—'Assuming a court to be constituted, its authority must be maintained, and the steps must be taken which are necessary for bringing to a conclusion a trial commenced before it. The king's demeanour was most noble; and he displayed such real dignity, such presence of mind, such acuteness, such readiness, such liberality of sentiment, and such touches of eloquence, that he makes us forget all his errors, his systematic love of despotic power, and his incorrigibly bad faith. He did so when the commissioners stood up, in token of assent to the awful sentence of beheading. Instead of hurrying him to the scaffold, we eagerly desire to see him once more on the throne, in the hope that misfortune might at last induce him sincerely to submit to the restraints of constitutional monarchy.'

VII.

THE SEVEN BISHOPS AND SACHEVERELL.

THERE are perhaps no hymns better known in the household, the closet, and the church than 'Morning,' 'Evening,' and 'Midnight,' by Bishop Ken. 'Had he endowed three hospitals, he might have been less a benefactor to posterity.' When dwelling in quiet thought upon the sentiment of the hymns, and listening to the plain solemn melodies to which they are sung, few perhaps think of the pious prelate who wrote them, and fewer still, of his connection with one of the most exciting scenes ever witnessed even in Westminster Hall—that theatre of surpassing excitement for so many centuries. Ken was one of the seven bishops there tried, in 1688, on the eve of the Revolution—*that* event being in no small degree produced by *this* proceeding. He was a man of pure devotion and intrepid honesty; and an anecdote is told of his refusing to admit to his lodgings the infamous Nell Gwynn, when she accompanied Charles II. and his court to Winchester. The king, instead of resenting his boldness, bestowed on him a mitre, giving him the see of Bath and Wells.

Lloyd, Bishop of St. Asaph, was another of the seven, 'a proficient in philology, history, philosophy, and divinity, as if each of these had been the sole object of his application.' He was a distinguished preacher and controversialist, and materially assisted Burnet in his 'History of the Reformation.'

Turner, Bishop of Ely, was another. He was 'an affected writer,' and in no way remarkable except as the early and intimate friend of Ken. Lake, Bishop of Chichester, was another, who, notwithstanding his share in the resistance of James, declared on his deathbed his belief in the doctrine of passive obedience. Trelawney, Bishop of Bristol, was another—a man of ability, 'of polite manners, competent learning, and uncommon knowledge of the world.' White, Bishop of Peterborough, was another—a person who seems to have been distinguished only by his connection with this trial.

The leader of the band was Sancroft, Archbishop of Canterbury, whose usually timid and irresolute disposition was overcome on this occasion. It is curious that, after being placed, as it is said he was, at the head of the Church, because he was of a recluse and meditative turn, and not likely to disturb the Court in their designs upon the people, he should appear at the head of a proceeding which served so greatly to put an end to the reign of arbitrary power. Refusing to take the oaths at the Revolution, he was deprived of his bishopric, and retired into obscurity, which he preferred to the cares and trials of office; and when living in a private house in London, after being accustomed to Lambeth Palace, it is said he was visited by the Earl of Aylesbury, who was affected to tears on seeing him come to open his own door. 'Oh! my good lord,' observed he, 'rather rejoice with me; for now I live again.'

Ken, Lake, White, and Turner, as well as Sancroft, after opposing James, proved nonjurors under William—advocates of an invariable legitimate succession, as well as High Churchmen—teachers of the divine right of kings, and of passive obedience, though professing themselves friends to toleration. Their conduct as nonjurors was more in harmony with their abstract political principles than the course which they pursued towards King James. That brought them into Westminster Hall as culprits, before the tribunal of a despotic prince, and so made them popular with multitudes of their contemporaries, who, in other respects, would not sympathize with them; at the same time it has rendered their names illustrious in the eyes of posterity, notwithstanding the repugnance of modern opinion to their conscientiously cherished maxims.

James issued a declaration of indulgence on his own simple authority; thus, indeed, by relieving from penal statutes against religion, conferring a benefit, but then doing it at the expense of a fundamental principle—that the king has no power to set aside any of the laws of the realm. 'The motive of this declaration,' observes Mr. Hallam, 'was not so much to relieve the Roman Catholic from penal and incapacitating statutes (which were virtually at an end), as by

23

THE SEVEN BISHOPS ON THEIR WAY TO THE TOWER.

extending to the Protestant Dissenters the same full measure of toleration, to enlist under the standard of arbitrary power those who had been its most intrepid and steadiest adversaries.' This declaration James commanded the clergy to read in the churches. This led to the petition of the seven bishops, who prayed for the withdrawment of the order, and that no alteration might be made but by consent of the whole legislature. The objection they felt to reading the declaration rested, they said, not on any want of duty to the king, nor any want of tenderness to the Dissenters, but on the dispensing power which it involved, so often declared to be illegal. The king was angry at this petition, which was soon printed and extensively circulated.

On the day appointed for reading the declaration at church, few complied. One clergyman preached from the text, 'Be it known unto thee, O king, that we will not serve thy gods, nor worship the golden image thou hast set up.' Another announced, 'My brethren, I am obliged to read this declaration, but you are not obliged to listen;' so out the people went, and the minister proceeded to repeat the royal decree to empty benches. James resolved to proceed against the refractory prelates for a seditious libel, into which the Crown lawyers were to construe the petition.

The seven bishops were committed to the Tower on the 8th of June. They went there by water; and the people, whose sympathies were with them, lined the banks and cheered them by the way, rendering their imprisonment a perfect ovation. 'The concern of the the people,' says Evelyn, 'was wonderful; infinite crowds on their knees begging their blessing, and praying for them as they passed.' The soldiers of the garrison received them most reverently, and went down on their knees to beg an episcopal blessing. The seven went to the Tower Chapel, it being the time of evening prayer, and there the deep excitement of the hour was at once heightened and softened by a passage which occurred in the second lesson, so full of comfort and hope to the prisoners: 'I have heard thee in a time accepted, and in the day of salvation I have succoured thee. Behold, now is the accepted time; behold, now is the day of salvation.'

All over London and the country the talk was of the captives. Ten Nonconformists came as a deputation from their brethren, with an address of condolence. Twenty-eight peers offered to bail them. Messages, too, came from Holland, expressing the interest of the Prince and Princess of Orange in their fate.

On the 15th, the bishops were brought to Westminster to the Court of King's Bench. The papal nuncio saw the procession, and informs us:—'Of the immense concourse of people who received them on the bank and followed them to the hall, the greater part fell upon their knees, wishing them happiness and asking their blessing, and the Archbishop of Canterbury laid his hands on those that were nearest, telling them to be firm in their faith; and the people cried out that all should kneel, and tears were seen to flow from the eyes of many.'

Westminster Hall has raised its huge form many a time, like an old rock out of the bosom of the sea, as crowds on crowds of excited people have surrounded it. On this occasion the ocean of heads was more immense than ever, while surges of feeling rose and rolled and broke every moment. All London seemed on the spot, and all the spirit of the nation concentrated there. Within were the lawyers arguing. The Attorney-General required the prisoners to plead forthwith, to which the counsel for the bishops objected. However, the objections were overruled, and the bishops put in the plea of 'Not guilty,' and were then released on bail. This the people took for a triumph, and set no bounds to their joy when 'the seven' came out. Huzzas rent the air; the Abbey bells rung; the streets were thronged all the way the bishops went; bonfires were lighted at night; Roman Catholics were maltreated; and execrations poured on all false bishops.

On the 29th of June, the grand trial took place in Westminster Hall. One of the most worthless men that ever sat on the bench, Lord Chief Justice Wright, the *protégé* of the infamous Jeffreys, presided on this occasion. Oddly enough, Sawyer and Finch, two lawyers who had been the state prosecutors in the reign of Charles II., and had conducted the proceedings against Lord William Russell, now appeared on the side of the prosecuted; while Williams, the Whig advocate, now Solicitor-General, with Powys, the Attorney-General, and others, acted on the side of the king. This strange confusion of parties led not only to remark and raillery among the bystanders, but to fierce attack and recrimination among themselves; one charging another with gross inconsistency, and each having the best of it in assault and the worst of it in defence. Lords and gentlemen attended the accused into court, and barons in abundance sat ranged in rows beside the judges, severely scrutinizing the acts of their lordships, and keeping Wright in something like order: for he did not know but that they might be *his* judges before long, so that, it is said, he looked 'as if all the peers present had halters in their pockets.' Such was the deep feeling produced in the audience, that there was no maintaining the usual order of a court: witnesses and counsel even cheered; the men on the bench could not repress the bursts of applause; and did not dare to make an example of the offenders.

The prisoners were charged with writing and publishing a seditious libel in Middlesex; but neither of those points could be legally proved, though the presentation of the petition was admitted. Indeed, the Chief Justice was about to direct a verdict of acquittal, when the imprudent interruption of Finch gave a new direction to the business. Lord Sunderland, President of the Council, was sent for to give evidence, and in passing down to Westminster Hall, in a sedan chair, was exposed to the insults of the mob, who called him 'a popish dog;' and when he appeared in court, it was with manifest terror. He proved the publication according to the indictment. Then came a grand struggle as to the lawfulness of the king's dispensing power. Wright tried to prevent the discussion of this point, but in vain. The counsel for the defence fought it hard, and had public opinion with them.

'We shall be here till midnight!' exclaimed the Solicitor-General.

'They have no mind to have an end of the cause, for they have kept it up three hours longer than they have need to have done,' rejoined the Chief Justice. 'If you say anything more,' he added, to the opposing counsel, 'pray let me advise you one thing: don't say the same thing over and over again; for after so much time spent, it is irksome to all company as me.'

Williams out-heroded Herod in his course of argument, when it came to his turn to reply. 'The Lords,' he said, 'may address the king in Parliament, and the Commons may do it; but therefore that the bishops may do it *out of Parliament* does not follow. I'll tell you what they should have done; if they were commanded to do anything against their consciences, they should have acquiesced, till the meeeing of the Parliament.'

The people in the court hissed at this. The summing up of the Chief Justice was not so bad as might have been expected; and on the legal point, as to whether the petition was libellous, there was a difference of opinion among the puisne judges.

At the end of this part of the proceedings, his lordship, who presided, said: 'Gentlemen of the jury, have you a mind to drink before you go?' To that they had no objection, and therefore wine was brought, and they had a glass apiece; after which they were shut up in the dark, without meat or drink, till they could agree on a verdict. The secrets of their prison-house have been told, and we learn that Mr. Arnold, the king's brewer, opposed the rest all night, and that unanimity was secured at six o'clock the next morning, by a juryman saying: 'Look at me, I am the largest and strongest of the twelve, and before I find such a petition as this a libel, here I will stay till I am no bigger than a tobacco-pipe.'

At nine o'clock the verdict was given, *Not guilty*. Up rose a shout of joy that made the old hall ring again, and the echo was prolonged from one end of London to the other, and from one end of the country to the other. It went rolling along the streets and along the river, and when the bishops came out, it was caught up, and as they entered the barges it burst out afresh. The people again knelt down, and begged the bishops' blessing. Money was thrown about to drink their healths, and that of the king and the jury. There was bell-ringing again, and bonfires again, and the pope was burnt in effigy. James was at Hounslow reviewing the troops, and, on hearing a great noise, asked, 'What was the matter?'

'Nothing but the soldiers shouting for the acquittal of the bishops.'

'Call you that nothing?' he might well ask; 'but so much the worse for them,' he insanely added.

The judges on this occasion did not please their master. Two were dismissed, and the wretched Chief Justice was nigh being cashiered; but he kept his seat a little longer, only to lose it at the Revolution, and then to be sent to Newgate, where he died in a few days of fever, brought on by intense vexation. He was buried with felons, not in a decent grave, but in a common pit.

The trial of Sacheverell, in the reign of Queen Anne, was another of the remarkable scenes in Westminster Hall; but, while in excitement it rivalled the trial of the seven bishops, their character and that of the individual who was now arraigned were far as the poles asunder. Whereas their resistance to arbitrary power was on principle, and did honour to their conscientious motives, the conduct for which he had now to answer was inspired by a morbid craving after popularity, mingled with the most rabid fanaticism. The seven bishops for the most part were men of learning, piety, and reputation; but Sacheverell was as weak, ignorant, unprincipled, and, until his violence made him notorious, as obscure and unknown a creature as ever entered a pulpit. They throughout acted on their own convictions, as persons of perfect integrity and honour; but he was employed as the tool of a miserable political faction, to serve the most selfish and unworthy ends. We introduce the trial of Sacheverell as a contrast to that of the seven bishops, and we would particularly point to the lesson which it reads of the worthlessness of popularity obtained by dishonourable means.

Sacheverell was a clergyman in the Borough—a Tory and High Churchman, with stentorian voice, which he lustily employed in the abuse of toleration and of the Whig party. Employed to preach in St. Paul's Cathedral before the Corporation, he gave vent to his furious zeal, by denouncing the means which brought about the Revolution, by condemning those who favoured liberty of conscience, by declaring the Church of England to be in danger under the existing administration, and by vilifying the ministers of her majesty, reprobating their acts, and calling them by odious names. The sermon was published, and had a large circulation; when, instead of allowing the man's bombast and rant to die away, the Government took steps for his prosecution. The matter was dragged before Parliament; Sacheverell was impeached, and his trial was arranged to take place in Westminster Hall.

The trial opened on the 27th of February, 1710, with a wonderful deal of show and ceremony. A box was prepared near the throne for the queen, who attended in a private character. On the one side of the hall benches were erected for the Commons of Great Britain, and accommodations were provided for noble ladies and gentlewomen. There was a kind of platform raised for the managers of the impeachment, and another for the doctor and his counsel. There were galleries erected at the end for the people, who flocked thither in such vast numbers as to excite a dread that the whole erection would come toppling down upon the heads of those beneath. The noble ladies who attended the trial were very much afraid lest somewhat in their dress or behaviour there should give occasion to the *Tatler* or *Observator* to turn them into ridicule in its papers; they came thither to see and to be seen, or else out of groundless opinion that the Church of England would be ruined by the punishment which was to be inflicted upon this one priest. The Whig ladies and the Tory ladies took the deepest interest in the trial, and might be easily distinguished from each other, at least by practised eyes, according to the arrangement of the little black patches on their faces, or the colour of their hoods—things then among the signs of political opinion, as declarative as the cockades in the old borough elections. Of the fair bevy on the Whig side, the Countess of Sunderland, a daughter of

Marlborough, might be counted a leader, the Duchess of Hamilton being one of the most conspicuous dames of the Tory chair.

Several eminent lawyers were employed to conduct the prosecution; Sacheverell also had the aid of distinguished counsel, and, moreover, Smallridge and Atterbury appeared at his side during the trial. Walpole, then rising into fame, made an eloquent speech, he being one of the managers for the Commons. 'I hope,' said he, 'that your lordships' just judgment will convince the world that every seditious, discontented, hot-headed, ungifted, unedifying preacher (the doctor will pardon me for borrowing one string of epithets from him, and for once using a little of his own language), who has no hope of distinguishing himself in the world but by a matchless indiscretion, may not advance with impunity doctrines destructive of the peace and quiet of her majesty's Government and the Protestant succession; or prepare the minds of the people for an alteration by giving them ill impressions of the present establishment and its administration. This doctrine of unlimited unconditional passive obedience was first invented to support arbitrary and despotic power, and was never promoted or countenanced by any government that had not designs some time or other of making use of it. What, then, can be the design of preaching this doctrine now unasked, unsought for, in her majesty's reign, when the law is the only ruling measure, both of the power of the Crown and of the obedience of the people?' Sacheverell's defence was prepared for him, as it displayed an ability of which, every one knew, he was not the possessor. He called God and the holy angels to bear witness to his innocence, at which my Lady Sunderland wept, and her Grace of Hamilton burst into rapture.

The trial lasted for more than three weeks, during which nothing could exceed the uproarious demonstrations made in favour of the doctor by the mob. He came daily to the hall, escorted by the multitude all the way from the Temple, where he lodged, while people crowded balconies and windows, showering down expressions of regard, sometimes even substantial presents. He rode in a sedan chair, nodding and bowing like a Chinese mandarin. One day, when the queen was going to witness the proceedings, the populace gathered round her chair, crying out, 'Bless your majesty and the Church we hope your majesty is for Dr. Sacheverell! Members of Parliament, going along in their coaches, were sometimes forced to take off their hats, and cry, 'Sacheverell for ever!' Party was pitted against party. It was a trial of political strength between the two grand political divisions of the country; and the Tories, having got the mob on their side, failed not to encourage their boisterous enthusiasm. But that enthusiasm rose to an excess and took a direction which at last frightened its instigators, for a tremendous riot occurred. Meeting-houses were attacked, and an Episcopal chapel was destroyed, because, having no steeple, it was taken for a conventicle. Burnet's house, too, was attacked, and the Bank of England threatened. The riot, however, was happily put down without bloodshed, and at last the miserable trial came to an end by Sacheverell being found guilty.

Kneeling at the bar, the Lord Chancellor pronounced sentence:—'You, Henry Sacheverell, doctor in divinity, shall be and you are hereby enjoined, not to preach during the term of three years next ensuing; and your two printed sermons shall be burnt before the Royal Exchange, at one of the clock in the afternoon, by the common hangman, in the presence of the Lord Mayor and Sheriffs of London.' Of course this was a punishment which the doctor was proud to receive. Sacheverell's party exulted, and had illuminations and bonfires and regalings on barrels of beer.

At the end of the three years' silence, his printer gave him £100 for his sermon; the House of Commons ordered him to preach before them, thanked him for his discourse, and the ministry gave him the Rectory of St. Andrew's, Holborn. Such were the consequences of this great trial, which, neither on the part of the prosecution nor the arraigned, had any associations of moral dignity to save it from the contempt and ridicule of posterity.

VIII.

JACOBITES AND AN INDIAN VICEROY.

WESTMINSTER HALL was built in the days of feudalism. Its earliest history is full of feudal associations. As we look upon its noble architecture, we are irresistibly carried back to feudal times. The chivalrous sentiments, born and bred of feudalism, often prompting to acts at once honourable and wild, generous and lawless, self-denying and violent, are forcibly brought to our recollection while we now walk up and down the old pavement which, for so many years, led to the line of courts devoted to the peaceful administration of English law, order, and justice. In this last chapter on the Hall, we shall behold the expiring flashes of mediæval chivalry; we shall catch echoes of its dying voice, and also witness signs of the inauguration, or rather proofs of the establishment, of another and totally different order of things, involving the system of modern civilization.

Among the distinctive traits of the chivalrous spirits of the Middle Ages, was the strong devotion of a liege to his lord. It was not devotion to a principle or an office, to an order of things revered and preserved from considerations of convenience or from calm convictions of duty, but devotion to a person—a strong, unreasoning, passionate kind of instinct, which bound the inferior to him whom he deemed his lord—bound him to his fortunes, prosperous or adverse—bound him in bonds of strong and hearty sympathy for life and death. The loyalty of the old barons to their king and his family was of this chivalrous stamp. It was not attachment to the crown and the throne and the constitution, with feelings of affection to the person of the sovereign, growing out of that impersonal sort of attachment; but it was, first and foremost, attachment to the person of a particular monarch and his race, deemed to have divine right to rule, not deriving his authority in any of the ways pointed out in modern theories of political government, but getting and holding it in some mysterious and direct way from Heaven itself. The loyal knights of the Henrys and Edwards were thus chivalrous in their loyalty; and it was this chivalrous love for particular persons and families, regarded as legitimate heirs to the royalty of England, which alone redeems the Wars of the Roses from the character of a mere factious squabble. A good deal of the spirit of chivalry survived the extinction of its forms; and nowhere did it linger on so long as in Scotland, where the relations of clanship, so akin to feudalism, even still exist. At the bottom of the great rebellions of 1715 and 1745, when so many Highlanders took up arms in the cause of the Pretender, lay not a little of this sentiment of chivalrous loyalty. There were other sentiments, personal, political, and religious, most base and unworthy, selfish and vindictive, superstitious and tyrannical, blended with this; but not so as to destroy, not so as to prevent, its supreme authority in the breasts of many of the unhappy adherents of the Stuart line. They had no notion of a constitutional claim to the throne. Acts of Parliament and the will of the people could not set aside, in their estimation, the descent of inheritance. The Stuarts were still their kings, as they had been the kings of their fathers despite of unconstitutional acts. They would fight for them; they would die for them. Adversity only endeared their persons the more. Not a whit less was Prince Charles a king because he was crownless. The enthusiastic Jacobite saw a kind of celestial halo playing round the brow of the outcast heir, brighter than the gold and jewelled diadem on the head of a son of the house of Hanover.

Distinguished among the state trials in Westminster Hall are those of the noblemen who, in 1716 and 1746, were placed at the bar for taking up arms in the service of the Pretender. The Earl of Derwentwater, Lord Widdrington, the Earls of Nithsdale, Winton, and Carnwath, Viscount Kenmure, and Lord Nairn, were the culprits on the first occasion, and were formally arraigned, all pleading guilty but one, and throwing themselves upon the mercy of King George. Two of them only were executed — Lord Derwentwater and Lord Kenmure — the former declaring that he died a

Roman Catholic, and that he regretted having pleaded guilty on his trial. Lord Nithsdale effected his escape from the Tower, through a stratagem of his wife, who changed clothes with her husband, and thus enabled him, in her dress, to pass the sentinels undetected.

After the second rebellion, in '45, Westminster Hall was employed for the trial of the Earls of Kilmarnock and Cromartie and Lord Balmerino. These noblemen appeared at the bar on the 28th of July, 1746. 'Three parts of Westminster Hall,' Horace Walpole tells us, 'were enclosed with galleries and hung with scarlet, and the whole ceremony was conducted with the most awful solemnity. No part of the royal family was there, which was a proper regard for the unhappy men who were to become their victims. One hundred and thirty-nine lords were present. I had armed myself with all the resolution I could, with the thought of the prisoners' crimes and of the danger past, and was assisted by the sight of the Marquis of Lothian, in weepers for his son, who fell at Culloden; but the first appearance of the prisoners shocked me, and their behaviour melted me.' 'Kilmarnock and Cromartie pleaded guilty; the latter especially professing remorse and shedding tears. Balmerino played a very different part, and endeavoured to defend himself. He was a man of wit; and when asked a question by Mr. Murray, Solicitor-General, he inquired who he was, and then added: "Oh! Mr. Murray, I am extremely glad to see you. I have been with several of your relations: the good lady your mother was of great use to us at Perth."' Walpole, speaking of Balmerino, observes: 'He is the most natural, brave old fellow I ever saw; the highest intrepidity, even to indifference. At the bar he behaved like a soldier and a man; in the intervals of form, with carelessness and humour. At the bar he plays with his finger on the axe, while he talks to the gentleman gaoler; and one day, somebody coming up to listen, he took the blade and held it like a fan between their faces. During the trial, a little boy was near him, but not tall enough to see; accordingly he made room for the child, and placed him near himself.'

When brought up for sentence, Kilmarnock and Cromartie sued for mercy; the former pleading with much eloquence, the latter with greater effect, from his allusion to Lady Cromartie, who was on the point of confinement. 'My own fate,' said he, 'is the least part of my suffering; but, my lords, I have involved an affectionate wife, with an unborn infant, as parties of my guilt, to share its penalties. I have involved my eldest son, whose youth and regard for his parents hurried him down the stream of rebellion. I have involved eight innocent children, who must feel their parent's punishment, before they know his guilt. Let the silent eloquence of their grief and tears supply my want of persuasion.' The lady herself earnestly pleaded for the life of her husband, and other influence was employed on his behalf. The consequence was that he was saved; but it is curious to learn that the child to whom his wife gave birth just afterwards was marked on the neck with an impression like that of a broad axe.

Balmerino did not attempt to awaken pity or ask for mercy. He avowed his loyalty to King James with chivalrous devotion; spoke of his holding a commission under Queen Anne as an act of treason to his lawful prince; and declared that with his full heart he drew the sword in 1745, though his age might have excused him from doing so. Not any intercessions were employed for saving him, whence George II. exclaimed, 'Will no one say a word on behalf of Lord Balmerino? He, though a rebel, is at least an honest one.' He and Kilmarnock were executed.

There were many besides tried for their share in the rebellion; but there is only one other connected with Westminster Hall whom we would notice—that is, Charles Radcliffe, brother of the Earl of Derwentwater, who was executed in 1716. He was engaged in both rebellions, and was twice tried and twice condemned at Westminster. In the first instance he was arraigned on the 8th of May, 1716, and a few days afterwards received sentence of death. When going through Fleet Street, he happened to meet George I. starting for his first visit to Hanover after his accession to the throne of England; and it is related that this obliged Mr. Radcliffe's coach to stop, 'which happening opposite a distiller's shop (the third door on the right hand towards Temple Bar), he called for half a pint of aniseed, which he and his fellow prisoner drank, and then proceeded to Westminster, where sentence of death was pronounced upon them.' He managed to get out of prison during a grand entertainment he gave to his friends, and escaped to France, where he for some time lived in indigence. He returned to England subsequently, and, though unmolested, remained unpardoned.

In 1745 he a second time embarked in rebellion, was captured, and, on the 20th of November, 1746, was again carried to Westminster to be arraigned for high treason. He puzzled the Court by challenging them to prove his identity. This occasioned delay; but at length the point was established by certain persons, who recognized in his face a scar, which he received from a piece of iron, when he was a boy, playing in a blacksmith's shop at Dilston, in Northumberland, where he had been brought up on his ancestral domains.

The following pathetic letter was written by him in the Tower just before his execution, thirty years after sentence of death was first pronounced.

'*From the Tower*, Dec. 7th, 1746.

'The best of friends takes his leave of you: he has made his will, he is resigned. To-morrow is the day —love his memory—let his friends join with you in prayer—'tis no misfortune to die prepared—let's love our enemies and pray for them. My blessing to them all; my kind love to Fanny, that other tender mother of my dear children.

'Adieu, dear friend,
'DERWENTWATER.'[1]

'The age of chivalry is gone,' said Mr. Burke; and true enough such chivalry as that we have just been describing *is* gone, and Westminster Hall has heard the last of it. Appropriately may the remark just quoted introduce us to the last of the great historical associations of the old edifice. We propose to notice that very memorable trial, of which Mr. Burke had the chief management—the trial of Warren Hastings; involving questions of a different kind from any which arose in the chivalrous days of England—charges of another order and spirit from those brought against the Jacobite lords, and principles and views indicative of a new order of civilization, that which belongs to an empire rich in colonial possessions, retained indeed by the power of the sword, but acquired and valued for purposes of commercial enterprise.

Mr. Hastings was for eleven years Governor-General of India, being appointed to that high position in 1774 and quitting it in 1785. There can be no doubt that he greatly contributed to the consolidation of the British empire in the East; but the principles of expediency which he adopted, and the maxim expressed and

---

[1] Charles Radcliffe assumed the title of Earl of Derwentwater after his brother's execution.

defended by him—that Indian statesmen were not to be judged by European rules of morality and justice—would of themselves raise the darkest suspicions as to the manner in which the ends of his policy were secured. Charges of corruption and cruelty were publicly rumoured against him before his return to this country; and soon afterwards Mr. Burke commenced the institution of an inquiry into the Governor-General's conduct. In 1786, articles of impeachment were produced in Parliament, accusing him of injustice towards the native princes and people, the impoverishment and desolation of the British dominions in the East, the acceptance of presents, contrary to law—influence or connivance with regard to unfair contracts, together with enormous extravagance and bribery. In 1788, the great trial began in Westminster Hall. Belonging to modern times, almost within the memory of some living, being so fully described and alluded to by contemporaries, then in the zenith of life, having employed the talents and oratory of men of whom many of us heard so much in our boyhood, being mixed up with so many household names, the proceedings and their associations become to us most vivid pictures, and we seem to be living at the time, to be familiar with all that took place, and even to be present at the august spectacle, for august most certainly it was.

We enter the Hall at eleven o'clock of the 13th of February, 1788. Grand have been the preparations; and the cold, grim-looking old place is transformed into an immense judicial theatre—a House of Lords enlarged to a gigantic scale, and fitted up for hosts of spectators. Scarcely any part of the building can be seen, except the enormous ribs of the roof and the tops of the windows, all the rest being covered by seats and galleries, rich in scarlet and green. A huge deep gallery runs up in front of you, concealing most of the large window at the end. Just in advance of that is the throne, with royal boxes on each side. Running down on either hand, as you look up the hall, are lofty galleries, and underneath them, far projecting into the area, are raised seats, with a partition at the bottom between them and the open space in the middle of the Hall. There are the benches for the House of Lords. Below the bar are boxes for counsel and the conductors of the trial. All these galleries are crammed from bottom to top, with people of rank and wealth—many of importance, and a few of world-wide celebrity. Ladies of fashion and beauty are there. Men of erudition, genius, and taste are there. The famous political Duchess of Devonshire is there. Mrs. Siddons, the actress, is there. Mrs. Fitzherbert, privately married to the Prince of Wales, is there. Gibbon, the historian, is there. Dr. Parr is there. Reynolds, the painter, is there; and Gainsborough too, is there, who, by the way, is catching his death of cold. In the royal boxes are Queen Charlotte and her daughters; on the middle benches, in front of the Lord Chancellor, who presides, are the twelve judges in their robes of state, and about a hundred and seventy peers, in their crimson velvet mantles, gold and ermine, marshalled to their places by heralds in splendid tabards. The conductors of the trial, including the great names of Burke, Sheridan, Windham, Fox, and Grey, the latter then rising into fame—a youth of promise among veterans who have won the highest honours—occupy the appointed compartment by the bar, dressed in court suits; and near them are lawyers in their gowns and wigs, among whom may be seen Law, Dallas, and Plumer, destined to be high legal officers afterwards.

The Serjeant-at-Arms calls for silence; Warren Hastings, Esquire, is summoned to appear; and, amidst the alternate buzz and hush—the thousand eyes directed to the bar, the glittering of uplifted glasses, and the pomp and ceremony of a stately introduction—in comes a small thin man, with intellect, self-possession, care, and sorrow depicted on his countenance, as he kneels before this supreme court, and listens to the further proclamation of the Serjeant-at-Arms, that he, 'Warren Hastings, stands charged with high crimes and misdemeanours by the Commons of England, who are now to come and make good their charges.' Whereupon Lord Chancellor Thurlow makes a short speech, assuring him of a full impartial trial, and Hastings replies that he is equally satisfied as to his own integrity and the justice of the Court. The charges and answers then begin, the clerks of the court reading them on and on; till it is a quarter past five, and the old Hall is getting dark on this February afternoon, and everybody is tired, and yet only the seventh charge is reached, and there are thirteen more to come. So the Lord Chancellor moves that the Lords do adjourn. The assembly separates, and all London is full of the great event of the day.

The next day is taken up in a similar manner, and not till the third day does Mr. Burke rise to deliver his opening speech. Gentle reader, you may have heard some long speeches in your life: here is a man delivering one that lasts four days; but, then, he is a man as rare in the annals of oratory as the length of the speech. With a knowledge of India which makes you think he must have been there all his life, though he never stepped on its shores; with an imagination and mastery of graphic, picturesque words, which enables him to paint in thought as Reynolds and Gainsborough paint on canvas; with a power of philosophical analysis and acute logical argument which perhaps no other man in the Hall can command; and with strong moral feelings, wrought up into violent passion and even frenzy by the description of the crimes he charges on the illustrious prisoner at the bar; he produces every now and then—with of course, in so long a speech, intervals of weariness, inattention and indifference—scenes of excitement scarcely paralleled. Ladies are fainting; sobs and tears are heard all over the Hall. Old Thurlow himself is affected, and even Hastings acknowledges: 'For half an hour I looked up at the orator in a reverie of wonder, and during that space I actually felt myself the most culpable man on earth; but I recurred to my own bosom, and there found a consciousness that consoled me under all I heard and all I suffered.'

The four days' speech over, there come debatings about the manner of conducting the trial; that settled, sixteen days are consumed hearing evidence; at the end of which, what with previous arguments and delays, summer is come; and instead of a cold February morning, Sheridan has the morning of the 3rd of June to begin the summing up of evidence. The Hall is as crammed as ever. It is said, fifty guineas have been paid for a ticket to get in. There are no bounds to the excitement. The orator, as great in his own way as Burke in his, declaims elaborately, yet with immense impression, for two days, and then falls back exhausted, with a rhetorical, 'My lords, I have done,' into the arms of his great colleague, who hugs him with admiration.

The prorogation of Parliament advances, and as yet only two out of the twenty items of impeachment have been heard. The proceedings linger through years; and not till 1795, seven years after the trial began, is the business finished, and the verdict given. Excitement has abated; opinion has changed. There has come a reaction since the astounding speeches of Burke and Sheridan were delivered. Cross-questioned evidence has produced a very different effect from warm, glowing, impassioned oratory. An acquittal is expected, and it comes.

In the spring of 1795 there is again a crowd in Westminster Hall. The peers vote, *Not guilty*. The Lord Chancellor on the woolsack informs Hastings of this; he bows, and retires. The charges of his defence have amounted to more than £76,000; but the East India Company lend him £50,000, and grant him a pension of £4,000 per annum. He devotes himself to quietude and study; but once again, in 1813, appears in public, to give evidence to the House of Commons on the question of renewing the East India Company's charter. The members simultaneously rise to show honour to the man their predecessors had arraigned for high crimes and misdemeanours between twenty and thirty years before.

We have done. The echoes of Westminster Hall awaken solemn thoughts—thoughts of man and time —thoughts of nations and Providence—thoughts of the great ocean into which time is pouring its streams —thoughts of the Infinite Ruler and Judge who governs all beings and events—thoughts 'of the silent waiting-hall, where Adam meeteth with his children' —thoughts of the great tribunal, at which all shall be arraigned, and where so many earthly judgments shall be reversed. These are thoughts for deep, deep pondering, which may well wake up in the hearts of all echoes of faith and prayer.

INDEX.

Abney, Sir Thomas and Lady, 140, 142.
Abney Park, 136, 159.
Addison, Joseph, 101-20.
Aldersgate Street, 25.
Allhallows Church, Bread Street, 22.
Andrew Marvell and Lord W. Russell, 73-87.
Anne Boleyn, 286.
Anne, Queen, 361.
Annesley, Sir John, 336-40.
Archbishop of Canterbury, 310.
Archbishop of York, 279.
Arnold, Dr., 66.
Art, remarks on the history of English, 179.
Artillery Walk, now Artillery Place, west, Bunhill Fields, 35.
Arundel, Archbishop, 295, 314.
Ashmole, the antiquary, 69.
Axe and Hammer, 265-76.

Bacon, Lord, 328.
Balmerino, Lord, 370-2.
Barbican, 26.
Barristers, 321; Barristers' wigs, 323.
Barrow, Isaac, 105.
Baxter, Richard, 38-55.
Beaufort, Cardinal, 296.
Bench and Bar, 318-35.
Ben Jonson, 111.
Berkeley House, 95.
Bishops, the trial of the seven, 356.
Blackstone, Judge, 175.
Bloomsbury Square, 50, 85.
Bolt Court, Fleet Street, 216, 220.
Borough Compter, 258.
Boswell, Mr., 203-9, 216.

Boydell, Alderman, 197.
Brambre, Sir Nicholas, 325, 326.
Bread Street, 21, 22.
Bridewell, 255.
Brus, Robert de, 323.
Bunhill Fields, 158.
Burke, Edmund, 194, 223-41, 374-8.
Button's Tavern, Russell Street Covent Garden, 114.

Canonbury House, Islington, 170.
Canute, 269.
Carnwath, Earl, 369.
Catherine, Queen of Henry V., 283.
Cave, the publisher, 203.
Cavendish, Lord, 80.
Chancellor, origin of the name, 292.
Chancellor and Lord High Chancellor, 292.
Chancery Lane, 56, 318.
Charles I., 342-9.
Charles II., 34, 74, 350.
Charles Street, 239.
Charing Cross, 336.
Charterhouse Square, 52, 53; Charterhouse School, 102.
Chaucer, 16.
Cheapside, 15, 46.
Christ Church, 54.
Christ's Hospital, Newgate Street, 101.
Clapton, 243, 245.
Clerkenwell Bridewell, 255; St. John's Gate, Clerkenwell, 203.
Coke, Sir Edward, 328.
Confessio Amantes, by Gower, 17.
Courts of Exchequer, Common Pleas, King's Bench, and Chancery, 291, 292.

INDEX.

Cowper, the poet, 40.
Covent Garden, 74.
Crabbe, the poet, 239, 240.
Cranmer, 61.
Cromartie, Earl, 370.
Cromwell House, Brompton, 240.
Cromwell, Oliver, 26, 139, 287.

Danby, Lord, 74.
Day, Judge, 176.
David, King of Scotland, 14.
Davy, Sir Humphry, 123.
Dean Street, 176.
Derwentwater, Earl of, 369.
Devil's Tavern, the, 111.
De Wayland, Lord Chief Justice, 144.
Doddridge, Dr., 149-54.
Donne, Dr., 63.
✓ Drury Lane, 74.
Dryden, 33.
Dymoke, the Champion of England, 283; Robert Dymoke, 285.

✓ Echoes of Westminster Hall, 265-380.
Edward the Confessor, 269, 271, 290.
Edward II., 305, 313.
Edward III., 313, 317.
Edward the Black Prince, 14.
✓ Eleanor, Queen, 293.
✓ Elizabeth, Queen, 15.
✓ Elizabeth, Queen of Henry VII., 285.
Ellwood, the Quaker, 31.
Erskine, Mr., 334.
Evelyn, of Wotton, John, 93, 97.
Exeter Street, Catherine Street, Strand, 202.

Flamsteed, the astronomer, 130.
Fleet Market, now Farringdon, 166.
Fleet Prison, 253.
Fleet Street, 56, 178.
Foxe, the martyrologist, 35.

Gascoigne, Lord Chief Justice, 327.
George I., 133.
George IV., 288.
George of Denmark, Prince, 130.
Gibbons, Dr., 143, 156.
Godolphin, Margaret, 88-100.
✓ Goldsmith, Oliver, 161-78, 188, 194, 219, 230.

Gough Square, Fleet Street, 204, 205.
Gower, the poet, 16.
Grattan, 176.
Great Ormond Street, 260.
Great Queen Street, 181.
Green Arbour Court, 167, 169.

Hale, Judge, 330.
Hallam, the historian, 228.
Hannah More, 218.
Hartopp, Sir John, 138.
Havelock, Sir Henry, 102.
Henry III., 278, 281, 291, 309.
Henry IV., 283, 314.
Henry V., 283, 296, 327.
✓ Henry VI., 15, 284.
Henry VII., 285.
Henry VIII., 57, 286.
Hogarth, 181.
Holborn, 26, 204.
Holland House, Kensington, 117.
Hone and Goldsmith, 172.
House of Commons, old, 231, 232.
Howard, John, 242, 264.
Hudson, the painter, 182.
Humphry Davy, Sir, 123.

Inner Temple Lane, near Temple Bar, 207.
Inns of Court, old, 57.
Isaak Walton and his friends, 56-72.
Isle of Thorney, 268, 274.

Jacobites and an Indian Viceroy, 367-80.
James II., 34, 352, 355.
Jeffreys, Judge, 329.
Jermyn Street, 131.
Jerusalem Chamber at Westminster, 135.
Jewin Street, 31.
✓ Johnson, Dr. Samuel, 119, 173, 175, 177, 178, 185, 186, 192; memoir of, 199-222.
Johnson's Court, Fleet Street, 209, 211.
Judicial combat, description of a, 336.

Katrington, Thomas, 337.
Ken, Bishop, 350.
Ken, Anne, 69.

INDEX.

Kenmure, Viscount, 369.
Kensington Palace, 133; Orbell's Buildings, Bullingham Place, 134.
Kilmarnock, Earl of, 370.
Kings in ancient London, 14.
Kings, acting as judges, the, 289.
King's Bench, Southwark, 257.

Lambeth, 68.
Lavington, Rev. Samuel, 153.
Leicester Fields, 181; Leicester Square, 186, 198.
Lincoln's Inn Fields, 26, 77-84.
✓ Literary Club, the, 194, 220, 229.
London Wall, 42.
Long Lane, Smithfield, 242.

Maiden Lane, 74, 76.
Mansfield, Lord, 333.
Marshalsea Prison, 257.
Marvell, Andrew, 73-87.
Matthew Henry, 51.
Matthew Paris, 281.
Mellitus, Bishop of London, 268, 269.
✓ Memories of Great Men in London, 9.
Men of the Marble Chair, 289-303.
Middle Temple, 223, 225.
Milk Street, 46.
Millington, the celebrated auctioneer, 32.
Milton, John, 21-37.
Milton Street, Fore Street, 32.
Monmouth, Alderman Henry, 19.
Montague, Chief Justice, 329; Mrs. Montague, 194.
Montfort, Simon de, and Henry III., 313.
(More, Sir Thomas, 296-303.

Nairn, Lord, 369.
✓Nell Gwynn, 107, 350.
∫Nelson, Lord, 122, 198.
Newgate Prison, 252.
New Ludgate, Bishopsgate Street, 254.
Newport Street, 184.
Newton, Sir Isaac, 121-35.
Nithsdale, Earl of, 369.
Northcote, the artist, 183, 188.

Old London, 9-20.
Old Parliaments and Policy, 304-17.

Old St. Paul's, 17, 41.
Onslow, the Right Honourable Mr., 154.

/Palgrave, Sir Francis, 304.
Parker and Dr. Watts, 156.
Parliament, the new Houses of, 275.
Parliament Street, 234, 235.
Paternoster Row, 69, 70.
Percy, 167, 186.
Petty France, now York Street, Westminster, 27.
Picard, Henry, 14.
Pope, 113, 183.
Poultry Compter, 254.
Public Schools, 101, 102, 105, 106.

✓Queen Anne, 363.
✓Queen Anne Street, 229.
Queen Catherine, 283.
Queen Eleanor, 293.
✓Queen Elizabeth, 15.
✓Queen Victoria, 288.

Radcliffe, Charles, 372.
Ranelagh Gardens, 177.
✓ Reynolds, Sir Joshua, 179-98.
Reynolds, Miss, 184, 186, 205.
Richard Cœur de Lion, 279.
Richard II., 272, 282, 313, 337.
Richard III., 284, 316.
Robin Hood Debating Club, 170.
Rosewell, Rev. Samuel, 145.
✓ Royal Academy, 195.
✓Royal Feastings, 277-88.
✓Royal Society, 123-9.
Russell, Lady, 85-7.
Russell, Lord W., 73-87.

Sacheverell, Dr., 366.
Sancroft, Archbishop, 351, 356.
Sandford Manor House, 107.
Savoy Chapel, the Savoy Conference, 43.
Scotland Yard, 27.
Sebert, King of the Saxons, 268.
Serjeants-at-law, 321.
Seven Bishops, the, and Sacheverell, 350-66.
Shades of the Departed, 21-264.
Shakespeare, 17.
✓Sheridan, Mr., 379.

INDEX

Sion College Almshouse and Library, 42.
Somerset House, 121, 129, 195, 196.
Southampton House, Bloomsbury Square, 84.
Spectator, the, 109-11.
Speed, the historian, 35.
Star Chamber, the, 342.
State Trials, 336-49.
Steele, Sir Richard, 105.
Stowe, John, 242, 278, 291, 315.
Strafford, Lord, 342-5.
Stratford, Archbishop, 294.
St. Bride's Church, 46; St. Bride's Churchyard, 24.
St. Catherine's Gaol, 256.
St. Clement Danes Church, 212.
St. Dunstan's Church, 44.
St. Giles's Church, Cripplegate, 35.
St. John's Gate, Clerkenwell, 203.
St. James's Coffee House, 115.
St. James's Park, 29.
St. James's Square, 202.
St. Lawrence Jewry Church, King Street, Cheapside, 46.
St. Margaret's Church, 30.
St. Martin's-le-Grand, 26; St. Martin's Street, Leicester Square, 131; St. Martin's Lane, 184.
St. Paul's Cathedral, 198, 319; St. Paul's Churchyard, 249; Old St. Paul's, 41; St. Paul's School, 23.
St. Swithin, 293.
Surrey, Earl of, 323.

Sutton, Thomas, 105.
Swan, in Golden Lane, the, 61.
Tatler, the, 111.
Temple, the, 57, 173; Temple Bar, 56, 170, 219; Brick Court, Temple, 174; the Temple Church, 178.
Thorpe, William, trial of, 295.
Tothill Fields Bridewell, 257.
Tower Hamlets Gaol, Wellclose Square, 256.
Tresilian, trial and execution of Judge, 325, 326.
Victoria, Queen, 288.
Vintry, Henry Picard's Mansion, 14.
Voltaire, 76.

Warren Hastings, the trial of, 236-8, 374-80.
Watling Street, 245.
Watts, Isaac, 136-60.
Wesley, John, 102.
Westminster Abbey, 119, 135, 159, 219, 222, 266, 269.
Westminster Hall, 50, 236, 265.
Whitechapel Prison, 256.
Whitehall, 26, 38, 93, 236.
Widdrington, Lord, 369.
William I., 271, 290; William Rufus, 271; William IV., 288.
Wimpole Street, Cavendish Sq., 228.
Winton, Earl, 369.
Wolsey, Cardinal, 58, 296, 302.

www.ingramcontent.com/pod-product-compliance
Lightning Source LLC
Chambersburg PA
CBHW030358230426
43664CB00007BB/640